Disintegration and Political Action
The Changing Functions of
City Governments in America

This is a volume of

Quantitative Studies in Social Relations

Consulting Editor: Peter H. Rossi, University of Massachusetts,
Amherst, Massachusetts

A complete list of titles in this series appears at the end of this volume.

Disintegration
and
Political Action

The Changing Functions of
City Governments in America

Roland J. Liebert
Department of Sociology
Florida Atlantic University
Boca Raton, Florida

ACADEMIC PRESS   *New York*   *San Francisco*   *London*

A Subsidiary of Harcourt Brace Jovanovich, Publishers

ACADEMIC PRESS, INC.
111 Fifth Avenue, New York, New York 10003

United Kingdom Edition published by
ACADEMIC PRESS, INC. (LONDON) LTD.
24/28 Oval Road, London NW1

Library of Congress Cataloging in Publication Data

Liebert, Roland J
    Disintegration and political action.

    (Quantitative studies in social relations series)
    Bibliography: p.
    1.   Municipal government–United States.   I.   Ti-
tle.
JS331.L53   1976   352'.008'0973   75-36651
ISBN 0–12–449650–4

To Derek and John
who arrived as bookends

Contents

Preface

This study of city governments for 668 of the largest American cities is centrally concerned with the causes and consequences of the range or scope of functions (education, welfare, hospitals, etc.) that each one performs. The basic proposition is that the functionally inclusive broad-scope municipalities approach the dimensions and character of what is here associated with the idea of *community*, including broad citizen participation, accessible "unreformed" leadership, and a kind of free wheeling innovativeness and high investment in public services.

This general proposition has another side: In its narrow scope manifestations, where a city government has few if any major functions, municipalities approach the dimensions and character of what is associated with *bureaucracy*, including reduced client participation, reformed leadership by inaccessible experts, reluctance to innovate without demonstrably great need, and economic low investment in on-going programs.

Using U.S. Census and governmental records data, the empirical analysis tests a causal model that links the nature of the urban context of cities through their governmental forms to the political and service activities of the city governments. A principal finding is that the recency of development of cities is the strongest identified determinant of both functional scope and political action.

A major implication of this study concerns prospects for local political systems in the future. It seems that newer cities, and probably those that are now being founded, are withdrawn from public view for want of functions, participation, performance, and politics; while a dwindling proportion of older cities brink fiscal and political crises both because of their full house of service functions and because of an associated intensity of political action and public costs. These patterns and their implications for the future are the principal concerns of the final chapter of the study.

It should be made clear from the very start that the focus here is always on *municipal* governments and on *their* scope of functions, their development since founding, their political behavior, and their citizens. This is not a study of all governments operating locally. It is a study of only one institution, city government, as it is found in some 668 cities across the United States.

Although largely undertaken as "pure" research, this study might usefully be read by those in policy making circles who are concerned with the fate of city governments in America. Local and state officials can choose between comprehensive community government and functionally fragmented jurisdictions for bureaucracies. In the past, the governments that have been established for cities have largely reflected unplanned drift, leading to more fragmentation and disintegration. These governments and their citizens could be made more attentive if not more responsive to analysis and evaluation of the costs and benefits of each way of organizing local political systems.

One policy dilemma before Americans is whether to continue to sustain the participatory politics and organizational growth dynamics of the financially collapsing broad-scope giants that characterize the Northeast. If they are to be sustained, can the political and financial resources necessary for aiding them be recruited from the opposing political culture found in the emerging newer urban areas of the South and Southwest? Although the answers lie in the future, the questions themselves may be formulated by viewing unfolding inter-urban political differences from the perspective developed here.

Yet, policy questions have comprised only a small part of the focus of this research. Much more important and intriguing has been the repeated evidence of limits on policy choices arising from continuity and tradition as major forces shaping city governments and local political cultures. Far more research and documentation than has been attempted here is needed on the changing and enduring cultural heritages of American cities. The present study succeeds if it has the effect of further stimulating such research.

Acknowledgments

Within the broad objectives for this study, its accomplishments are modest and not entirely of my own making. I must, of course, take full responsibility for my methods and interpretations of the data. What I have attempted, however, would surely have been more thoroughly frustrated if not abandoned were it not for the tremendous encouragement from my very competent friend and wife, Pat. It is a pleasure to record my great appreciation and affection for her.

My substantial intellectual debt to Robert Alford should be acknowledged. Nothing in the following pages will survive longer than as a footnote to Alford's work on urban bureaucracy, participation, voter turnout, "reformism," city age, and public program innovations, organization, and delivery. In pressing beyond these discrete topics to find broader patterns of political culture, Alford has blazed trails that unify an entire area of study.

Along with Alford, Michael Aiken deserves special note for showing how to discipline a skeptical curiosity about differences in the scope of city governments. For their suggestions and encouragement concerning an earlier version, I am also grateful to Warren O. Hagstrom, Leo F. Schnore, David Elesh, and Philip G. Altbach.

From Gerald Hage, always the exceptional teacher, I learned anything of value in my methods of theory construction and conceptual analysis. My requests of Robert Hauser for clarification of some issues in the use of path analysis were met with very helpful and affable responses, for which I remain most appreciative. I take full credit for any methods or their use that remain opaque, improper, or plain wrong.

Others whose constructive comments and encouragement helped to make this volume perhaps a little better include Terry N. Clark, Charles Tilly, and Peter Rossi. I am indebted to Rolf Blank, Judy Brock, and Thom Niffenegger for their very competent assistance in the preparation of the bibliography and indexes.

The data for this study are from the Government Units Analysis (GUA) data files that were compiled by Professors Michael Aiken and Robert Alford in the mid-1960s and is now maintained by and available from the Data and Program

Library Service (DPLS), University of Wisconsin, Madison. The particular GUA file used here is for the 676 cities (reduced here to 668 after deleting a few "missing data" cases) having 1960 populations of 25,000 or more. The assistance of Professors Aiken and Alford in providing access to this data and of the DPLS for data reproduction is gratefully acknowledged.

In a substantially revised and shortened form, the main ideas in Chapter III of this volume appeared in the *Social Science Quarterly* (Liebert, 1975).

I.

An Approach to the Study of Political Action: Functions within the Scope of Government

"The scope of government," wrote Agger, Goldrich, and Swanson (1964:6), is "the core of politics." By this, the authors of *The Rulers and the Ruled* meant that most political action is oriented toward maintaining, expanding, contracting, or otherwise altering the functions of government (pp. 38–41). This conception, they suggested, implies a general continuum of political action from a nadir where government has virtually no functions, an "apolitical condition," to higher levels of political activity as the scope of government expands over ever more functions, programs, and services. The differences are in the *pervasiveness* of the government, in how many *other* institutions of organized life it enters, in the degree to which government alters the social consequences of other institutions, and ultimately in how much of people's activities can be mobilized by or through government.

This imagery recurs often in modern social theory and policy analysis, as well as in political ethics and ideology. In the everyday lore of ordinary politics, the "scope of government" becomes one way of stating the familiar American folk distinction between

1

"limited" and "big" government. The former has relatively few functions, and is expected to have a low leadership profile and an efficient low-cost performance record that eschews aggressive and expensive new social programs. The latter, the "big" government, has many functions, and is expected to have an activist leadership style and a tendency to set its performance records both in the elaboration of established programs and in experimentation with new ones. Images such as these have long provided the principal guideposts for identifying the direction in which American government is headed.

SOME ISSUES ABOUT THE SCOPE OF GOVERNMENT

As a matter of ideology, issues about the proper scope of government divide much of modern-day conservative from liberal thought. Ladd (1969) found, in the diverging images of scope, America's "most enduring and comprehensive ideological dichotomy," competing only with cosmopolitan–local values for hegemony in contemporary civic culture. In American conservatism, narrow scope is promoted as a way of maximizing the share of a society's resources controlled by nongovernmental institutions. This goal entails limited public functions, the most technically efficient and rationalized public administration, and the relative isolation of public function administration from the diffuse political demands of mass constituencies. In American liberalism, broad scope is advanced as an elixer for nongovernmental institutions, as an American tradition "to promote the general welfare," and as a symbolic incorporation of common bonds and shared fate in a community that is politically responsive to all.

This ideological dichotomy is restrained within a rather general consensus renouncing the extreme points of reference implied by each pole. In the American context, where neither pole is fully developed, a principal strategy of compromise is to avoid the polar positions of a fully communal *or* laissez-faire society. Because strategies, compromises, and the balance of power differ from place to place and over time, the various governments in the American federal system will most certainly differ in scope.

The importance of differing governmental scope in the American context is further developed by social science theory. Broad-scope government is one meaning for the concept of "community" as the ultimate, inclusive arena where diverse interests and all of their activities and functions find common focus (Warren 1963, Gutman and Popenoe 1970:9–12). This diffuse corporate breadth identifies a form of community integration through a locally inclusive and inter-actionally dense system, and as such is presumed to have certain outcomes that raise the level of political action by way of broad participation in decision making, considerable conflict, accommoda-tion, and generous program expansion (Warren 1970, Turk 1970).

Arising at the opposing pole from community as a form of social organization is the special-purpose bureaucracy. With its distinctive property of a specific goal and its formal autonomy from organiza-tions having other goals, each bureaucracy has, in theory, certain associated or consequent properties involving constraints on action. These include a narrow interest base for decision inputs, a routiniza-tion of decision processes, and a technical competence and control that closely circumscribe performance within parameters of pre-dictability and rationality (Weber 1946:196ff, especially p. 228; Warren 1967).

There is, in short, substantial theory that the breadth and density of action in general, and that decision-making processes and perfor-mances in particular, vary with the scope of organizational functions. There is really a surfeit of such theory, but a scarcity of applica-tions and tests in empirical research, for research tends to assume a focus on one type of organizational system or the other. A reason for the selective focusing of research may be that the prevailing forms of organization, including governmental organization, clearly change over time. Research on what currently exists must make (even if it does not always test) assumptions about the form or forms now in phase.

One of the more authoritatively reported long-term trends in the structure of American society is a movement away from organiza-tional forms modeled on the inclusive community and toward spe-cial-purpose bureaucracies modeled on limited goal attainment (Broom and Selznick 1973:52–54). This trend is evident in govern-ment with the fragmentation of jurisdictions and functions within the local context and, perhaps to a similar extent, with the develop-ment of autonomous and semiautonomous public agencies, authori-ties, and commissions within the more centralized state and national contexts. This would produce the narrow-scope type of government and its corresponding bureaucratic pattern of action.

Yet, even with this first trend toward independent specialized structures, a second one is also evident. Many governments do expand their functions and, in some instances of great recent impor-tance, seem to grow well beyond the capacity of their funders to support them. Even with specialization, the expanding big government is very much with us. By no means distinct from this second expansionist trend are traditions of maintaining the big-government prototypes of the past, for the increment that produces tomorrow's giant is an addition to yesterday's near giant.

There are important issues of public policy in the unfolding of these two trends. The first trend promises, in theory, both low-cost efficiency and reduced capability and enthusiasm for public mobilization or leadership, while the second promises political access, innovation, and costs approaching or surpassing available resources. Fulfillment of either of these promises, or a combination of them, has clear implications for future policy choices regarding the organization of government. One possibility in the long run is a dilemma of extremes, or a choice between government vanishing from political view behind technical specialization and government collapsing on its tax base under the weight of open expansion. If we are to assess the actual direction of organizational change and outcomes, the balance between the two trends and its consequences needs to be determined for particular governments. This would seem to be a major item on an agenda of research issues in modern political development.

It is somewhat surprising, then, that the scope of one of America's most troubled types of government, the municipality, has not been subject to very careful scrutiny. A wide range of scholars and policy analysts (e.g., Adrian and Press 1968, Friesema 1966, Campbell and Sacks 1967, Bollens and Schmandt 1970, Hawley and Zimmer 1970, Committee for Economic Development 1970, Liebert 1974a) have called attention to the maze of governments in urban areas, many of which have limited sets of service functions and, therefore, have less than full capacity and authority to confront urban problems and make a city move. The scope of some municipal governments is, by these accounts, further narrowed wherever state governments directly administer local programs, or indirectly do so through special administrative districts and quasi-governmental public authorities. Facts of this sort are fairly well known, but they are generally presented in an analysis of metropolitan-area governmental fragmentation and cooperation, or as distorting "noise" in studies of service delivery, rather than in terms of implications for the political activity of individual cities.

There has, of course, been widespread concern and some research about the leadership and performance of city governments, perhaps because these matters have always been of some immediate interest both to the urban polity and to its reform movements. But little is known about whether and how these matters are affected by the historically accumulated scope of municipal government. Moreover, with the partial exception of the metropolitan fragmentation literature, community studies generally take little or no cognizance of any major differences between city governments with respect to their scope of functions.[1]

This study is an exploration into the measurement and implications of *municipal scope*. In Chapter II, this variable is defined as the number of major governmental functions performed by city governments, and is found to vary considerably among the cities over 25,000 in population (1960 Census) that are included in the study. Much of the variation in scope is found to correspond to historical patterns of settlement from the earliest communities in America to some of the newer and more specialized suburbs. This historical development, which will be discussed in Chapter III, helps to interpret not only the transformation of the American community but also some of the ways in which cities have not changed very much at all.

The more general concern of this study is, however, with the implications of differences in municipal scope for the character and outcomes of political action by municipalities. To help guide this inquiry, a set of assumptions and propositions about how city governments work are developed in Chapter IV, using what might best be called an "interorganizational perspective," which produces conclusions similar to the folk imagery about "big" and "limited" government. This chapter also raises the question of whether political processes are determined more by the social and organizational context and origins of the government than by governmental scope. Chapters V and VI then explore the empirical relationships between municipal scope and indicators of four aspects of political action—the formal leadership system, voter participation levels, program innovativeness, and fiscal performance of municipalities. The analysis persistently points to the importance of historical differences in the origins of city government as a determinant of both scope and political action. The final chapter summarizes the findings and suggests some of their implications for future trends, intervention policy, and social theory.

Before entering the more analytical portions of the study, it seems

---

[1] Even the community studies by Agger (1964) and his associates, which made considerable use of the concept of governmental scope, largely bypassed the question considered here by focusing not on city governments but on all governments serving four separate countywide areas.

important to get a firmer grasp of what is meant by the notion of municipal scope. To achieve this objective, several suggestive illustrations of differences in scope are presented in the remainder of this introduction.

DIFFERENCES IN SCOPE: SOME EXAMPLES

Among the studies of metropolitan governmental fragmentation, two are particularly relevant as illustrations of one possible component of municipal scope. Hawley (1957) and Kasarda (1972) set out to test the urban ecologist's proposition that suburbanites use central city governmental services without paying for them. They found, as expected, that the per capita size of the central-city municipal budget is strongly correlated with the absolute size of the *suburban* (i.e., nonpaying user) population. They reasoned that these findings reveal the extent to which central-city municipal governments must beef up current programs such as police protection or road maintenance, as well as add new functions such as recreation and museums, as a service to suburbanites who almost diurnally enter the central city. This adding-on of new functions to serve a larger metropolitan or regional area is certainly one way in which the scope of some city governments becomes broadened while their neighbors retain narrower sets of responsibilities. Yet, this is probably not the major component of variation in scope, nor do these studies provide the best understanding of its meaning.

Many of the central cities included in the Hawley and Kasarda studies are somewhat peculiar in the American system of local government, for they are in effect consolidated city–county governments. Such municipalities include cities like Baltimore, New Orleans, St. Louis, Denver, and San Francisco, as well as all the large cities in Virginia. Unlike their neighbors, these city governments have budgets that include funds for what elsewhere are generally county functions, e.g., judicial services, welfare, sometimes education, and, of course, the county roads, sheriff's, health, sanitation, and other departments. Moreover, cities in some of the more urbanized and suburbanized parts of the nation, namely the region stretching from Portland, Maine, to New York City, are also in effect consolidated city–county governments, due to the virtual absence of functioning counties in New England.[2]

---

[2] Data and references supporting these statements are presented in Chapter II.

All of this means that many cities in the center of large metropolitan areas have tremendous budgets and, more to the point, broad functional scope. Some of this inordinately broad scope may be due to what Hawley and Kasarda identified as intermunicipal inequalities leading to assignment of certain area-wide functions to central-city governments. But, in a more general sense, what is important for an understanding of municipal scope is that many other kinds of governmental assignment are involved, including consolidation with counties, absorption of the school system under the municipal government, or state action that adds or takes away functions like public welfare.

From this stance, we can see that a central-city—suburban distinction, or even a big-city—small-city distinction, is not a self-evident corollary of differences in scope. A small New England city may have basically the same number of general functions as Boston, Providence, or New Haven has. A major city that has an effectively consolidated city—county government, such as New York City, can hardly escape having a broader scope and a more pervasive involvement in community affairs than would be true of another major city where county and special district governments carry most of the local government responsibilities. It turns out, in fact, that the cities of New York and Los Angeles provide one of the most interesting comparisons in this regard as retrospectively viewed from the mid-1970s.

One of the great problems before New York City and its leaders and constituents is how to meet the many public welfare needs of the disabled, the aged, unsupported children, and the unemployable. Federally funded programs help out, but they are designed to leave some of the real issues of "who gets how much?" for resolution at the local level and in the state capital (see Piven and Cloward 1971). The administration of the welfare programs by New York City authorities seems to be constantly at issue if one were to judge by reports in *The New York Times*. One might suppose, in sympathy with the welfare officials, that even if the administration of these programs fully met the letter and spirit of the law, there would be interests demanding a change in city government policy.

Similarly, New York has been one of the cities that have been shaken by the conflicts over school desegregation and neighborhood control of schools, and it is the New York City government that once again provides this function. Rogers (1967) has written extensively about New York City's response to these school issues. Although he was sharply critical of the mayor's office for not intervening in these issues during their early stages, he nonetheless considered the city government's school bureaucracy (rather than the mayor) to be the principal source of resistance to change. Rogers argued that change would come only with eventual intervention by "the most significant levers to social change," namely, "the mayor, the state education department, and the federal government (p. 183)." The hope that Rogers held for intervention by the mayor or superior governments was based on his observations that these higher-level "levers to social change" experience a broader base of pressures and have a wider range of resources and authority than do the specialized professionals in the city's school bureaucracy.

In contrast, the mayor's office and the entire city government of Los Angeles do not worry themselves much about welfare or school issues, for they have no official responsibility over these matters. To expect or hope or even demand that the mayor would intervene would be quixotic politics. In Los Angeles, as in most of the rest of the nation, counties or special-purpose governments take care of the administration of most welfare and public education functions.

These and other differences between New York City's functional scope and that of Los Angeles City were brought out in more dramatic form during hearings of a U.S. Senate Subcommittee on Executive Reorganization (1966). The subcommittee's report, *The Federal Role in Urban Affairs,* is worth noting at length for the suggestions that it contains regarding implications of these differences for the character of political action in New York and in Los Angeles.

The Senate investigators, Abraham Ribicoff of Connecticut and Robert Kennedy of New York (formerly of Massachusetts) had evidently assumed that the mayors of major cities were in a position to take leadership in the resolution of a wide gamut of urban problems. The testimony from New York's Mayor John Lindsay went as expected. Lindsay reported, or perhaps overstated in some cases, that his administration was active on all of the issues raised by the subcommittee, particularly in the more needy areas of the city. He and his administration would welcome more federal aid for new programs and to supplement old ones.

The testimony from Los Angeles' Mayor Sam Yorty, on the other hand, was a surprise to the subcommittee. To nearly every question of concern to the Senators, Yorty reported that he lacked jurisdiction over the issues. He could not account for activities and needs of other governments operating within his city. The subcommittee would have to consult with these governments directly. Nor could Yorty supply information about how overlying governments perform in such "needy" parts of the city as the Watts area, "because they [the other governments] do not break it [their information] down this way." At last, exasperated with Yorty's apparent lack of leadership, the Senators resorted to challenging him:

Senator Kennedy: *But are you not mayor of all of the people in Los Angeles?*

Mayor Yorty: *Of the people of the city of Los Angeles, yes.*

Senator Kennedy: *Then if they have a problem, do they not look to you for some leadership?*

Mayor Yorty: *Yes. They get leadership, too, evidenced by the last election. But whether or not I can solve a problem may depend on my jurisdiction.*

Senator Ribicoff: *As I listened to your testimony, Mayor Yorty, I made some notes. This morning you have really waived authority and responsibility in the following areas: schools, welfare, transportation, employment, health, and housing, which leaves you as the head of the city basically with a ceremonial function, police and recreation.*

Mayor Yorty: *That is right, and fire.*

Senator Ribicoff: *And fire.*

Mayor Yorty: *Yes.*

Senator Ribicoff: *Collecting sewage?*

Mayor Yorty: *Sanitation, that is right.*

Senator Ribicoff: *In other words, basically you lack jurisdiction, authority, responsibility for what makes a city move?*

Mayor Yorty: *That is exactly it.*

Senator Ribicoff: *I would say that the city of Los Angeles right now, from your testimony, does not stand for a damn thing.*

Mayor Yorty: *Well, it stands for a lot.*

Senator Ribicoff: *I believe that there will be federal programs that will be initiated in the next two years that will really put America on the road to start doing something about the cities in America . . . .The one city that won't be able to take advantage of any of these programs will be Los Angeles, because you are not organized to do so.*

Mayor Yorty: *The only way we can organize is . . . to . . . do it by a joint powers agreement with the other jurisdictions that are involved, so at that point we can work together. When you get to solving the problems of the cities, in our community we probably have to work countywide.*

[Exerpted and adapted from U.S. Senate Subcommittee on Executive Reorganization, *The Federal Role in Urban Affairs*, 1966:775–77]

Throughout his testimony, Mayor Yorty made a small but symbolic distinction between "our community" and "my city." It is
reasonable that to Yorty the community is organized into multiple
jurisdictions and autonomous powers, the boundary of which is best
understood as that of the largest major local unit, the county. The
city as municipality is just one of the political units in this community, and a minor one at that. Its functions may be more than
ceremonial, but not much more. Opportunities for leadership are
correspondingly narrow. It is in the nature of this county community
that record keeping and decision making in one unit are neither
accessible nor particularly useful to another unit. Yet, informal
collaboration occurs, and on occasion several units share resources or
decision making through ad hoc agreements.

The senators, on the other hand, made no distinction between
communities and cities. They talked solely of cities, like Kennedy's
New York or Ribicoff's New Haven, where the city is an inclusive
political system for virtually every decision made locally about local
government. At least some of these decisions are channeled back and
forth between the sprawling legs and central body of a single overall
hierarchy. There may be ad hoc agreements, but there are also lasting
commitments and greater potentials for interagency coalitions, cooperation, and of course conflict. Centralized records attempt to
keep tab of these commitments, of decisions that are made, and of
the allocation of resources. The mayor is the leader of all of the
people, for he is equipped with a bureaucracy that stands for something for everyone.

If the drift of this bureaucracy is, as Sayre and Kaufman (1960)
point out in their study of New York, toward self-controlled and
self-directed agencies, there are nonetheless both legal—administrative
and public pressures running in the other direction. When new
challenges or opportunities arise, there are a host of organized
interests available to facilitate some efforts, to block others, and to
bargain over still others. Innovation may be far from speedy and may
have to satisfy the claims of many partisans, but such integration of
these partisans and their resources as the broad-scope city provides
would seem to give them a greater probability of getting together on
innovative new programs than would be true in the narrow-scope
city. At least the mayors seemed to think so.

If these inferences are not too overdrawn, they suggest that the
American folk imagery distinguishing "limited" from "big" government may have some validity as applied to municipalities of differing
scope. New York and Los Angeles are both big in one respect; they

are the two largest cities in the nation in terms of population. Partly for this reason, they are not the most dissimilar cities in terms of functional scope. The extreme cases of narrow-scope cities include some that are also located in Los Angeles County, such as Lakewood City, which receives virtually all major local governmental services from the county, from some other government, or does without them (see Cion 1971). The important question about all of these cities is whether organizational differences resulting from the scope of their governments impose limits or press opportunities upon the uses of leadership and its relevance to urban problems.

The U.S. Senate subcommittee hearings of the mid-1960s gave a pro-activist bias to the significance of this question. Such a trend was characteristic of the times. In substantive urban programming, it was a time of heightened funding for and attention to the great innovative projects of an era of rehabilitation, urban renewal, and public housing. In the more symbolic politics of participation, demands for involvement seemingly arose from every quarter. They rose highest in evoking the marvelous Great Society promise of a participatory democracy that would signal the coming solution of even the most vexing social problem of cities: poverty. Activists of all kinds were looking for a confrontation of interests in a setting where interests could be confronted, power wielded, and decisions made. For the Senate activists of the mid-1960s, an exemplary setting that was "organized" for this purpose might well have been the inclusive-scope New York City government, as distinct from the government of Los Angeles City in which many decisions were not made, nor powers wielded, nor interests confronted.

Within a decade, by the mid-1970s, the exemplary organization of New York City had more fully revealed its own problems. The national participatory disposition had waned, costs of government had risen while resources fell, and New York City had become the model of the overcommitted city. The organization of government no longer took its principal policy significance from a pro-activist bias, for there now was much to recommend the city government of limited roles and political restraint for the accolade of being well organized.

The nation's economic and political cycles produce times of governmental feast and times of famine. An analysis of the responses of governments of differing scope may identify those cities best organized for each temper. The cities of New York and Los Angeles are only illustrative. If they exemplify different problems and capacities, analysis of the consequences of the varying scope of all city governments. The data to be used in this analysis were mostly taken from documents and surveys from the recent period of activist ascendency, in the early and mid-1960s. If we can identify the patterns that distinguish those city governments most seized by this animus from those that lagged behind, perhaps we can also better understand the basis for the currently salient problems of overcommitment and accountability.

ORGANIZATION OF THE STUDY

There are several ways of defining the scope of a government. Some possible definitions and empirical measures, such as general expenditure levels, go beyond the widely overlooked issue of whether a government has *any* responsibility for various functions. Such definitions and measures also deal with how and how much a government responds to the basic tasks that it has. When applied to municipal governments, these approaches cloud the important distinction between *performance* and whether a government even *enters* various arenas of political issues. Differences in the number of functions under municipal control are so great and so elementary to any notion of scope that they probably impose stringent limits on levels of performance and other possible notions of scope.[3]

Chapter II develops the functional measure of scope used in this study, discusses alternative ways of measuring and defining scope, and concludes with a statistical analysis of the strong relationships of alternative measures with the functional measure. Of the 12 major functions of government identified in Chapter II, only police, fire, and highways enjoy status as fairly universal functions of all 676 municipalities that had a population of at least 25,000 residents in 1960. Some of these cities have had responsibility for only the 3 "common" functions, while others have had responsibility for all 12, including schools, general-assistance welfare, categorical-aid welfare, hospitals, health, sanitation, sewers, parks, and recreation, and general judicial functions.

Chapter III is an account of how contemporary American cities have acquired responsibility for their varying sets of service func-

---

[3] For a critique and partial revision of some of the expenditures literature that overlooks this issue, see Liebert (1974a, 1974b).

tions. The central-city–suburban distinction is considered as a source of variation in scope, as is the size of the city in terms of population. But the most interesting findings concern the relationship between the age of the city (when it first reached a population of 10,000) and its scope. This relationship suggests that the older-style inclusive political community survives in modified form as a relic of the past, even while newer and functionally narrower, more specialized city governments emerge in recently urbanized parts of the nation.

By this point in the study, there is a firm basis for going into the theoretical implications of the "big" versus "limited" government imagery. Chapter IV attempts to do this by spelling out why variability in scope might affect the character of leadership, public participation, innovativeness, and fiscal performance of municipal governments. A model of decision-making processes is built along lines suggested by interorganizational theorists. The municipal government is seen as a kind of *focal* organization (Evan 1966, Warren 1967) that receives human and capital resources commensurate with its scope, and responds in like manner, innovating and spending more as its scope expands. The theory also holds that a broad range of functions performed by municipal government results in greater accessibility to the formal leadership structure by a broader range of interests and centers of power in the city. Overall, the general thesis hypothesizes that as the scope of city governments broaden, such cities develop a more dynamic and more politically active civic culture. Several complementary theories about the activation of other organized systems suggest some consensus about this perspective. Also considered is a somewhat different perspective suggesting that activation may depend in part on the nongovernmental social structure and historical origins of the community in which the government is located.

An empirical analysis of some of the consequences of variability in municipal scope is presented in Chapters V and VI. Specific indicators of relatively more dynamic municipal govermnents include: (1) the extent to which the formal leadership system permits wide accessibility by special interests (or absence of such reform mechanisms as a city manager and at-large election of councilmen); (2) the level of citizen participation through voter turnout in municipal elections; (3) the level of municipal innovativeness through new program adoption (e.g., urban renewal and public housing adoption), and the responsiveness of innovative change to relevant interests and needs in the city; and (4) the level of municipal fiscal performance as measured by expenditure levels within specific functional areas.

The findings lend some support to the scope-centered theory that motivates and directs this inquiry. At least as important, however, is an unexpected emerging theme of a slightly different character. The data increasingly require that the historical origins of cities and their modern-day residues in both scope and political activation become the concluding focus of concern. The summary in Chapter VII centers attention on the evidence and implications of diverging cohorts of civic culture rooted in generational age differences between cities. Widening scope and politicization seem to be the fate of early cohorts, while narrow purpose and technocratic administration seem to characterize recent community development.

The data used in the empirical portions of this study have, in most instances, been taken from the Alford and Aiken Governmental Units Analysis data bank on the 676 cities with a 1960 population of at least 25,000. This data is on file at the University of Wisconsin (Madison) with the Data and Program Library Service. The measure of municipal functional scope was constructed from this and other data sources and will be discussed in detail in the next chapter. The original data sources for the variables used in this study will be identified as they are introduced.

It should be noted from the outset that this study is, of necessity, only preliminary to a full understanding of the meaning and implications of the scope of government. The issues on which the study focuses, and the conceptual framework and empirical data, are hardly exhaustive of those that might apply. Theory about political action and organization clearly needs development beyond what can be provided here. Data sources and measures need closer examination to find those that better identify theoretically important concepts. Interpretations should be taken with the usual critical scrutiny, which research of this type merits. While always admitting to limitations in the present effort, I have not been wholly reticent in drawing inferences from the evidence. The reader is encouraged to seek and draw others.

II.

Measuring the Scope
of Municipal Government

The greatest advances in the sphere of the social sciences are substantively tied up with the shift in practical problems and take the guise of a critique of concept-construction [From Weber, Max, *The methodology of the social sciences.* Copyright © 1949 The Free Press, New York, p. 106.]

To focus on the differing scope of individual city governments, it is necessary to dispense with any assumptions that our units of analysis are in any sense "inclusive" communities. They are organizations. City governments in modern America are often organized to *exclude* most community problems from their agendas. At issue is the extensiveness of the powers included in the domain of each city government. Analysis of this question requires making a choice of one of the several heuristically useful definitions of the scope of government. A brief discussion of four possible definitions will serve to illustrate the distinct meaning of the definition and operational measure used here.

DEFINITIONS OF SCOPE

The most elaborately developed parameters on scope might be found by a *legal charter* definition, pertaining to the legally mandated, granted, or reserved authority and powers of a city. This definition views city government as a creature of higher formal law, and developing within that law. As a legal creation, scope extends beyond all activities that are mandated and enacted, and includes the very limits of permissible legal action or the full potential of the city's formally vested authority.

This rather ideational notion of scope is never firm or discrete; with the characteristically glacial momentum of formal law, it changes with changing legal interpretations and precedents. Those who have written about the legal charters of cities (e.g., Winter 1969: 78–164) stress that there is constant intergovernmental bargaining for delegated autonomous powers, that cities are nonetheless fully subordinate legal entities, and that any traditional expectations regarding the distribution of powers persists at the pleasure of the state. B. Clark (1970) documented the slow unfolding of another type of legal charter, for four colleges having distinctive original missions, and suggested that the organizational "saga," or function-actualizing history of each college, revealed a persisting role and mission that captured some essence of the initial charter in every new era encountered.

Despite its heuristic value, scope by the legal-charter definition is fairly intractable to direct measurement on a large comparative scale. This is so partly because it concerns a potential limit rather than a realized one. More crucially, the relevant constitutions, legislative statutes, charters, codes, and case law are rather resistant to synthesis, let alone access, by social scientists. The scope of a city's "legal charter" might be inferred from its historical development and current actual commitments, as we attempt to do in the next chapter, but it cannot be directly measured.

A *social charter* definition of scope is also conceivable, if only in passing. The *scope* of a city government's social charter is the extent of its legitimate authority as derived from the approval or consent of all relevant power groups and constituencies. Scope by this definition would probably be narrower than by the legal definition, due to the limits on authority imposed by significant nongovernmental veto groups. Indeed, the social charter may reduce to precisely what the government does, with the relevant power groups getting, by definition, what they want. This forces concern with definitions expressly dealing with enacted scope.

One way to view enacted scope is to define it as the full quantity of *manifest resources* possessed or controlled by the government. Manifest resources might include its budget, its manpower, its expert staff, or all of its specialized tasks. This is a viable definition in that it points to readily measurable aspects of a government's performance in the sense of controlled resources. There is, however, considerable value in keeping much of the detail about performance out of our definition of scope. It is one thing for a government to take on a role, and quite another to perform that role with greater or lesser resourcefulness. As distinguished from performance, scope as a set of enacted roles or functions implies an established *capacity* that may be performed at various levels. It is this last definition that is used here.

This study operationally defines the scope of municipal government in terms of *functional* differentiation, or the number of functionally distinct issue arenas in which a branch or component of municipal government exercises some measure of coordination and control. In contemporary American cities, these functional components generally take the form of departments or bureaus that have distinct staff, clientele, and objectives. In less organizationally developed cities, and certainly during an earlier and simpler era, these functional components may be found fused into relatively few organized subdivisions.

In a nominal sense, it is in terms of functional components that officials, citizens, and government records alike refer to the different units of activity by municipal government. The familiar ones with their usual titles include the police, fire, roads, and health departments; the sewage and school systems; the hospitals; the sanitation, parks and recreation, and welfare departments; and in some cities the clerk's office or courthouse. This is simply a listing of the major traditional service functions of local government as identified by U.S. Census records. The number of these functions that are performed by any given city government is the estimate of municipal scope constructed in this chapter and used throughout the study.

Before this estimate was adopted, three alternative procedures were considered, each based on more detailed performance data. These alternatives are actually indicators that other writers have used for more general phenomena such as the organizational *complexity* of a government (Hage and Aiken 1970), the extent of political *integra-*

tion by a government (Jacob and Teune 1964; Turk 1970, 1973a, 1973b), and the *inclusiveness* or "singleness" of government for a given area (Campbell and Sacks 1967). This is a tightly knit set of concepts by some measures and meanings. Each draws on elements of the previously mentioned four definitions of scope, and each provides another perspective on what it means for a government to have many different rather than a few limited tasks. This commonality is discussed again at the end of this chapter, particularly with reference to certain indicators of the concepts. The chapter concludes with an analysis of the statistical correlations between the functional measure of scope and some of the other performance-based measures.

LISTING THE FUNCTIONS

State laws, interlocal agreements, and governmental records all keep tab of municipal responsibilities in terms of functional categories. Yet there exists no universally accepted listing of these categories. It is nonetheless possible to devise a list of major categories from the U.S. *Census of Governments* 1962 and 1967 reports on municipal general finances and employment. This list would include ten of the categories noted earlier: education, welfare, health, hospitals, sewage, sanitation other than sewage (mostly refuse removal), and parks and recreation, as well as police, fire, and highways. All of these are traditional functions; none are recent innovations. These ten functions accounted for approximately 82.5% of municipal government general expenditures in 1962 for all city governments in the nation (*U.S. Census of Governments, 1962*, Vol. IV, p. 2). The remainder belong to an "other" category which, if known, might empirically widen and conceptually strengthen the measure of functional scope that was constructed.

The Census Bureau's listings, therefore, provided the formal criterion for selection of "major functions." Inspection of these listings and of other sources suggested the wisdom of making several exceptions. Welfare was split into two functional categories, an additional function indicating "judicial" responsibilities was added, and the three "common" functions of police, fire, and highways were deleted from the list.[1] The reasons for these adjustments are described below.

[1] Also implicitly removed from the list were all common functions which might appear in the "other" category, such as general central administration.

The basis for determining whether or not a municipality had administrative and some financial responsibility for a function depended to some extent on the kind of data available. In each case, data for or close to the year 1962 were sought. Using the sources and procedures described below, the presence or absence of major functional responsibilities was estimated for each of the 676 cities with 1960 populations of 25,000 or more. Four of these 676 cities were eventually dropped from the study because of missing data on their functional responsibilities.[2] Washington, D.C. and the three cities listed for Alaska and Hawaii were also eliminated due to their unique histories and governmental status. This left 668 cities located within the contiguous states for which the following information was available and was coded.

For education, the 1962 *U.S. Census of Governments: Governmental Organization* provided most of the information on whether school systems were dependent agencies of city government or were governmentally separated from city hall and under county or autonomous administration. A few cities with municipal colleges but no dependent public schools were coded as having the education function.[3] Cities for which the determination of public-school responsibility remained ambiguous were coded as having the school function if they had expenditures in the education category during 1962 that exceeded one dollar per capita. This one-dollar figure is arbitrary, but it was deemed useful to avoid miscoding a few cities that may have reported a tiny educational expenditure arising from interbudgetary transfers between the city and an independent school system, or for a host of financial reporting irregularities that could put in the educational category an expenditure that is wholly insufficient to support any major aspect of the function.

For welfare, *The Public Welfare Directory* (Martin 1966) was consulted as the best source indicating which of the major welfare programs were administered by an agency of the city government. In the early 1960s, municipal administrative jurisdiction implied fiscal responsibility for the local share contributed to such federally subsidized programs as old-age assistance, aid to dependent children, and aid to permanently and totally disabled. These federally aided programs were counted together as one function. Separate from the federally aided welfare programs are the general assistance programs,

---

[2] The four cities were Belleville and Bergenfield, New Jersey; Elyria, Ohio; and Maywood, Illinois.

[3] These cities are Akron, Cincinnati, and Toledo, Ohio; and Louisville, Kentucky.

which have traditionally been funded by local and state governments and are often provided solely on local initiative. The welfare *Directory* was not complete with regard to general assistance programs, making it necessary to check for about 20 cities the same expenditures data for welfare as was carried out for education.

Surveys published in the *Municipal Year Book* (Nolting and Arnold 1963, 1965) provided the best source of information on whether or not a city government owned and operated a sewage system. Missing data for 60 cities were replaced with data provided by earlier editions of the *Municipal Year Book,* taking for each city the most recent available data.

For the remaining functions, determination of governmental responsibility was based on inferences from census data. Estimates of municipal responsibility for hospitals, sanitation other than sewage, and parks and recreation were made from *U.S. Census of Governments* (1962, 1967) data on employment within these functional areas. The criterion was whether or not the city had a minimum of five full-time-equivalent employees assigned to the function. In the case of health, for which employment data were unavailable, cities were considered to have the function if they spent at least $10,000 on it during fiscal 1967.

These estimates are consistent with the reasoning that if a city possesses one of these major functions, that function is probably large enough to be a division or agency at some level in the government. Smaller expenditure or employment levels would have a high probability of being token intergovernmental or private-agency transfers, or of supporting a liaison activity rather than an operating program. Future researchers might readily take this assumption one step further and determine the presence or absence of governmental responsibility solely on the basis of minimal employment or expenditure levels for each function. My attempts to seek more direct information on governmental organization only served to increase my confidence in the relative reliability of the latter approach. Yet, caution is more in order. We simply know so little about the intergovernmental allocation of formal authority and its enactment that all estimates at this point can at best be good inferences.

Making a final inference, I added one more function to the previous list of eight. It actually consists of the set of judicial and clerical duties that accrue to a city when it lacks any general-purpose overlying government such as a county. Such matters as legal records and documents; administering elections, tax, and assessment laws; supervising miscellaneous minor state programs; and having court jurisdiction over some state criminal and civil laws might fall into this category. It indicates exclusive municipal jurisdiction over all non-special district governmental functions performed locally. It was identified by using the *U.S. Census of Governments:1962, Governmental Organization* information on whether or not a city has a functionally active and governmentally separate county overlying its boundaries. Counties in New England were considered functionally inactive at the local level because they are comparable to state court districts in many other states, with the exception that New England counties relinguish some judicial responsibilities to cities and towns (Updyke 1913, Nuquist 1964:199–230).

The major functions excluded from this list of nine are the familiar police, fire, and highway functions. No data were coded for these functions on the assumption that they were common to all cities, as was suggested by Brazer (1959) in his study of expenditures on common functions. An inspection of 1962 expenditures data indicated that only 9 of the 668 cities spent less than $10,000 on any of these functions. However, when employment data were inspected, a handful of cities, amounting to as many as 30 in the case of fire, were found to have fewer than five employees listed for each of these functions. It was ultimately decided to continue treating these as "common" functions despite the possibility of a few cities having city-aided volunteer fire departments, county road crews, or non-municipal police protection. It is assumed that the deletion of these three items from the final list of variable functions has the simple effect of scaling down the number of functions found in nearly all municipal governments.

The resulting list of nine variable functions is presented in Table II-1. No claim can be made that this list is exhaustive, or satisfies everyone's definition of "major" functions. It represents only one effort to achieve the latter objective. Table II-1 also gives the percentage and number of cities found to have responsibility for each function. Again, the measurement of responsibility is open to question. I would have preferred the immoderate time and resources necessary to check other local-government documents for indisputable evidence that cities have and exercise some authority for each of the functions. Others might prefer looking for evidence of enacted authority simply by determining whether each city has a minimal expenditure or employment in each census category. Attempts at either approach, or the present combination of them, can result only in approximations. The approximations used here should not differ greatly from others that might have been used.

TABLE II-1
Number and Proportion of Municipalities with Responsibilities for Each Function[a]

Function	Municipal governments (%)	Number
Welfare, Federally Aided	9	57
Judicial	12	81
Hospitals	13	87
Education	22	146
Welfare, General Assistance	24	159
Sewers	60	402
Health	70	468
Sanitation	72	483
Parks and Recreation	89	597
Total number of cities	100	668

[a]Source: See text.

There are two ways of viewing Table II-1. The first is to look at particular functions and to note the proportion of municipalities having responsibility for them. From this viewpoint, it is notable that no function (excluding the omitted police, fire, and highway functions) is universal, and that only one (parks and recreation) is a municipal function in more than three-quarters of the cities over 25,000 in population. This is strong empirical evidence of how varied the American system is in providing public services through local governments.

Further inspection of Table II-1 suggests a distinction by type of function. Note that each of the more *people*-oriented functions (welfare, education, hospitals, and judicial) is a municipal responsibility in fewer than 25 % of the cities, whereas each of the more *environment*-oriented functions (sewers, sanitation, health, and parks) is a municipal responsibility in 60–90 % of the cities. The two most prevalent municipal functions, health and parks, may be the most heterogeneous in their orientations. Public health services are primarily directed toward communicable disease control, which does not necessarily involve health care or direct contact with patients. The ubiquitous municipal parks function involves limited constituency contact by way of any recreational programs in the city's domain, as well as any museums, zoos, gardens, parks, and beaches. These differences in the relative incidence of *types* of functions may play some role in explaining variations in the *number* of functions performed by municipalities.

ADDING THE FUNCTIONS

Measures of differentiation, of which functional scope is a special example, are rarely reported in ways that permit one to determine whether the different component items or elements in the measure are related to each other. This question is of more than passing interest in the present instance due to the difference in the incidence of people- and environment-oriented functions and to the rather interesting prospect that each of these may tend to occur in clusters. The final measure for each city, a simple counting of functions, may take shape along substantively different patterns of service programs from city to city.

The strongest reason for *not* reporting relationships among items in a differentiation measure was stated by Blau (1970). He held that organizations, such as the state-wide employment agencies that he was investigating, can be equally differentiated even if they possess totally different substantive components. The only thing that matters is how many components they have, for this tells us how extensively the system is ramified and subdivided as opposed to its existence as a simple homologous unit. One can accept this standard without taking the additional step of asserting, as Blau did, that substantive organizational traits such as technology, goals, or kinds of tasks are irrelevant to the measurement of differentiation. They may be very relevant in determining how the items in that measure cluster, as well as in explaining variation in the measure.[4]

With this in mind, Tables II-2 and II-3 are presented here to show something about how major municipal functions are empirically related to each other. Intercorrelations between dummy variables, each indicating the presence or absence of a function, are presented in Table II-2. Approximately two-thirds of the coefficients are positive and significant at the 5 % level, and the remaining third are insignificant in either direction at the same level.[5] Two of the

---

[4] Klatzky (1970) illustrated this point using Blau's data on employment agencies for a different study. She found that the larger, more differentiated agencies emphasized the technologies, goals, and tasks of providing relief aid, while the smaller, less differentiated ones emphasized job placement.

[5] In studies of a universe, as here, there is no sampling error, though there may be error in measurement. In this situation, significance tests are used to judge between "appreciable" and "negligible" relationships (Gold 1969, Morrison and Henkel 1969, Winch and Campbell 1969). It is, however, always important to introduce the reader to one's own less systematic judgments as to the substantive significance of empirically identifiable relationships in a universe. This is done here for relationships that are generally presented in the form of standardized slopes which, when squared, provide a measure of shared variance (Cain and Watts 1969, Blalock 1967).

TABLE II-2
Zero Order Correlation Matrix of Nine Major Functions[a]

Function[b]	1	2	3	4	5	6	7	8	9
1. Welfare, Fed. Aid	——								
2. Judicial	.71	——							
3. Hospitals	.22	.17	——						
4. Education	.47	.64	.16	——					
5. Welfare, Gen. Asst.	.55	.67	.18	.75	——				
6. Health	.19	.22	.15	.31	.31	——			
7. Sewers	-.07*	-.06*	.02*	-.04*	-.07*	.14	——		
8. Sanitations	-.05*	-.06*	.04*	.00*	-.02*	.22	.17	——	
9. Parks and Recreation	.05*	.05*	-.03*	.10	.10	.08	.13	.10	——

[a]Source: See text.

[b]Each function in this matrix is a dummy variable with scores of "0" indicating the absence and "1" indicating the presence of the function for the 668 cities.

*When tests of significance are applied to these zero-order, product-moment correlation coefficients, all those less than an absolute value of .08 are insignificant at the .05 level.

TABLE II-3
Functional Scope: Item to Total-Less-Item Correlations and Item to Total Correlations[a]

X = Function[b]	Y = Functional scope less X[c]	Functional scope
1. Welfare, Fed. Aid	.48	.59
2. Judicial	.54	.66
3. Hospitals	.20	.38
4. Education	.57	.71
5. Welfare, Gen. Asst.	.58	.72
6. Health	.38	.60
7. Parks and Recreation	.11	.30
8. Sanitation	.07*	.35
9. Sewers	.02*	.33

[a]Source: See text.

[b]Dummy variables indicating presence or absence of each function for the 668 cities.

[c]Computed by adding together the number of functions for which the municipal government was responsible, and subtracting the score for the "X" variable.

*p > .05.

functions, sewers and sanitation, have between them seven slightly negative correlations with other functions.

Despite these differences, there is no strong tendency for a given function or set of fundtions *not* to occur in cities having other functions. Yet, there is a distinction between the more people-oriented and environment-oriented functions. The former tend to collect together, while each of the latter tend to be dispersed more randomly with respect to all others. The only exception to this pattern is the somewhat heterogeneous health services function, which is consistently related to all of the other functions in a positive direction.

Table II-3 presents correlations between each individual function (labeled the "*X* variable") and the number of the eight remaining functions under city government control (labeled "Functional scope less *X*"). If the validity of a differentiation measure rested on the interrelatedness of its component items, then the item to total-less-the-item correlations in Table II-3 would be a check on how strongly and consistently each of the various items is related to all of the *other* items when scaled (see Bohrnstedt 1969; Heise and Bohrnstedt 1970). Table II-3 shows that each of the nine functions has a positive and usually quite strong relationship with scope as measured by the remaining eight functions. Another way of stating this is that a government having a wide scope on any set of eight functions is likely to have the ninth one as well. An exception may be made for the two most environment-oriented functions, which come close to being randomly distributed with respect to the total-less-the-item variables.

Another way of calculating the relationship between a scale and its components would be to use the entire scale, or all nine items in this case, even though the relationships would be contaminated by the presence of the item. What this procedure does indicate is the amount of common variance between each of the items and the entire scale. These relationships, also presented in Table II-3, show that the presence or absence of the clustering health, education, welfare, or judicial functions has very strong effects on the entire scale. Yet, even the other functions, including sanitation and sewage, contribute greatly to the overall scale when they are included in it.

In general, these data suggest the significance of distinctions between types of functions for any explanation of variations in functional scope. The *number* of components may be analytically isolated from the *type,* but here—as probably in all organizational studies—they are related empirically.

TABLE II-4
Frequency Distribution of Ranges of Functional Scope[a]

Range of functional scope (Number of functions)	Municipalities at each range (%)	(Number)
0	1.2	8
1	9.4	63
2	13.6	91
3	23.7	158
4	26.0	174
5	10.6	71
6	5.7	38
7	6.1	41
8	3.1	21
9	.4	3
Total	99.8[b]	668

[a]Source: See text.
[b]Does not add to 100% due to rounding error.

Finally, Table II-4 presents the distribution of cities by range of functional scope. Each "range" is simply a count of the number of functions performed by municipal governments. This variable has a low of no functions (for eight cities) and a high of all nine functions (for three cities). The distribution is nearly normal, although the curve is steep on both sides. Half of the cities fall in two of the middle categories indicating three or four functions. That the distribution is distinctly *not* bimodal, with some cities having most functions and the rest having little or none, takes some of the edge off of the importance of some functions clustering by type. There is, in short, not only wide variability in the functional scope of municipal governments, but also substantial diversity of functional composition.

"NONFUNCTIONAL" MEASURES OF SCOPE

One advantage of investigating alternative conceptions of the scope of government activities is that they might suggest measures and data sources that avoid the empirical difficulties of trying to identify functions and responsibility for functions. Instead, it was found that the alternatives have similar or greater problems of measurement, as well as more general meanings and implications for which functional scope is a basic determinant.

Organizational Complexity

One of the more traditional ways of measuring the scope of activities within an organized system might be to adopt one of the estimating procedures used by organization analysts in their operationalization of *complexity* or *structural differentiation.* Hage and Aiken (1970:16), for example, define complexity as the "number of occupations, especially those requiring knowledge," within an organization. By this measure, the scope of a government would clearly be wider if it employs teachers, welfare workers, and health officials than if it employs only policemen and firemen. Indeed, any increase in functions performed should entail an increase in complexity, although the reverse may not always be true due to the probability of differences in intrafunctional complexity.

A somewhat broader and equally applicable conception of structural differentiation was provided by Blau (1970:204).

> The term differentiation refers specifically to the number of structural components that are formally distinguished in terms of any *one* criterion. The empirical measures used are the number of branches, number of occupational positions (division of labor), number of hierarchical levels, number of divisions, and number of sections within branches or divisions.

In Blau's view, structural components become formally distinguished when differences in "status and social affiliation" formally designate those who "belong to different groups and subunits of various sorts [p. 203]." The direct effect of differentiation is to produce a "subdivision of responsibility" along lines of "specialized competence" or "function" [p. 203].

Any one of Blau's empirical measures, or an index constructed from all of them, might offer the best estimate of the range of specialized *activities* and *affiliations* within municipal political systems. Useful as this might be, the necessary data are simply unavailable. Data compilations such as the *Municipal Year Book* or the *U.S. Census of Governments* do not include information on any one of Blau's empirical measures. The closest measurable approximation would be to count the number of functional areas in which each municipality has some staff.

A counting-of-the-functions measure might be made to correspond more closely to Blau's definition of differentiation by weighting each function according to some "expected degree of structural differentiation" within that function. This would produce a scale that would tap both interfunctional scope of activities and intrafunctional subdivision of responsibility. This would require data not only on the functions performed by municipal governments, but also on the probable or actual range of specialized occupations, sections, branches, divisions, or programs within each functional area. Again, however, the latter types of information are not available in any standardized form for all municipal governments.

It nonetheless seems reasonable to assume that structural and functional measures are at least modestly associated within modern municipalities. That is, the range of functions should impose relatively stringent limits on the level of structural complexity. In this sense, functional differentiation, as defined here, may be a prior condition for the emergence of divisible structural units. Although both measures may provide estimates of the range of activities, issues, and affiliations within municipal political systems, the functional measure identifies the contexts or arenas within which this range may be expanded through the subdivision of activities.

Political Integration

Another possible measure of the scope of an organized system is very simply and easily calculated from available data. As applied to political systems, this measure is merely the level of expenditures or tax revenues of governing institutions. Jacob and Teune (1964) discussed this measure as an indirect indicator of political integration:

> A broad range of social activities carried out or supported by members of a community would indicate a high degree of integration among them . . . . Cohesion is politically integrative if the political unit acting through its governing organs, adopts public policies that commit the resources of the community to common purposes. Thus, if a high portion of total community income is spent by the government, this would indicate a high level of cohesion within the political community [pp. 5–6].

What Jacob and Teune seem to be saying is that political integration is positively related to functional scope, and that the latter may be measured by governmental expenditures per dollar of aggregate personal income of constituents. They may be making an even stronger case that expenditure levels are directly integrative, but on this point they are somewhat ambiguous. In general, however, they advance the contention that the important integrative mechanism consists of fiscal attachments to issue arenas institutionally identified as corporate (i.e., municipal) affairs.

To some extent, of course, very high or very low expenditure levels may stimulate, if not compel, integrative involvement on the part of some citizens and centers of power. The same point, however, suggests one of the disadvantages of using expenditure levels as an indicator of either the activities of government or its integrative capacity. *Both inordinately high and extremely low expenditures* on, for example, public schools may be associated with intense taxpayer involvement or even with the concerted integration of local centers of power. The crucial question is whether the government has institutionalized responsibility in the issue arena within which political action is mobilized to raise, lower, or maintain expenditure levels and other performances.

Turk (1970) made a somewhat more compelling case for using municipal *revenue* as an indirect indicator of "community integration." "Municipal revenue," he wrote, indicates "the degree of control the city's government has over community affairs [p. 9]." In support of this contention, Turk presented correlation coefficients for 130 cities in which municipal revenue was associated very strongly with expenditures for education (.76), welfare (.64), and a number of other functions. "Further analysis," Turk continued, "suggested that the size of the municipal budget was also associated with the city government's share (its autonomy) vis-a-vis county, state, and federal government in the provision of education, welfare, and health services—another measure of its capacity to integrate through control [pp. 9–10]."[6]

Whereas Jacob and Teune spoke of political integration through cohesion and common purpose, Turk referred to political integration through autonomous control. Turk's language is stronger, but he is probably talking about the opposite side of the same coin used by Jacob and Teune. Like the latter authors, Turk also combines a performance measure (revenue not attributable to the distribution of governmental functions) with a measure of responsibilities ("the city government's share" in the provision of education, etc.). If the composite expenditures or revenue measure is used to denote both dimensions, a high level of performance on a function such as welfare might obscure low levels of performance or control in other areas. More importantly, high welfare expenditure might even obscure the

[6] Turk's measure of "autonomy" or "the city government's share" of expenditures in the provision of services is virtually identical to an index of "inclusiveness" constructed by Campbell and Sacks (1967) and discussed below. This indicates the great overlapping of various concepts pertaining to an organized system's scope of activities, or at least reveals the limited choices that we have for empirical indicators of aspects of scope.

probability that the city government controls little more than welfare functions. This makes it more difficult to estimate either the scope of government activities or the extent of control implicit in those activities.

Inclusiveness

Another way of measuring the scope of a government might be to somehow calculate the percentage of governmental services provided by that government. In a major study of metropolitan fiscal patterns, Campbell and Sacks (1967) computed such an "index of inclusiveness," as they called it.[7] Perhaps because Campbell and Sacks were interested in fiscal rather than organizational or more purely political characteristics of cities, they constructed their operational definition of inclusiveness from fiscal data. It consisted of the "proportion of total local government expenditures made in the central city area by the city government itself [p. 114]."

They assumed that expenditures by overlying or coterminous governments could be prorated to the city, or were "made in the central city," on a per capita basis.[8] This assumption, of course, is probably partly in error in a number of cases. Overlying governments having welfare functions may spend heavily in central cities and little in suburbs, while counties or special districts having no poverty-oriented functions may spend little in central cities. Yet, the Campbell–Sacks index of inclusiveness gives some idea of the range in fiscal burdens that is a large part of the consequences of variations in municipal functional responsibilities.

The index was computed from 1957 fiscal data for the central cities in the 24 largest metropolitan areas. As reported by Campbell and Sacks, it ranged from around 95 % inclusiveness for Boston, Baltimore, and New York to 20–40 % inclusiveness for Los Angeles, San Diego, and Houston [p. 115]. In other words, by the Campbell–Sacks index the three large Northeastern cities carry about three

[7] This index differs somewhat from the measure of inclusiveness that I devised for some earlier work (Liebert, 1974a) where I was interested in the "singleness" or inclusiveness of *legal* responsibility rather than of *fiscal* responsibility.

[8] For each governmental jurisdiction operating within a given city, this prorating procedure involves calculating the proportion of that jurisdiction's population living within the city of concern, and then multiplying this fraction by the total expenditures of the overlying jurisdiction. The sum of all such prorated within-city expenditures, when divided into the city government's expenditures, yields Campbell and Sacks' index-of-inclusiveness score.

times the local fiscal burden as do the three Southwestern cities. The reason for this is that the Southwestern cities do not have public schools, welfare, and other functions in their budgets while the Northeastern cities do.

Campbell and Sacks never explored the implications of their index. It was presented as an illustration of some of the problems involved in comparing central-city expenditures. One is left wondering what difference this makes, for New York City to have its local public-service program come almost solely from city hall, and for Los Angeles to get only a third from municipal agencies. Yet, in one sense, it is sensible that Campbell and Sacks did not carry their concept further. Both the concept of inclusiveness and those authors' measure of it imply some notion of a totally self-sustaining system, a notion foreign to their study of intergovernmental fiscal exchanges. The index will be most misleading for cities receiving substantial direct aid from other governments, direct programs and services from nonlocal governments, or not receiving any part of certain services from any public agency. The expenditures ratio does not adjust for these deviations from "inclusiveness."[9]

RELATIONSHIPS BETWEEN FUNCTIONAL AND OTHER MEASURES OF SCOPE

The distinctiveness of the functional measure of scope is that it identifies the range of contexts or arenas of political action relevant to municipal affairs. It is within these arenas and in central administration that decisions are made regarding how to carry out the various functions. The other notions of scope are broader. They include some variance in activities attributable to what the government does in each functional area. Does the government subdivide functions and develop special programs? Does it spend heavily on its functions per capita, per dollar of aggregate private income, or in relation to what other local governments spend in the city? Some of these special programs and expenditure levels are better understood as *performances,* as opposed to the more elementary concept of capability to act as indexed by the number of functions performed.

---

[9] There is another less inherent problem with the inclusiveness index. It can be calculated only if one has information on the total and within-city population of each governmental jurisdiction overlying cities. Among the censuses of governments through 1967, only the 1957 census reports data in sufficient detail to permit construction of the index, and that data only applies to cities located within Standard Metropolitan Statistical Areas.

This distinction points to the most obvious and direct way in which the functional measure of scope is related to special program development (or complexity) and to fiscal performance (or integration and share of local fiscal load). Ordinarily, cities do not spend capital or develop programs within an issue arena unless they already perform the affected function. The functional measure of scope denotes certain critical conditions about governmental role that are necessary for and prior to the elaboration of such outcomes as spending, taxing, program development, and community integration. This obvious conceptual contingency of outcomes on roles may be stated in empirical terms. Given the knowledge that governments either have or do not have responsibility for a particular function, the expected outcomes for that function will be either a zero (for governments not performing it) or a non-zero group mean (for governments performing it). This model can be expanded to include all outcomes on all functions as the dependent variable, which would be contingent upon and largely explained by a series of indicators for the presence or absence of each function. If we disregard the series of indicators and take the single overall functional-scope measure alone, much of its relationship with the outcomes-based measures of scope would be simply due to the sum of expected outcomes on each function, given the presence or absence of each function.

A second possible relationship between functional scope and the other measures is also conceivable and is much more interesting. It would consist of any increment or decrement in special program development or fiscal performance, above or below the previously expected levels associated with a city having a certain number of functions. This would be a theoretically *indirect* effect of performing various functions, for it would indicate the extent to which the overall functional scope of a government affects *how productively or energetically* it performs its functions. This last question can be phrased in terms of the extent to which a broad-scope government will elaborate or spend more on a particular function than will a narrow-scope government having the same function. Or, put another way, for all cities that perform a function, what is the effect of functional scope on their level of performance for that function?

Finally, functional scope may affect outcomes of all kinds by affecting the probability of adopting a wholly new function. All of these issues will be analyzed in more detail in later chapters, but they are introduced here to illustrate the various ways in which the outcomes-based measures of scope can be, and must be, distinguished from functional scope and considered contingent upon functional scope.

The actual correlations between the functional-scope measure and several other measures of "integration" and "fiscal inclusiveness" are presented in Table II-5. The sources for the data are noted in the table. The "Index of fiscal inclusiveness" was computed according to the formula noted earlier, following coding rules used by Campbell and Sacks and described to the author through personal communication from Sacks. Note that this index applies only to the 201 cities in Standard Metropolitan Statistical Areas in 1957. Measures of complexity were not available and are therefore not presented in the table.

As expected, Table II-5 shows very high positive relationships between functional scope and all of the other measures. Approximately half of the variance in per capita municipal expenditures, per capita municipal tax revenue, expenditures per dollar private income, per capita municipal employees, and fiscal inclusiveness are associated with functional scope. Moreover, it really doesn't matter which of these measures is used; they all have nearly identical correlations with functional scope.

It is, of course, important to note that the relationships in Table II-5 are not perfect. There are variations in fiscal performance, in

TABLE II-5

Correlations between Functional Scope and other Measures of the Scope of Municipal Government

Other measures of scope	Zero-order correlation with functional scope
Per capita municipal employees[a]	.75
Campbell and Sack's index of fiscal inclusiveness[b]	.74
Per capita municipal expenditures[a]	.72
Per capita municipal tax revenue[a]	.74
Municipal expenditure per dollar of aggregate personal income[c]	.77

[a] *U.S. Census of Governments: 1962*, Vol. IV. ($N = 668$ cities; missing data for five cities were coded with the mean for the other 663 cities).

[b] Computed according to Campbell and Sack's formula (see text) from data contained in *U.S. Census of Governments: 1957*, Vol. III, Table 6. ($N = 201$ cities in Standard Metropolitan Statistical Areas).

[c] Although the municipal expenditures data was taken from the 1962 *U.S. Census of Governments* (see Note a), the aggregate personal income data is for 1959 as reported in the *County and City Data Book: 1962*, ($N = 668$ cities).

inclusiveness, in governmental manpower, and certainly in special program development as well, which are unrelated to functional scope. These unrelated aspects are due partially to various errors of measurement, but also to real differences in the conceptions and measures of scope. Those outcomes that are unrelated to functional scope, like those contingent on it, should clearly be treated separately from scope as outcomes to be explained by properties of the political system.

Yet, the strong relationships among the findings in Table II-5 also need to be stressed. The high correlations provide a kind of validation for the functional-scope measure, indicating that it has indeed much commonality with several more general governmental attributes that are, in theory, closely dependent on functional scope. It is here that we return to emphasis of the commonalities of the theoretical constructs themselves and not just their measures. In this very general sense, functional scope is one indicator among many for identifying a set of theoretically overlapping concepts concerned with the extent to which diverse activities are organized within a single, formal entity. Different aspects or images of this generalized conception are evoked by such notions as community political integration through municipal government, the governmental inclusiveness of a municipality, its complexity, and its functional scope. Each may raise somewhat different questions, but what they all share is an attempt to distinguish between political systems having many different tasks rather than a few limited ones. Here, we focus on functional scope as a necessary and generally overlooked precondition for the elaboration of most, if not all, of what may be called a government's role, scope, and activity.

There are other reasons why it is useful to step down from such concepts as "inclusiveness" and "community integration." These concepts are difficult to apply to the modern city, partly because of variation in functional scope. They are older concepts than the increasingly familiar reality of functionally and governmentally fragmented cities. They refer to ideal-type cities that are no longer typical. Yet, these older concepts have some use in interpreting the trends that have shaped American cities into highly varied and often fragmented political systems. The following chapter analyzes the trend away from inclusive, integrated communities, and the effects of this trend on differences in the functional scope of municipal governments.

III.

The Varying Functions of City Governments: Explorations into Origins[1]

[O] rganizational forms and types have a history, and . . . this history determines some aspects of the present structure of organizations of that type. The organizational inventions that can be made at a particular time in history depend on the social technology available at the time. [From Stinchcombe, A.L., Social structure and organizations, in *Handbook of organizations,* edited by J.G. March. Copyright © 1965 by Rand-McNally, Chicago, p. 153].

Why have some municipal governments acquired responsibility for a broad service program consisting of most major local government functions, while others have a far simpler and smaller set of functions? What accounts for variations in the functional scope of municipal governments in America? An examination of these questions entails an interpretation of three of the major forces that have shaped community development.

The first of these is the force of local tradition, deriving from historical political cultures and institutional forms, which may continue to shape the governmental systems in specific cities and

---

[1] This is an expanded adaptation of Liebert (1975).

35

regions. Sociologists do not generally explore historical references even in studies of change, partly because of the difficulties of acquiring quantifiable data from early records. Yet if the limited amounts of currently available cross-sectional data are to be interpreted properly, it is important to draw some inferences from less quantifiable observations on earlier political communities. Lipset (1970:3–34) discusses this approach at length in his comment on the recent "revival" of interest in historical sociology. He and others involved in this emerging literature stress that an historically informed sociology depends particularly on the historical application of the concept of social roles or, more precisely, on a concern with the expectations that any set of contemporaries holds for such social units as a status position or an organization (Cochran 1963). Through explicit comparisons of the role of current governments with the role of government in the past, the analysis on the following pages reveals the significance of tradition in producing the present situation with respect to functional scope.

A second force affecting community development, and one of the most widely discussed in the sociological literature (e.g., Boskoff 1970:23–25, Gist and Fava 1969:Part 3, Greer *et al.* 1968), concerns the growing national complexity and interdependency of the bureaucratic organizations affecting community affairs, with their tendency to turn some functions of government into specialized nonmunicipal governmental or private operations, and to turn many others into segmented branches of centralized state or national governing apparatuses. The battlefront for these trends, as for other major trends in community development (Lipset 1959, Ladd 1969), has been the growth of the state's power to intervene in the local scene with attempts to rescue an increasingly interdependent private economy and formally unrelated local polities from instability, stagnation, or social injustice. Weber (1946:183–194, 228), in discussing these and other organizational trends toward overcoming and supplanting autonomous community institutions, termed them the process of "societalization."

Most cities are certainly affected to some extent by these national developments, but the question is whether and how these trends lead to the location of governmental functions within some municipal governments, but not others. To answer this question, some institutional histories for particular functions are reviewed and then interpreted in light of current cross-sectional data on the national distribution of municipal responsibility for these functions. The findings show the emergence of city-age cohorts characterized by new types of municipal organization at each step in the history of the societalization of America.

A third force, to which urban ecologists and kindred students of the metropolitan area have given greatest attention, concerns the growth of urban population, and the dual pressures of urbanization on local government to provide more services and to splinter into the characteristic metropolitan mosaic of many separate governments. On this issue there are some quantifiable indicators of urban status, which will be introduced and analyzed towards the end of the chapter. The ecologists' contention that technological development, as well as population, affects organizational change will also be considered in this context. The inferences drawn from the entire analysis lend little direct support to either of these ecological postulates, while emphasizing instead the other two forces: (1) the generation of various cohorts of local organization by the superior force of progressively more interdependent nonlocal organization, and (2) the simple force of local tradition by which cities maintain the organizational residues of past cultural conditions.

The point of departure, or the character of American cities in the earliest cohort, is of immediate interest. Most theoretical notions about community political development implicitly *assume* something about the character of precontemporary cities. A familiar example, developed by such writers as Nisbet (1962), Greer (1962a), and Stein (1964), refers to a "loss of community," but provides little specific information about what that community was. Ostensibly new definitions of cities and urban places (as reviewed by Gutman and Popenoe 1970:9–17) or of communities (Hillery, 1968) abound, even though little evidence is ordinarily presented to sustain the claim that old realities resoundingly fail to fit the new definitions.

Here, we begin by briefly describing early municipalities in some detail, relying most heavily on Griffith's *History of American City Government: The Colonial Period* (1938) and on Glaab and Brown's *A History of Urban America* (1967). Attention is centered specifically on the *functions* of city government, and on inferences that can be drawn regarding the reasons for the scope of those functions. There is no comprehensive or definitive history of the development of municipal government functions, or of local government functions in general. Until such a history is written, rather general inferences such as the ones drawn in the following will have to serve as general guidelines to this aspect of our national history.

THE POINT OF DEPARTURE: COLONIAL CITIES

Most of the cities in colonial America were governed by a fairly simple and unitary political system. Public affairs in the incorporated cities, and even in the unincorporated towns in the northern colonies, generally devolved upon an inclusive municipal or town government, which had the responsibility for initiating and regulating the full range of service functions received by a community. The irony of colonial urban development, as Glaab and Brown suggested (1967:2), was that the cities and towns became model independent societies long before the American nation itself achieved independence (see also Bridenbaugh, 1955). Although colonial authorities were menacing in their mercantilist control over external markets and taxation policies, they tended to permit and even encourage the development of internally autonomous, inclusive and self-governing urban centers (Griffith 1938:51–74).

From the perspective of the British Crown, the colonies were primarily important as sources of raw materials and capital. To provide these benefits, there were only isolated craftsmen, merchants, and artisans in the urban areas, and scattered farmers, woodsmen, and traders in the hinterland. Lacking any other means of monitoring production and exportation, Britain and her colonial magistrates actively pursued the establishment of cities and towns as combination commercial and governmental structures. By granting city and town governments extensive powers over commerce and urban development, the Crown hoped to create a local agency that would use the powers of government to coordinate and stimulate commercial affairs.

British attempts to create these kinds of cities were felt in all of the colonies, but were particularly strenuous north of the Carolinas where settlements tended to occur in towns. In the Jerseys, towns and boroughs were granted broad municipal powers in the hope that each would develop as a market or port. These powers often included authority to outlaw or regulate competition in certain crafts and trades, exclusive right to products from the hinterlands, and authority to build and maintain any desired port facilities, public markets, and ferries and trade roads (Griffith 1938: 99–125). In New England, the tradition of powerful and inclusive local government was universally applied in the form of small towns that covered every acre of the settled areas. Colonial New England towns are celebrated in Zuckerman's (1970) study as "peaceable little kingdoms" that managed their own commercial and political affairs through "common communal governments."

In a general sense, however, the New England towns were not exceptionally different from most other colonial cities. The major difference was that most New England towns did not generally have legal charters of incorporation. With regard to the formality of incorporation, cities in Vermont and Virginia were polar cases (Paullin 1932, Bain 1967: 4–11). The Virginia colonial General Assembly readily incorporated cities, granting them the extensive powers elsewhere granted to cities, but was relatively unsuccessful in attracting large populations to them. Finally, scattered up and down the seaboard between Virginia and New England, a number of other major cities—Baltimore, Annapolis, Wilmington, Philadelphia, New York, and Albany in particular—were also incorporated with rather inclusive powers over internal affairs and with urban populations to use them as well.

The powers granted colonial cities and towns were eagerly sought and jealously protected by the townsmen. If the inferences Griffith draws from his analysis of colonial cities are correct, the townsmen who made a livelihood of commerce and crafts found the arrangement particularly suitable to the promotion and protection of their enterprises, although they resisted paying the Crown its share of the return. The economic fate of the commercial and craftsmen classes rested largely with the capacity of the town or city government to regulate competition, provide markets, and attract and compel traders from the hinterland to exchange their commodities in the town or city.

If this portrait of the colonial-period cities is translated into the language of the modern era, it describes a municipal government that had virtually exclusive jurisdiction over the full range of governmental functions that might be performed in the city. Of course, not all of the functions familiar to us today were then being performed by any government. Sewers were roadside gutters, sanitation and health tended to be private matters, "charities" were often voluntary contributions, and only in New England were "free schools" sometimes operated by municipal or town governments (Maclear 1967: 161–2, Griffith 1938: 266–91). Yet, to the extent that any of these were or might become public functions, the municipal government had the sole responsibility to assume the burden.

In most of these features, colonial American cities roughly resembled European cities of the same period. Stephenson's (1933) study of urban origins in England points to the emergence of a commercial class, the "burgess," and its acquisition of privileged self-government as the basis for the relative autonomy and governmental unity of English cities at the time of American colonization. Similarly, Max Weber (1958: 87–96) singled out the occidental cities of the seventeenth and eighteenth centuries as exemplary of a unique form of city that gained its distinction from its special stratum of "burghers" and commercial tradesmen. In Weber's terms, these burghers bonded together into a single "common communal association" through which they exercised "autonomous self-administration" over the commercial and governmental affairs of the city. Particularly important to Weber was the control that this government had over substantive and formal law. Weber believed that wherever civil disputes were within the jurisdiction of state-established "special administrative districts" and were no longer local and autonomous, the administration of city affairs could never be truely communal. Not surprisingly, both Weber and Stephenson reserved the special word "community" rather than our general words "city" or "municipality" for the governmentally inclusive and relatively autonomous cities they described.

NATIONAL GROWTH AND FUNCTIONAL DISPERSAL

What has happened to the American colonial cities and towns that once had this "community" character? What factors account for subsequent variations in the functional scope of municipalities? One perspective in which these questions might be considered focuses on the thesis that political and economic organizations have become increasingly interdependent on a national scale and in a manner that may be described as centralization. Three syntheses of the community studies literature, by Stein (1964), Greer (1962a), and Nisbet (1962), have contributed extensively to the development of this thesis.

The General Trend

Stein derived his synthesis largely from the urban studies of Park (1952), Lynd and Lynd (1929, 1937), and Warner (1963). Each of these researchers focused, in Stein's view, on the processes by which large-scale national organizations were produced. The growth of metropolitan areas, the development of new industrial technologies, and the emergence of efficient modes for organizing specialized occupations all produced new and diverse organizations in cultural, economic, and governmental fields. As the variety of organizations grew in number, they also grew in interrelatedness. Stein stressed the patterns of vertical interrelatedness, i.e., the linkage between local organizations and those not so local. He therefore found "the one underlying trend" in community development to be "toward increasing interdependence and decreased local autonomy [p. 107]." This trend, Stein emphasized, could be seen most clearly in the transformation of Yankee City's locally owned leather shops into branches of large bureaucracies that had central headquarters elsewhere. Similarly, Yankee City's welfare or relief programs, its eventual labor unions, and other activities became local adjuncts to nationwide bureaucracies.

Greer examined much the same literature that concerned Stein and came up with a slightly different interpretation. While Stein stressed the trend toward vertical interdependence, Greer stressed the complementary trend toward local differentiation into horizontally interdependent organizations and associations. Greer saw a growing national pluralism in the types of organized groups affecting community life, whereas Stein saw a growing external centralization in the various sources of influence or centers of power shaping community affairs. These perspectives do have a common point, however; and it is this commonality that is most important.

Both Stein and Greer agree that governments and organizations other than the common association of the "community" or municipality have come to play an increasingly significant role in the civic life of the city dwellers. Both refer to this trend in terms of increasing extracommunity organizational influences and attachments and growth in scale of separate organizations. In place of the political integration of an inclusive and relatively autonomous municipal government, there now exists a broader system, a national network of interdependent organizations, which is represented in any city's governing processes by several tiers of governments all providing or funding services of various types for the city.

This generalization and the community literature on which it is based provide few specific references to the kinds of governmental functions over which municipalities may have lost administrative control. They do imply, however, that no functions are administered any longer in a fully autonomous way, and that all are associated with centers of power—resources, regulatory bodies, planners and experts—located outside the city and often in national and state governments. These assumptions have come to be fairly widely accepted in the community-studies literature (e.g., Warren *et al.* 1974, Turk 1970, 1973b, Aiken and Alford 1970a, 1970b), yet they do not alone tell us why the functional scope of modern cities should vary widely. A closer inspection of what has happened to specific functions, particularly the ones least likely to be contemporary municipal responsibilities, would be helpful at this point.

The "Judicial" Function and Emergence of County Administrative Districts

The transformation of judicial and certain other minor administrative functions from predominantly municipal to predominately county responsibilities is related to the growth in scale, diversity, and bureaucratization of commercial affairs. During most of the colonial period, commerce and industry were primarily matters of individual enterprise by isolated townsmen, or at most were organized into small shops with strictly local employment. Municipal governments developed as associations through which these independent artisans and merchants could organize and secure protections, amenities, and (most significantly) a mutually acceptable judicial system for interpreting and securing civil agreements or commercial contracts (Griffith 1938: 102–3, 126–7).

As the date of the eventual rebellion neared, however, increasing numbers of townsmen were becoming agents or workers for growing local enterprises, particularly in the shipping and trading industries (Jensen 1963, Morgan 1956, Washburn 1840). These industries generally had only one main shop and headquarters; but they also had agents scattered throughout the hinterland and on ships calling on ports up and down the coast. So long as law was locally interpreted and made, the shippers and traders found their agents subject to nonuniform legal restraints. Contracts written in one place were sometimes not honored in another, for each locality sought to protect its own economy. This problem was exacerbated in areas under direct British rule, where the colonists' growing shipping and trading industries presented unwelcomed threats to the Crown's early monopoly over long-distance interlocal commerce.

The development of large, independent colonial commercial organizations meant three things: (1) The local municipal or community governments were already being partially "eclipsed," to use Stein's word, as the industries assumed some of the responsibility for coordinating commerce that the cities once had. Some strictly commercial functions of community government, eventually included the now rare public market, were lost to the new industrial organizations, to their owners, and to the not-so-communal associations that industrial leaders increasingly formed (Griffith 1938: 158–9). (2) Because the new industries greatly expanded interlocal commerce, they established some of the first forms of interdependence between cities and made clear the need for a uniform system of justice to protect this interdependence from insolvable legal disputes. One can reasonably assume that this need was felt not only in the cities, but also in the various hinterlands claimed by the cities and colonies. (3) The new industries met with resistance from the Crown's monopolies over interlocal commerce, and thereby helped to stimulate, if not lead, the drive for independence from Britain (Morgan, 1956).

Consistent with these generalizations, some of the first actions taken by leaders of the new independent nation were to begin establishing a uniform system of justice. The Supreme Court was constitutionally vested with jurisdiction over "controversies . . . between a State and citizens of another State." Much of the work of the early Supreme Court, from the Dartmouth case through the first interpretations of the Fourteenth Amendment, consisted of developing uniform applications of contract law among corporate "persons." In local government, the new system of justice means that cities no longer develop and administer autonomous law, particularly in the common law areas of contracts and agreements (Seasongood 1934: 1–24). Cities make contracts but no longer have the sole power to enforce or dissolve them. The federal constitution, as well as the state constitutions and statutes and certain generally accepted "due process" protections, are often applicable even in minor police-court proceedings.

The application of this system of justice took its most distinctive form in the expanding frontiers of the West. The standard procedure was for territorial governments, and later state governments, to establish the principal judicial system in areally-defined administrative districts even before settlement. These districts, or counties as they were officially identified, have never had a tradition of autonomy, but have always been creatures of the state having specifically assigned state functions (Porter 1922: 99–100, 156–157). By the time of the revolution, most judicial functions had become state or federal functions, and counties in the frontier were assigned the responsibility for administering many of them. Other related state functions, such as the keeping of legal records and the administration of elections, were part of this judicial package assigned to counties

(Porter 1922). As cities developed in the frontier, they typically remained subject to the judicial powers of the overlying counties. Often, however, narrowly construed police courts and specialized general trial courts were placed under the jurisdiction of municipal governments, with the more general common courts having county affiliation (Phillips 1954: 341).

Significantly, those cities for which a colonial tradition of judicial autonomy had been established often retained administrative responsibility for these state-supervised judicial functions. That is, counties and other districts were not generally superimposed on many of these ex-colonial cities. In this case, the prevailing system of local government was simply adapted to the standards of uniform justice within the judicial profession, without the complete disruption of this function from traditional local ideas about the appropriate functions of government.

This is particularly true in New England and Virginia, states which, as colonies, established general policies by which all cities were free from county jurisdiction. Several cities in the mid-Atlantic region had county districts superimposed on them for a period of several decades, but in the cases of Baltimore and New York City, they were eventually, in effect, reunited into one municipal government. Interestingly, the only cities outside the colonial states that lacked overlying counties according to the coding system used earlier are those that were most clearly Western commercial centers during the mid-nineteenth century. Although San Francisco, Denver, St. Louis, and New Orleans all have unique explanations for their exceptional status as cities without overlying counties (see National Municipal League 1930: 170–204), they also have a common status as cities that had significant control over patterns of commerce and trade during the nineteenth century. These exceptional cities do not contradict the thesis developed above. Several more recent city–county unifications, resulting from contemporary consolidation movements, are not included in the measure of functional scope, due to their recency (Winter 1969: 201–14).

Finally, it should be noted that the colonies south of Virginia had no cities that today possess the judicial function as defined here. These states were primarily plantation colonies before independence, and both townsmen and colonial authorities refused to subject the economy of the plantations to the broad powers of colonial cities (Griffith 1938: 51–74). Instead, the entire colony of Georgia was made into a single "municipal corporation," whereas the Carolinas were governed somewhat more locally by counties. In each case, the economy was too rural and spread out to permit coordination within compact community governments.

A somewhat different but wholly compatible account of the emergence of counties was reported by Stephan (1971). Stephan's central concern was with the areal *size* of counties, which he demonstrated to be larger as one moves west from the small towns of the New England area. He reasoned, following Durkheim's theory of *The Division of Labor in Society* (1933: 181–187), that the small community settlements of New England were organized when there was minimal diversity of social type and minimal interlocal exchanges or interdependence, as indexed in Stephan's study by the sophistication of the transportation system, a concept not dissimilar from that of the organizational scale of colonial shipping and trading industries. The simplicity of social structure was reflected in settlement units having general functions. Increasing division of labor and interdependence (i.e., sophisticated transportation to Stephan) produced larger settlement and administrative areas having, in the beginning at least, more specialized functions.

Education and Welfare Functions

Similar developments can be traced with respect to public education and welfare functions. The origins of the public education system were again in New England, with differing institutional forms developing in most other parts of the country. Katz (1968, 1970) interpreted the movement for educational reform that culminated in compulsory public schools as largely a drive toward a uniform system of instruction that would overcome the dissimilarities in the amount and type of learning imparted to the young in increasingly diverse types of voluntary or neighborhood schools. The voluntary, neighborhood school systems were suitable for an earlier period when social differences were minimal. But, as the cities became centers of new immigrant neighborhoods, the older schools failed to provide socialization in common ways, and were indeed held responsible by many reformers for the persistence of poverty, idleness, and rude manners among the immigrants who controlled their own schools or did not attend them.

The drive for a uniform system of instruction was led, in Katz's analysis, by schoolmen who saw in a professionally controlled, publicly supported school system the only appropriate alternative. In the older cities in the Northeast, the battle for school reform was fought at two levels. At the state level, there were mounting pressures from reform advocates to institute statewide standards. Within the traditional agencies of local government, the municipalities, school reform necessarily involved a political conflict between beneficiaries of the older system, particularly immigrant groups and other lower class citizens who perceived a threat to their cultural continuity, and the new advocates of a more homogenizing instructional system. In contrast, throughout most of the rest of the nation during the mid-nineteenth century, the objectives of the reformers were most easily obtained by appealing to state and territorial governments to create special school districts before other traditions of schooling could set in.

Wilensky and Lebeaux (1965) reported the development of public welfare programs in America in similar terms. They begin with the observation that early American, and particularly preindustrial forms of aid to dependent persons were generally intrafamily responsibilities or, on occasion, volunteer and local community responsibilities consisting of poor houses, insane asylums, and the like (pp. 49–89). These simple forms of "institutionalized" aid were serviceable for an economy that operated largely on a local scale, where productive skills could be learned within the family, and where unemployed dependents lacking attachments to families were few. Sustained in principle by the English cultural inheritance of the Poor Law, this early system prescribed that any public, governmental responsibility for aid "must be minimal, deterrent, local, and it remained so with remarkably little change in the U.S. until the depression thirties [p. 148]."

Certainly the greatest change in the American system of public welfare occurred during the 1930s as part of the New Deal federal intervention into matters of general domestic welfare. Yet, long before the Great Depression, there were other incipient developments that paved the road to the New Deal through the emergence of large area-wide organizations having some responsibility for welfare. Wilensky and Libeaux described the most important of these in the following way:

> During the nineteenth century state governments came to the fore as the major instruments of social welfare. "Welfare statism" was far from public consciousness. But under the stress of problems engendered by changed life conditions—cities growing, factories multiplying, heavy immigration—social services multiplied under the state auspices: asylums for the mentally disturbed (Virginia, 1773), schools for the deaf (Connecticut, 1817), reformatories for juveniles (New York, 1825). There were so many, finally, that

central supervisory bodies were forced into being (Massachusetts Board of State Charities, 1863). These, taking on administrative authority, evolved into the presently universal state departments of welfare . . . [p. 149].

The emergence of centralized state responsibility for many welfare activities may be traced, following Wilensky and Libeaux, to the effects of a growing urban industrialism on the integrity of the family and community as self-sustaining institutions. "The inability of the individual to provide fully for himself, or to meet all his needs in family and work settings, is considered a 'normal' condition [p. 140]." While values of this sort undergirded increased state intervention, there were additional and more formal organizational forces at work as well. One of these, noted above by Wilensky and Libeaux, was simply the growth in the number of specific social welfare services under the auspices not only of state governments, but also of local governments and of private or volunteer organizations. As the number of such service programs grew, so too did the pressure for public sponsorship, accountability, and professional standards to reduce possibilities of exploitation, degradation of clients, or ineffective piecemeal programs (pp. 140–5). These pressures for organization realignment came most strongly from some of the leading social workers of the nineteenth century, who were already bonding together into multicity, interstate, and programmatically comprehensive associations of professionals (p. 326).

Piven and Cloward (1971) carried this analysis further by emphasizing the growing political and economic significance of social welfare. To explain why relief arrangements exist and expand, they noted the important functions of maintaining civil order among people of marginal attachments and social utility, and of enforcing work among those marginal people who fail to meet varying standards of eligibility for welfare. The key to performing these two delicately balanced functions successfully rests in the capacity of the welfare system to vary standards of eligibility over time, so that civil order is only occasionally jeopardized for the sake of cheap labor. Control of this precision could not rest with individual local governments and still be effective. A trend toward supralocal control and funding of welfare provided greater stability for the increasingly interdependent economy and federal political system.

When, in response to these conditions and trends, state governments began exercising regulatory, supervisory, and fiscal powers over welfare activities, they typically worked through administrative districts (e.g., counties) covering the entire state. Fairlie (1898) noted that this transition occurred in New York State during the years 1820 to 1830, and that the resulting county-administered system of charities and poorhouses had the advantage of simplifying the number of different types of governments through which the state had to work (pp. 78–123). The chief exception to this pattern in New York and in other states was, once again, in those cities or regions where municipal government had already established traditional rights to administrative responsibility for most or all local government functions.

Summary of Trends Affecting "Social-Justice" Functions

As the American economy grew in scale from community craftsmen to nationwide organizational networks, certain unstable features of this economy became evident. The problem was one of securing and maintaining an increasingly interdependent private economy in the face of growing complexity and cleavages within the social structure. Solutions were sought in state and, increasingly, federal guarantees of elementary forms of social justice. Among these were a more uniform system of substantive and procedural law affecting corporate and commercial relationships or transactions; a more standardized system of childhood socialization (or education) to recruit productive participants from lagging sectors of the social structure; and a publicly supported and professionally directed system of social security for those who would continue to lag or would be displaced by ruptures of older institutions such as the family.

These social-justice functions were recognized rather early in the experience of the new nation as having implications that extended far beyond the parochial confines of a neighborhood or community. Emerging interlocal professional groups (e.g., lawyers, educators, social workers) were particularly vocal in advancing this perspective, perhaps partly because they envisioned greater professional leverage over the development of uniform standards through the elimination of strictly local, fragmented, parochial control. As a result, responsibility for general supervision and regulation of the social-justice functions became nested in higher-level governments throughout the United States.

This manner of centralization, although nowhere complete and autarchic, has nonetheless greatly reduced the significance of local *administrative* responsibility for carrying out the social-justice functions. Powers are now shared in such a manner as to make local administrative units partially dependent on state or federal agencies for regulatory supervision and some funding, even while the local units retain substantial discretion. Yet, for many city governments, the "loss" of power has been total. The centralizing trend with respect to some functions has removed any opportunity for many newer city governments to initiate or administer governmental responsibilities in the basic social-justice areas. Other state-created special administrative districts have been delegated this responsibility in places and regions of the nation where a tradition of city responsibility was not previously established.

Regional Location and City Age as Indicators of These Trends

Some empirical evidence supporting these general observations is presented in Table III-1. For eight regions of the nation, this table shows the percent of city governments in each region having responsibility for each of nine different functions during the modern era (the early 1960s). The eight regions may be considered somewhat distinctive from each other with respect to patterns of political development. That is, the regional categories are rough indices of (1) the stage of national development when political jurisdictions were first organized in the area, and more specifically, (2) the extent to which centralization and nonmunicipal assignment of functions had progressed when ideas about the appropriate scope of municipal government were ingrained in the traditions of local political culture.

The major social-justice functions (judicial, educational, and welfare) are most likely to be municipal responsibilities in New England, where the colonial tradition of broad-scope community governments persists. Somewhat less likely to have administrative responsibilities for these functions are cities in the Middle-Atlantic region, where functionally inclusive community governments occurred only occasionally during the colonial era. The East Border states, and particularly Virginia, have many cities retaining similar colonial traditions. Elsewhere in the United States, in areas that developed after the Revolution, municipal responsibility for basic social-justice functions occurs today in only a few rare instances. Most of these situations developed, as in New Orleans, St. Louis, Denver, and San Francisco, in cities that emerged as early regional centers of commerce, exercising broad governmental powers even before their hinterlands became organized under territorial or state governments.

It is interesting to note that the health function and, to a lesser extent, the hospitals function tend to follow the same pattern by regions as do the basic social-justice functions. As one moves west-

TABLE III-1

Percentage of Municipalities Having Responsibility for Each Major Governmental Function, by Region

	New England	Middle Atlantic	East Border	Deep South	West Border	Northwest Territory	Midcontinent Highlands	Far West
				Region[a]				
Welfare, Fed. Aid	55%	7%	32%	0%	1%	1%	2%	1%
Judicial	100	2	32	1	1	0	2	1
Hospitals	25	12	35	15	15	9	11	2
Education	98	37	59	4	4	13	2	0
Welfare, Gen. Asst.	100	43	56	1	16	9	10	1
Health	97	80	88	60	84	69	73	32
Parks and Rec.	92	91	82	96	90	79	92	95
Sanitation	56	77	94	94	84	73	67	47
Sewers	47	52	79	70	77	54	79	48
Total number of cities	(64)	(97)	(34)	(84)	(73)	(154)	(63)	(99)

[a]States comprising each region are as follows: New England = Maine, New Hampshire, Vermont, Massachusetts, Connecticut, Rhode Island. Middle Atlantic = New Jersey, New York, Pennsylvania, Maryland, Delaware. East Border = Virginia, West Virginia, Kentucky, Tennessee. Deep South = Louisiana, Alabama, Mississippi, Florida, Georgia, North Carolina, South Carolina. West Border = Texas, Oklahoma, Kansas, Missouri, Arkansas. Northwest Territory = Ohio, Indiana, Illinois, Michigan, Wisconsin. Midcontinent Highlands = Minnesota, Iowa, North Dakota, South Dakota, Nebraska, Montana, Idaho, Colorado, Utah, Wyoming, New Mexico. Far West = California, Oregon, Washington, Nevada.

ward from New England, the probability that city governments will exercise some responsibility for these functions declines. The health and hospitals functions might therefore be included in the set of basic social-justice functions which, in more recently organized areas of the nation, do not accrue to municipal government. In this light, it should also be noted that the health and hospitals functions, along with welfare and education, comprise Fairlie's (1898) list of major functions that underwent significant state centralization during the nineteenth century. This trend, of course, continues today, going beyond the state boards of health of the last century, beyond the county health agents organized under the New Deal, and increasingly involving federal and state health-care and insurance programs. There is even a tendency for the federally administered Veteran's Administration hospitals to be expanded and opened to more citizens, as proposed in legislation of the 1972 U.S. Congress (*The New York Times*, Oct. 14, 1972, p. 19) and approved in a rewritten and weaker form by President Nixon (*The New York Times*, August 3, 1973, p. 60).

The deviant functions in Table III-1 are the least people-oriented ones, sanitation and sewers. These have the greatest probability of being municipal functions, *not* in New England, but in some of the least urbanized areas of the nation—notably in the border states and in the South. In this instance, it seems probable that state centralization was not the prevailing response to problems of areawide coordination or standardization of these functions. Other more localized explanations for variations in municipal scope may be relevant here, and some of these will be discussed in the section that follows on urban growth and suburban status.

In addition to regional differences in functional assignment patterns, there is a second way of identifying the historical origins of municipal functional scope. The age of a city, dated from when it first achieved a certain minimal size, should be a fairly valid indicator of the level of state centralization prevailing at the time that unique local political cultures and institutional arrangements were established. The age of a city has implications somewhat different from those of its regional location in that the latter includes the broader contextual effects of a regional tradition, whereas city age more narrowly identifies traditions dominant when the city was organized. This distinction is particularly relevant for cities like St. Louis or San Francisco, which emerged under traditions that predated the organization of their respective territorial and state governments, and therefore differ distinctively from most other cities in their areas of the nation.

The city-age indicator may also be relevant to cities emerging more recently. America's increasingly national urban environment provides new cities with examples of how to organize local government that go beyond local, state, and even regional points of reference. Fads in politics, as in other domains, are now communicated nationwide. In short, the trend toward effacement of municipal powers discussed in the foregoing and indicated in the regional differences in municipal scope may be more fully specified by taking city age as another indicator of the stage in this trend when each city "inherited" certain parameters in relation to its functional scope. Newer cities should have inherited narrower scope than older cities.

A competing interpretation of city age should also be considered. One might argue that some, or even most, city governments accumulate functions as they age due to various factors. As distinguished from the "inheritance" theory, this accumulation or "achievement" theory would hold that cities add on new functions over time as they experience increasing need for protection of a deteriorating physical environment, and as they experience new demands for services from clients who establish increasing interface and involvement with, as well as reliance on, the government over time. One might even suggest that cities accumulate functions over time as a result of the general underlying trend toward increasing complexity of organization at all levels of our society.

There is, however, another side to this accumulation theory. Many functions are accumulated by some government, but become assigned to nonmunicipal governments often because of state centralization of functional supervision. This process imposes limits on the functional scope of municipalities emerging at various points in time. Since most of the major functions under consideration here are probably being performed by some government or quasi-government for modern cities over 25,000 in population, it is not likely that much variation in scope can be caused by new cities not yet generating functions performed by older ones. The best interpretation of city age, then, is that it indicates an inherited potential scope, much of which has probably been attained or always performed for major functions.

Table III-2 presents evidence on the relationship between city age and functional scope. Age cohorts are defined in terms of the decade when they reached a population of 10,000 or more. For example, the oldest age cohort in Table III-2 consists of cities that reached 10,000 by the time of the 1840 Census. The next four age cohorts are cities reaching 10,000 within each of the following four 20-year

TABLE III-2

Percentage of Municipalities in Each of Six Age Cohorts Having at Least "n" Number of Major Functions

Municipal age cohort[a]	Number of functions									All cities in the cohort[b]
	All 9	8 or more	7 or more	6 or more	5 or more	4 or more	3 or more	2 or more	1 or more	
(1) Before 1841	6.9%	24.1%	48.2%	62.0%	72.5%	82.8%	93.1%	100%	100%	100% (29)
(2) 1841-1860	1.8	10.6	31.7	45.7	63.2	89.5	94.8	100	100	100 (59)
(3) 1861-1880	.0	5.6	13.9	22.2	36.1	75.9	91.6	97.2	100	100 (108)
(4) 1881-1900	.0	2.3	9.2	16.1	32.1	60.3	87.8	96.2	100	100 (131)
(5) 1901-1920	.0	.7	3.5	7.0	16.7	46.6	79.2	95.2	99.4	100 (144)
(6) After 1920	.0	.5	.5	2.0	6.0	22.6	48.7	71.8	96.4	100 (199)
All cities	.4	3.6	9.7	15.4	26.0	52.1	75.7	89.4	98.8	100 (668)

[a]Defined by year municipality first reached 10,000 population. Source: *U.S. Census of the Population: 1960,* Volume I, Table 5.
[b]Number of cities in each cohort is given in parentheses.

intervals. The relationship with functional scope is stated in Table III-2 in terms of the percentage of cities in each age cohort having a minimal number of major functions. That is, the percentages are cumulative, beginning with 6.9 % of the oldest cities having 9 functions, proceeding to 24.1% having 8 *or* 9, and ending with 100.0 % having at least 2 of the major functions (not counting police, fire, roads, and central administration). This cumulative approach facilitates comparison across age cohorts.

As expected, the relationship between city age and functional scope is both strong and monotonic. Whereas about a quarter (24.1 %) of the oldest cohort have at least 8 of the functions and nearly half (48.2 %) have at least 7, comparable proportions for the newest cohort (those reaching 10,000 population after the 1920 Census) are about 1 in 200. Between these extreme age cohorts, the percentage of intervening cohorts having at least 7 functions steadily declines from 31.7 % of the cities in the 1841–1860 cohort to 3.5 % of the cities in the 1901–1920 cohort. These middle-range cities (in terms of age) have had at least 40 years to "accumulate" functions, which, given modern rates of social change, should or could be enough time to "catch up," were it not for differences in what has been called inheritance.

A more useful comparison for interpreting the monotonic relationship might be to consider the minimal number of functions over which a bare majority of cities in each age cohort exercise responsibility. For the oldest group (emerging prior to 1841) over half have at least six, almost seven functions. In the 1841–1860 cohort, the "wide-scope" majority includes cities with only five functions. This drops to four functions among the 1861–1880 and 1881–1900 cohorts, to three functions among cities in the 1901–1920 cohort, and among those in the 1921-and-after cohort a majority of wide-scope cities is reached only when we include some having only two functions. Similar patterns may be found throughout the table.

Finally, it should be noted that variation in the number of municipally performed functions is evidently not a unique product of such twentieth-century developments as the Great Depression, the New Deal, and the subsequent strong role of the federal government in urban affairs. The difference in scope between cities emerging after the 1920s and those emerging just before is similar to other differences between adjacent cohorts in Table III-2. If, as argued here, city age indicates the stage in the processes of "eclipse of community," of interlocal interdependence, and especially of state centralization when the city's scope was set within limits, then the effacement of municipal powers was under way long before the development of massive urban intervention programs by the federal government. By the time the federal government entered the scene, its role was largely, but not exclusively, partnership arrangements with existing governing institutions. The problem had become, for the most part, how to manage existing urbanized areas rather than how to establish governments for them.

URBAN GROWTH AND SUBURBANIZATION

The thesis presented in the foregoing is not what most scholars think about when, and if, they compare cities in terms of scope. Instead, the tradition of research on metropolitan-area growth and on the concomitant fragmentation of local government provides most of what is generally known or believed about differences in the functional scope of municipalities.

Scholars from McKenzie (1933) through Bollens and Schmandt (1970) have called attention to an apparent connection between population growth of cities and the emergence of more extensive pressures for public services. These scholars have also noted certain public-service consequences of cities becoming locked within boundaries set by smaller neighboring cities or suburbs. Suburbanization is presumed to generate more pressure on central cities to provide services for suburban areas having partial dependence on central cities for work places and for some patterns of consumption. This perspective on the effects of urbanization actually includes three separate propositions. Two have to do with the distinction between central cities and suburbs, and the third is more elementary and concerns the presumed effect of population size, itself.

The first of these propositions, called by Neenan (1970) "the suburban–central city exploitation thesis," holds that suburbs are nonpaying "dependents" of central cities, exploiting them for services not provided by the suburban governments. For example, Kasarda (1972: 1119) argues in his study of this thesis that "the suburban population makes regular use of central city streets, parks, zoos, museums, and other facilities; its routine presence in the central city increases problems of the sanitation department and contributes to the costs of fire protection; the daily movement in and out of the central city of the large commuting population requires services that constitute a large part of the operating budget of both the police and highway departments."

This thesis is only partially relevant to the present issue, for it deals largely with the effects of "exploitation" on budget levels. The same thesis may, however, play some role in explaining the presence of certain functions in the central city (e.g., parks and recreation and lesser functions not enumerated in this study), which may be provided for a metropolitan-area clientele. In this case, suburbs may not find it necessary or even desirable to provide any amenities that can be acquired by simply crossing the suburban boundary into the central city. What is important here is not the relative size of the suburban and central-city populations, nor even the size of the commuting population, but simply whether a given municipality is a central city or a suburb.

A second proposition about suburban qualities seems more relevant to the present issue. Suburban communities may not only have bilateral exploitative relations with central cities, but they may also define smaller less internally diversified areas for which the administration of some public affairs becomes part of the larger web of multilateral metropolitan-area coordination. Suburbs are often described (e.g., Walton, 1968; Winter, 1969) as semiautonomous balkanized jurisdictions that depend at least as much upon their neighbors and on overlying governments for certain public services as upon the central cities. As writers in Maass's theoretical volume on *Area and Power* (1959) point out, some functions such as sewage and sanitation are often most efficiently provided on a large-area basis, particularly in suburban areas, due to the absence in many suburbs of waterways and disposal sites. The same thesis may apply to welfare, where clients are lacking, or to various other functions not planned for suburbs. The presumed result is an effacement of suburban functions through the emergence of local (not state) coordination of some functions within special districts, a cooperative county, or perhaps even private organizations that cross jurisdictional lines.

Aside from these organizational pressures toward superordinate local coordination in suburban areas, one may wish to add to this thesis Greer's (1962a, 1962b) observations on the normative character of many suburban polities. Because suburbs often have internally less diversified social structures than central cities, they also often attain substantially more consensus about the role of government. A principal component of this consensus, according to Greer, is that the government should be of such small scale as to present citizens with "limited liability" in its affairs. Many suburban governments are evidently founded with this limited role in mind.

We have here, however, a "chicken and egg" question. Should we argue that suburban municipalities might have relatively narrow scope because their founders and current residents conceived of their towns in this light, or because the social communities and political organizations that they hatched are too interdependent with neighbors to permit autonomous development of certain functions? Although either interpretation is defensible, it is clear that both depend on the emergence of suburbs as small, socially specialized and governmentally balkanized areas. Such a situation may result from aspirations for "limited liability" governments, or it may produce them.

The third proposition in the metropolitan studies literature (e.g., Bollens and Schmandt, 1970; McKenzie, 1933) is that city size itself may, as it increases, create demands for more service functions. This proposition is fairly straightforward at this point, for it is largely a corollary of the more general hypothesis, noted earlier, that growth in scale entails growth in organizational complexity with widening demands and needs for social services. Once again, however, we must question whether the effects of urban growth were uniquely felt within individual urban centers, or whether they were felt more generally at the state, regional, and federal levels. That is, was the political response to urban growth to allow all of the established and growing cities to multiply their functions, or to assign certain functions in newly emerging areas (and therefore less populated ones) to state-supervised administrative districts? More succinctly, can we expect large cities to have many functions, and small cities to have few functions, because of their size or because of their age?

To answer this question and to explore the propositions about the significance of suburban status, Tables III-3 and III-4 are presented. Table III-3 shows correlation coefficients between measures of population size, age, suburban–central-city status, and functional scope of municipalities. The population-size variable is for the 1960 Census, the closest one to the data sources used to measure functional scope, and was transformed (log N) to reduce skewness. The age-of-city variable is a count of the number of decades since the census reported that the city first reached 10,000 population, meaning that old cities have high scores. The "suburban dummy" variable was dichotomously coded to assign a score of one if the municipality was a suburb, and a score of zero if the municipality was a central city or was not located in a metropolitan area.

Table III-3 shows that age of city is most strongly correlated with functional scope (.56) among the three predictor indicators. Al-

TABLE III-3

Matrix of Correlations between Functional Scope and Indicators of Contextual Forces Shaping Functional Scope (N = 668 Cities)

	(1) Age	(2) Size	(3) Suburb	(4) Scope
(1) Municipal age[a] (High score = old)	—			
(2) City size[b] (1960 population)	.53	—		
(3) Suburban status[c] (High score = suburb)	-.45	-.28	—	
(4) Functional scope	.56	.34	-.37	—

[a] Defined as the number of decades since the U.S. Census first reported that the city had reached 10,000 population. Source: See Table III-2.

[b] Natural logarithm of 1960 population. Source: *U.S. Census of Population: 1960.*

[c] Suburbs are defined as cities located within the 212 Standard Metropolitan Statistical Areas (SMSAs), excluding the largest city in each SMSA for the 1960 census. Conversely, non-suburbs are the 212 "central" cities in the 1960 SMSA's plus all cities not located within SMSA's (adapted from a classification used by Jones, Forstall, and Collver, 1963).

though the other two indicators have lower correlations with scope, they are both strong and in the expected direction. Suburbs have narrower scope than central cities ($r = -.37$), and large cities have broader scope than small ones ($r = .34$).

Yet, each of these indicators is strongly related to the others, for small cities tend to be new and suburban. To partially disentangle the relative influences of each indicator, Table III-4 presents statistics computed from a multiple regression predicting municipal functional scope from population size (log N), suburban status, and city age. First, attention should be drawn to the multiple R, or the coefficient of determination indicating the combined effect of all three indicators on functional scope. At .58, this multiple R is only slightly higher than the zero-order correlation coefficient between city age and scope (.56). Population size, suburban status, city age, and functional scope are all so closely correlated that the first two of these account for very little variance in scope not associated with city age.

To break out or decompose this common variance among the three indicators, Table III-4 shows partial correlation coefficients and standardized regression coefficients for each indicator controlling for

TABLE III-4

Multiple Correlations and Regression Analysis of Indicators of Contextual Forces with Functional Scope (N = 668 Cities)[a]

Independent variable	Zero-order correlation coefficient	Second-order partials	
		Correlation coefficient	Standardized regression coefficient (STD error)
Municipal age	.56	.41	.469
(High score = old)			(.040)
City size	.34	.05	.052
(1960 populations)			(.038)
Suburban status	-.37	-.15	-.141
(High score = suburb)			(.036)
			$R_2 = .577$
			$R = .332$

[a]Sources: See Tables III-2 and III-3.

the other two. These statistics show that while there is substantial common variance, population size has a small unique effect that is virtually negligible but in the expected direction. Status as a suburb has a relatively small but notable effect in the expected direction when the other indicators are controlled. And city age retains distinctiveness as the strongest predictor among the indicators. After all of the variance in functional scope that can be attributed to city size and to suburban status has been statistically removed, city age still has a partial correlation coefficient with scope of .41.

DISCUSSION

The generalizations that follow must still be taken as somewhat tentative. As historical urban studies become increasingly more empirical, the theoretical alternatives explored here can be more fully tested. For now, the following discussion seems consistent with available institutional histories and with some initial empirical evidence.

Three basic statements summarize our inferences. First, we note that the growth in the population size of cities is related to the number of basic functions performed, mostly because large cities were often the first cities and were infused with a broad scope at an early date. Secondly, the older cities generally fulfilled much of their original, diffuse functional mandates as the nation modernized, while newer cities were established with far more specialized roles. Lastly, suburbs emerged as municipal examples of specialized governments, having both narrow functional mandates and little viability to expand those mandates.

The analysis and findings that support these statements extend the work of institutional historians, treat Weber's version of community as a historical type of organization, and modify the strong emphasis on population factors found in the work of urban ecologists. The analysis takes the nation-state, not the metropolitan community, as the final inclusive system and the appropriate unit of analysis for assessing the environmental determinants of organizational change in the urban community. The metropolitan area is a setting in which national trends toward "societalization" (or specialization and centralization of units of organization) are played out. As for the metropolitan context itself, it has little effect on that aspect of organization that we call the functional scope of municipal governments. Federal urban programming adds to the importance of the nation-state context without constituting a sharp break with previous trends.

The analysis also supports the inference that organizational change in functional assignment to governments varies over time by function. Some functions have been more rapidly responsive to specialization than have others, especially those social-justice functions that were most sensitive to early displays of inequality and conflict under conditions of growing free-market interdependence. In making this point, I have stressed the social factors of increasing industrial scale, socioeconomic differentiation, and political centralization of functions of government rather than the underlying population and technological changes stressed by ecologists. The immediate cause of narrowing scope of newer municipalities has traditionally been the fiscal and administrative power of the state in standardizing interlocal contract law, recruitment to the labor force, and unemployment security. With considerable success in newly organizing areas, the elites who control resources necessary for the performance of the social-justice functions have separated control over the goal-setting apparatus of these functions from the diffuse demands of general urban government. This trend is more recently encompassing other functions of government that lack private regulation and that manifest growing interlocal inequality, particularly health, hospitals, and, with the widening concern over biophysical ecology, perhaps even sewers and sanitation. If the trend extends to police and fire protection, the new municipality of tomorrow may be comprised of little more than symbolic functions.

Lastly, I have stressed the importance of "historical residues" in the organization of city government. Older forms persist where they were constituted. Schnore (1965: 311–323) made a similar point in his analysis of public transportation systems as historical residues that are today more extensively used in older, pre-automobile cities. Mass-transit systems were generally not scrapped by cities that had them when the automobile came along. Yet, we cannot place singular emphasis on antiquated physical technology as the cause of residues. Schnore's own data show no discontinuities in the probability of mass-transit use by city-age cohorts, but like our data, show gradual changes in the relation between city age and governmental functions. These changes may begin earlier for some functions than for others, and may proceed at different paces for different functions. But there is clearly more to the effect of age on functional scope than discontinuities in the types of residues left by changing physical technology. At least equally important are gradual changes in the overall social engineering of a society. The roles of any newly emerging organizations are shaped in large part by the kinds of social technology (e.g., specialization, bureaucracy, professionalization) developed to provide a viable existence for the new organization within its broader social environment.

For this reason, the concluding emphasis must be on reiterating a somewhat more historically informed interpretation of city age as an indicator of a kind of charter written in the organizational and cultural context of the city's founding. The nature of this charter, as denoted by age, concerns the way in which the proper and potential role or scope of local government organization is to be defined. The relevant contextual factors shaping this charter will, of course, have many particularities unique to each time and place. In general, however, the organizational context within which each new organization must define itself has been changing in a trend away from support for independent, autonomous, inclusive community-like organizations, and toward support for interdependent, specialized, limited-purpose organizations. If the former type is anywhere to be found, it is more because of tradition than because of innovation. This interpretation of organizational age is similar to the one developed by Stinchcombe (1965) to explain such matters as the persistence of distinctively nonbureaucratic modes of organization in craft industries. Like Stinchcombe's analysis of organizational age, the present one has implications leading into an analysis of organizational control, decision making, and outcomes for all organizations emerging during a particular era.

FURTHER IMPLICATIONS

If the explanation for municipal functional scope is to be found principally in the organizational context of the municipality's founding, then surely the same context should have broader implications as well. For city governments, the trends toward effacement of powers among the newer municipalities seem to be due largely to contextual factors such as state centralization of supervisory responsibility for major social-justice functions and, to a lesser extent, to interlocal specialization of municipal communities in new suburban areas. These contextual factors may shape more than the functional scope of municipal governments; they may also establish various *cohorts of civic culture* that differ in how the proper role and scope of most community-action organizations are defined.

Indeed, following Stinchcombe, one of the more general implications of these findings is that they may apply to an understanding of variability in the functional scope (or program specificity, integrative capacities, or structural complexity) of various kinds of corporate organizations other than municipalities. That is, older organizations, born in an era of diffuse *Gemeinschaft*, or community-like organization, may become modern-day giants in both the mass of their memberships and in the extent of their activities largely because they have fulfilled in time their inherited potential scope. Newer organizations, born in an era of specialized *Gesellschaft*, may be constrained to a narrow scope and role both by charters of incorporation and by other, new, specialized organizations operating in areas of possible expansion.

A case in point may be colleges and universities. The broad mandates given to many older institutions of higher education have often led to vast multiversities, whereas the narrower scope of newer junior colleges seems unlikely to lead to any Berkeleys or Harvards (Kerr, 1963; Riesman, 1958). In some instances, location of a newer institution in a growing urban context may stimulate functional expansion beyond what would be expected from knowledge of the *institution's* age cohort, and some older colleges in small towns or suburbs may never develop broad functional scope in more than token ways. These apparent exceptions to development by institutional-age cohort may be due in part to contextual differences in community size and suburban status, and in larger part to different generalized traditions regarding the proper role and scope of many types of organizations in the community, as indexed by *municipal* age.

In short, an analysis of organizational development within cohorts of local civic culture may have far more general applications than to municipal governments alone. Many domains of social organization within American communities may vary in functional scope, diffuseness of purpose, and breadth of integrated activity for roughly the same reasons that the range of municipal functions varies and that are indicated by the age of the community. This may be true of cultural, educational, religious, and economic as well as civic, political, and governmental institutions. Diverse elements or "functions" in each of these institutional domains may be subject to similar development of comprehensively interlinked modes of social organization within older communities, and to tendencies toward more splintered modes of organization—if any organization at all—within newer communities. Large city size may add greater diversity to each domain, and suburban status may imply little diversity in any domain, but our analysis would suggest that neither of these latter two contextual factors contributes as much to the organized inclusiveness of diverse elements within each domain as do the broader traditions and trends indexed by municipal age.

In the specific case of municipal governments, one consequence of long-term trends has been to fragment rather than to consolidate local governance systems. Big government at the local level is no new invention. The notion of broad-scope city government is very old fashioned and almost antiquated, like that of a "community." It is the specialized and limited-purpose government that is really new.

Municipal governments of simple purpose and function seem to be products of increasingly complex patterns of differentiation and interdependence within the larger environmental context of the nation, region, state, and metropolitan area. The expanding roles of federal and state government and of various professional groups have brought about some hierarchical coordination at superordinate levels of authority, but only at the price of fueling the drive for multiplying the numbers of distinct local governments. It is further suggested that not only government, but other domains of social organization in the immediate environment of the city itself have been similarly affected, such that within the old-style community there is a broader reach by local coordinating mechanisms for any domain than would be found within the newer city. The question that now arises is whether these changes have brought about municipal governments that, by differing in scope, also differ in their efficacy as instruments of political action.

IV.

The Active City:
Theoretical Perspectives on
Decision Making and Performance
by Municipalities of Varying Scope

With the advancement of societal complexity, the political context of American cities has increasingly become a multinucleated patchwork of diverse organizations and institutions. Political disunity, especially in the form of specialized interests and governments, now seems basic to the contemporary city and a chief barrier to concerted political action. Having lost their "common focus," the public affairs of a city's citizens are often not the affairs of its government. Meanwhile, urban problems mount, and city governments appear to be increasingly unable to mobilize resources to meet the challenge.

TWO PERSPECTIVES ON POLITICAL ACTION

Scholars who observe the modern urban condition rarely attribute signs of political inaction to the growing diversity of the social and

65

economic understructure. Instead, this underlying diversity is often applauded. To Sennett (1969:6), differentiation with respect to status and life style "encourage(s) social individuality and innovation, and is thus the instrument of historical change." To Warren (1970), a broad distribution of community decision-making power among many different social units is one of the basic values or desiderata often affirmed in the community literature. And to Mumford (1961), summarizing a number of humanistic sentiments, the city of social variety is a city of great social resources that provide challenges and opportunities for "continued enlargement . . . of the cultural heritage." If these claims are taken without substantial qualification, they suggest that at least some types of dynamic mobilization of city government might be attributable chiefly to differentiation and diffuseness of the community context in which the government is located.

Many scholars, including some advancing the latter perspective, nonetheless question whether government in the city provides an integration of this underlying structure into an orderly and viable political community. It is often and quite appropriately asserted that governments fail to bring diverse interests into some common focus for collective action. This assertion has a particularly long history as a guiding principle behind the metropolitan reform movement and in scholarly critiques of urban-area governmental fragmentation (Richards 1954, Sayre and Polsby 1965, Friesema 1966, Hauser, 1967, Committee for Economic Development 1970). Literature in this tradition essentially states that as governments in urban areas proliferate and become more specialized, citizens lose simple unitary loci for involvement, leadership responsibilities become narrowly constrained, and independent governments fail to coordinate their programs or share their resources with each other in innovative ways. Hawley and Zimmer (1970: 2) are not atypical in their characterization of the result as "governmental chaos" and "administrative impotence."

This familiar critique of metropolitan-area fragmentation has been highly provocative in both scholarly and public-policy circles. As if developed in the shadow of imminent urban crises, the critique offers a diagnosis of failing urban political organization as ostensibly symptomized by inefficiency, short-sighted planning, unintegrated programs, and limited capacities and goals. Much of the research making this critique has illustrated urban fragmentation, in particular metropolitan areas (e.g., in studies as diverse as Hoover and Vernon 1962, and Miller 1975) or has elaborated the logic of the indictment or certain prescriptions for reform (e.g., the authors in Crecine 1970).

These tendencies of metropolitan-area analysis have meant that, in advancing the critique of fragmentation, little of national generality has been tested or explained. The explicitly reformist tradition in metropolitan studies has been criticized (e.g., by Greer 1962a, Warren 1974, and Banfield 1974) for having an implicit normative assumption, which, in a nutshell, holds that "coordination" is a "good thing" in itself. These same critics point out that, in the absence of evidence to support any other assertion that coordination would matter, it is at least as reasonable to assume that the present arrangements give to elites, if not also to the general citizenry, roughly the outcomes that they want and deem to be "good." This may well be true, but such an assumption addresses an issue quite different from that of trying to resolve the original public-policy question of the effects of governmental organization on governmental behavior. To formulate this policy question in theoretical terms amenable to empirical investigation, it is necessary to go beyond the normative concerns of the prescriptive and reformist tradition.

Empirical studies of metropolitan governmental fragmentation, including some of a largely prescriptive nature, tend to suffer from another problem. They generally emphasize only one dimension of fragmentation, namely the proliferation of *adjacent* cities, suburbs, and unincorporated areas, and the problems of intergovernmental cooperation and competitiveness engendered by this type of fragmentation (see studies in Governmental Affairs Foundation 1958, and in Bollens and Schmandt's text 1970). This is the most distinctive dimension in the local contexts of metropolitan-area case studies. Often overlooked is a second dimension of fragmentation, the emergence of overlying governments and quasi-governments that efface the powers of each affected municipality, and which have a more direct bearing on the political activities of each municipality. This dimension would be more evident in interlocal comparisons. It is interesting that where the problem of interlocal differences in the assignment of functional responsibilities is recognized, it rather oddly takes on the conceptual status of "noise" and actually deters some researchers (as noted by G. Wilensky 1970: 202–203) from developing a theory and method for analyzing the effect of this dimension of fragmentation on local government behavior.

This chapter develops a theoretical model of municipal activity that focuses on the roles that individual municipal governments play as integrative loci for political action. The key term in this model is variability in the scope of major governmental functions performed by municipal governments. The discussion begins with an interpretation of interrelated decision-making contexts, and proceeds to a set of propositions concerning the probable effect of broad or narrow scope on five universal, but variable, aspects of political activation of municipalities: the accessibility of formal leadership, voter participation levels, fiscal performance or expenditure effort for public programs, program innovativeness, and freedom from narrow standards of program accountability. The propositions state, in effect, that there will be greater, broader, or more flexible political action on each of these dependent variables among municipalities having wider scope.

After this perspective is elaborated rather extensively, it is placed in partial opposition to the hypothesis that a diffuse environmental context, particularly in the underlying social structure of the community, activates city government. This hypothesis opposes the scope-centered theory only partially, for both perspectives suggest that the key to activation is some type of diversity or differentiation in the relevant political system. The difference between the perspectives is that the scope-centered one, as developed in the following, focuses more narrowly on the integration of differentiated units within the official municipal organization rather than on differentiation and webs of affiliation in the broader environmental context of the host community.

The central issue is whether the actions of city governments can be substantially determined by the way in which such governments are organized, or whether the "social context" of the governments determines their behavior, regardless of how their structure, role, or scope is engineered. The first of these views or perspectives includes an implication of direct policy relevance: Governmental behavior may change if we organize governments differently. The second calls attention to the dependence of governments on their social contexts, and raises the more implicit policy question of whether major changes or reforms are possible without strong intervention by some previously latent or external power.

The present chapter is almost entirely conceptual and theoretical in nature. Measures of dependent variables, analyses of their empirical relationships with functional scope, and consideration of possible confounding and control variables are presented in Chapters V and VI.

BASIC ELEMENTS OF DECISION-MAKING NETWORKS

In a major assessment of community studies, Walton (1966) noted that attempts to explain community political action generally begin with assumptions, or meta-hypotheses, about how decisions are made. For example, a long tradition of community studies focused largely on the assumption that a small group of men makes most major contemporary government decisions. By means of sociometric techniques for identifying those who are reputed to be the most powerful persons in town, this tradition documented the phenomena of perceived power elites in numerous published (see Gilbert's list and critique, 1966) and unpublished case studies.

Somewhat more recently, the pendulum has swung to the other extreme, and some scholars are expressing doubt that any assumptions about centralized decision making are appropriate. Norton Long (1958), for one, has suggested that no single power structure, individual, group, or institution makes the decisions affecting a given polity. Community decision making, he proposed, is really a loose "ecology of games" played by diverse actors having no overall common purpose or focus. Going somewhat further, Greer (1962a: 20) lumped Long's perspective together with that of urban ecologists who see some form of governmental fragmentation in most urban areas, and suggested that the urban polity that they portray is actually little more than an atomized " 'dust heap,' organized only in the myriad competing and accommodating subgroups whose arbiter is the market." Those who assume this pluralist imagery generally document the phenomena of fairly distinct clusters of decision makers within various issue arenas.

These two extreme and partially valid notions of decision-making processes can and have been reconciled or merged in various ways (e.g., by Clark 1971, Laumann and Pappi 1973, Burt 1974, Miller 1975). I will shortly suggest a reconciliation appropriate to the present study. Traditionally, however, the elitist and pluralist approaches have not only rested on quite distinct assumptions and methodologies, but for what may be ideological reasons, they have also roughly corresponded to the two previously noted perspectives on the relevance of a community's formal political organization. Elitist assumptions about the macrodimensions of unified power structures have tended to issue in the conclusion that the significant wielders of power always control government and that power can be significantly reallocated by willful change in the government. The pluralist view, in its most simplified form as a theory of rationally pursued microexchanges, more easily supports a deduction that the organization of local government is, in practice, nothing more than a reified formality of little consequence in itself. As Mills (1940:330) noted some years ago, "Pluralist causes are easily carried to a point at which no action is possible; revolutionary manipulation calls for belief in a monistic cause." Fortunately both for inquiry and for its application, thought-models increasingly entertain aspects of elitist as well as pluralist assumptions, and permit a more thorough test of the importance of manipulable variables.

Without accepting in full the assumptions of either extreme view, a middle course having some prima facie appeal can be charted and tested in the context of the present concern with functional scope. Following Long (1958), it can be reasonably assumed that no single group or institution makes all or even most of governmental decisions in any community. But rather than accepting the further assumption that the actions of political actors generally lack common purpose or focus, we should pursue Rossi's (1960:394) contention that these actions are directed toward ultimately influencing the behavior of some governmental institution. This "referencing" of influence and of resources toward an institution is itself a mode of integrative collective action involving some common focus leading in the end to an outcome having at least the official sanction of a common purpose. While individual actors may seek to attain their own ends, they do so through institutionalized governmental mechanisms at least to some extent.

By this conception, decision making for municipalities is seen as occurring throughout networks of community (and extracommunity) political actors. If the units in this network are to be at all effective and relevant, they must ultimately form direct or indirect linkages with organized units of government. Because most of these actors are likely to be organizations or organized groups in modern America, the resulting imagery is similar to what Warren (1967) once called an interorganizational field, with the municipal government serving as a kind of "focal organization" (Evan 1966). The following discussion elaborates this conception further.

Interfaces between Centers of Power

Expanding on Levine and White's (1961) exchange framework for studying interorganizational relations, Aiken and Alford (1968) developed two elementary concepts having general utility as building blocks for a theory of political decision making. Interfaces between centers of power may be considered some of the most generic forms of political interrelatedness. As defined by Aiken and Alford (pp. 6–10), these terms refer to an "exchange relationship" between "coalitions of interests and/or values." The center-of-power concept identifies social units having "a relatively high probability of acting as homogeneous entities." Examples would include any organization or group, and in some instances, perhaps, individuals who represent or symbolize organizations or groups having a unified stance.

The interface concept identifies an exchange of "any valued resource which the centers of power may hold: information, personnel, goods, services, money, clients, protection, or promises of future reciprocity with respect to any of these resources." This "mutual exchange" conception of political coordination assumes no integrative mechanisms other than the "actions of two or more actors seeking to attain their own ends." It also assumes no inclusive goals, no collectivity orientation, no formally structured division of labor, and no commitment to a single set of leaders. This is what Warren (1967) termed a "social choice" context of decision making, and is simply an arena within which social units interact with respect to a particular issue.

The centers-of-power and interfaces concepts are generic enough to include most, if not all, of the types of influentials and patterns of influence that may shape governmental behavior. They include, for example, federal and state officials, neighborhood groups, and economic elites having some involvement in a particular issue. The question that arises is whether and how the participants in an arena of issues are integrated with municipal government.

In some cases, most centers of power may never acquire interfaces with municipal governments for lack of an issue in common with that government. In other cases, most centers of power may have extensive interfaces with municipal government due to the pervasiveness of its activities. The ultimate context of municipal decision making may be either narrow and unresourceful, or broad and rich with the resources of political exchange. What will make the difference here is the institutional location of certain special types of centers of power, namely the administrative units of government toward which issue arenas are referenced.

Issue Arenas and Governmental Functions

Issue arenas should be defined rather liberally to include all of the possible controversies that might be raised in a community. Aiken and Alford (1968) define the arena portion of the term as follows: "The number of centers of power which possess interfaces with each other and which must be activated on a given issue to effectuate a decision constitutes the necessary arena with respect to a given issue [p. 11]." To this might be added one minor qualification. Some issues find no adequate arena for a decision (except in the sense of a nondecision or refusal to act), while others may activate centers of power that are not normally essential participants in decision making. A *necessary* arena may be limited to the parameters suggested by Aiken and Alford, but an *actual* one may be much larger.

In matters of political action, at least one unit in each issue arena will be a component of a government. The only sensible exception to this might occur where an issue is sufficiently new or exotic for no government to exercise authority over matters pertaining to it. Even in this case, it seems highly probable that if an arena is formed by extragovernmental centers of power, they will rapidly try to recruit some governmental participants. Often, especially on newer issues, the participating governmental components will include members of the legislative council or the executive leadership. The participation of some functional branch will be almost certain for established and somewhat routinized issues.

The importance of the functional branch is threefold. By its performance, it defines most issues or sets the standards (e.g., output levels, public image, etc.) against which others define the issues. It also provides opportunity for interfaces between extragovernmental centers of power and the government itself. And it creates channels of interaction and communication through which various centers of power might develop interfaces with each other as they jointly seek to influence policy.

If we add up the number of functions performed by a municipal government, those governments having wide scope also have more administrative officials whom citizens and centers of power can contact to demand that something be done, more administrative officials who can (independently of any citizen action) pressure political leaders to do something in their own or their department's interest, more administrative officials who maintain contacts with federal or state officials, and more resources available at these levels of government. The plurality of these linkages encourages the self-selection and formation of those specific coalitions having the capacity to attain their goals (Aiken and Alford 1968; 1970a, b, c), while the inclusive goal framework of the host government will likely legitimatize their actions and aims, or those of a stronger contending coalition, or both. In addition, a broad-scope government is more likely to bring a greater number of administrative officials, their staff, and other centers of power into contact with each other over various policy issues than would a narrow-scope municipality whose functional components are distributed among several independent governments. This facilitates the emergence or use of formal coordinating instrumentalities to express overarching, shared norms. All of these factors increase the set of interrelated resources that might be mobilized for collective action.

It is important to note that although functional components may be in close liaison with each other and with political officials of their municipality, they often have some of the attributes of semiautonomous unitary organizations. School systems, hospitals, health bureaus, and sanitation departments are generally organized for the achievement of specific goals, have a well structured division of labor, and possess a relatively rigid hierarchy of authority. There is, of course, great variation in this regard, with some functional components looking more like a set of organizations and others sometimes appearing to be little more than subdivisions of a larger organization. Functional components probably vary widely in complexity, centralization, and formalization. These factors are undoubtedly relevant to their behavior and outputs, but are really beyond the range of this study. Of central importance here is the assumption that each functional component is itself a center of power, or, at most, a small set of centers of power.

Although these administrative components are relatively small in number compared with extragovernmental organizations and groups, their weight, as direct or indirect channels of influence, becomes multiplied enormously beyond a mere count of such components, because they are major gate keepers or bridges at the outer limits of the formal structure of municipal government. By servicing clients, soliciting resources, participating in interlocal exchanges with other governments, gaining information and professional guidance from national associations, and keeping tab of pertinent federal and state regulations, the professional administrators and technical staff of each component multiply the number of municipally referenced centers of power participating in particular issues.

The Formal Leadership of Municipal Government

A final notable feature of functional components, and one that also permits them to be so often characterized as unitary organizations, is that while they may have many interfaces with external centers of power, they nonetheless tend to maintain an official stance of nonpoliticized administration. Department and bureau heads, as well as staff, only rarely make public entry into issue arenas, despite many backstage involvements. Their role is generally interpreted as a technical or professional one, requiring the specialized skills of a trained manager or the organizational loyalty of a bureaucrat. Their interests formally represent those of the bureau that they work for, rather than those of any other sector or coalition in the city.

Superimposed on these semiautonomous units is the more diffuse and publicly political context of formal municipal leadership. Responsible for coordinating multiple budgets and integrating a wide range of extragovernmental and internal interests, municipal leaders are more openly subject to the pressures of coalescing with sectors and factions in the city. Administrative components that compete for scarce resources, such as revenue for salaries or program expansion, often come into conflicts that only central political leaders have authority to resolve. Conflicts of this sort may also be generated by various extragovernmental centers of power seeking to influence resistant administrative components, or attempting to resist influence by such components. The role of central political leaders, therefore, often becomes one of conflict resolution, requiring an open and accessible stance to those generating such conflict. The interests that such leaders represent may vary from occasion to occasion and from issue to issue as they join in coalition with one faction or another to settle disputes. This is essentially the same view of central political leaders that Banfield (1961) and Sayre and Kaufman (1960) portray in their studies of Chicago and New York City, and that Kotter and Lawrence (1974) apply in their study of 20 big city mayors. In these studies, the mayors and their aides are seen as highly politicized power brokers atop what might best be described as a sprawling confederation of periodically warring organizations and changing coalitions of interest.

On the other hand, where there are relatively few administrative units in a municipality, the competition for resources and conflict over policy reduces to a minimum. Indeed, the entire government becomes more nearly like a single, unitary organization, having relatively specific and limited goals and little probability of disputes disrupting the routine used to achieve those goals. In this instance, the power brokerage functions of central political leadership would be minimized and largely supplanted by the same kind of technical and professional roles of the bureau chief. The few bureaus in such a limited-scope government would require only very infrequent services or skills in conflict resolution from central executive and legislative branches. Incidents demanding nonroutine attention would not only be limited in number and frequency, but in type as well. In this respect, central executive and legislative officials would be reduced to performing largely routine and ceremonial tasks, interspersed on occasion with selected, but limited, policymaking chores. Similarly, relations between the formally structured bureaus and the central officials would be more repetitive, goal specific, analyzable, and rationalized than in wide-scope cities, with the effect of producing a more systematically structured governmental hierarchy. This arrangement more formally specifies the central authority of executive and legislative personnel in these narrow-scope cities than do the vicissitudes of the interagency conflict and power brokerage arrangements of wide-scope cities.

A Summary

Municipal decision making can be understood as occurring throughout networks of community and extracommunity political actors. At the most elementary level of network integration, any single point, interface, or decision probably identifies an exchange between two or more relatively autonomous actors or corporate agents seeking to attain their own ends or the ends of their corporate interests. One way in which these elementary "social-choice" processes become integrated within a higher-level network of such processes is through participation in a common issue arena or, more specifically, through the focusing of political behavior on influencing the performance of a functional branch of a government. Finally, the functional branches and issue arenas are themselves integrated, albeit with varying scope of units and stability of bonds, within the broader focal context of executive and legislative policymaking through which legitimacy is bestowed on the entire multifunctional municipal enterprise. These statements come together in the central assumption that municipal decision making of any sort ordinarily involves all three levels of integration at once. Exchanges between relatively autonomous (or autonomy seeking) centers of power occur within and among issue arenas having functional programmatic reference, with the intent of receiving the overall government's certification of legitimacy.

More important for the present study is a principal theoretical implication of this assumption. As the range of municipally referenced linkages expands with expanding scope, so too does the diversity of legitimate actions and the turbulence of relationships among the centers of power that seek legitimacy for favorable decisions regarding available resources. As the network of linkages with the government narrows with narrowing scope, so too does the specificity of legitimate goals and the definition of procedures and relevant input for attaining those goals.

HYPOTHESES: SCOPE AND POLITICAL ACTION

Implicit in this discussion of the integration of decision-making processes are a number of theoretical hypotheses about differences in the political action of wide- and narrow-scope cities. These implied differences may be elaborated along various lines. For the most general elaboration, the differences implied here closely parallel a very extensively developed distinction between communal (broad scope) and formal (narrow scope) organizations, which Hillery (1968) proposed and Gottschalk (1975) applied to an analysis of alternative community types. Their typology might be consulted for a vision of the logical (and, it may be presumed, utopian) theoretical models pertaining to all aspects of community life that might be explored in more exhaustive inquiries. Within the present, limited focus on government, the previous discussion leads to several specific hypotheses about the relationship between municipal functional scope and various aspects of political action. These hypotheses are presented as follows with brief explanations.

Hypothesis: The Broader the Functional Scope of a Municipal Government the Higher the Probability That the Government Will Engage in Program Innovation

The adoption of wholly new programs by governments having the legal or jurisdictional authority to do so may well be one of the most difficult forms of collective action to carry out because the initial stages of such innovation are not guided by repetitions of previous routines; that is, the innovation does not yet have a formal organizational home. Decision makers who interact across organizational boundaries, and who can therefore combine partial resources from various organizations in a new context, provide a particularly strong basis for successful new program implementation (Levine and White 1961, Emery and Trist 1965, Hage and Aiken 1967, Aiken and Hage 1968, Turk 1970, Hage 1972). The density of resourcefulness among these interrelated "boundary spanners" would, by the previous discussion, be highest in municipalities having broad scope, thereby increasing the chance of an innovative combination of interests and their resources.

This hypothesis is largely a more specific restatement of a similar, but more general, thesis developed by Aiken and Alford in their studies of federal programs in cities. In an early essay where they most extensively discuss the notions of interfaces and centers of power, Aiken and Alford (1968) presented this hypothesis:

> The more centers of power there are and the more interfaces established among them, the higher the probability that a collective decision will be successfully implemented. There are several reasons for this assertion. First, the greater the accumulation of knowledge in a community system (i.e., the greater the number of interfaces), the greater the probability that centers of power most relevant for a given issue will have a history of prior contact. The centers of power that are both the most relevant and also the most likely to be favorable to a given issue can be activated first and brought into a coalition in the issue arena. Second, the greater the number of centers of power, the less likely that any one center of power can dominate in an issue arena (assuming that community differentiation means fragmentation of power). Third, under such conditions centers of power are more likely to know which other centers are potential opponents. They can then take steps to either avoid that center of power or artfully co-opt it [Reprinted from Community structure and mobilization: The case of the war on poverty by Michael Aiken and Robert Alford by permission of the authors and the Institute for Research on poverty, October, 1968, Discussion Paper No. 29–68, p. 12].

The major qualification that the present discussion brings to this earlier formulation is a selective emphasis on only those interfaces and centers of power indicated by the functional scope of the government. Whereas Aiken and Alford discussed the interfaces and centers-of-power concepts as general properties of communities that might be manifest or denoted in a number of ways (e.g., diversity and continuity of the underlying social structure), these concepts are discussed here principally in a narrower sense. We are most concerned with those interfaces and centers of power that the scope of the government "recruits" or "screens" into participation in the interorganizational system comprising the municipality as a political institution. As such, scope is a way of denoting that specific portion of the centers of power in the city's immediate environment, as well as those outside it, which, by virtue of the government's own organizational span, have a history of prior contact within or with the city government and can therefore mobilize for action in ways stated by Aiken and Alford.

In subsequent published studies by Aiken and Alford (1970a, b), it was hypothesized that the differentiation and integration of the *formal organizational* structure of a city produced essentially the same dynamics as the general interfaces–centers-of-power thesis proposed, and might be a specific means of testing that thesis. The authors then specified the theory even further, suggesting that data on "crucial" types of organizations, such as local city government, might be applied to a test of the thesis if such data were available. Because the scope variable provides this data, it affords an opportunity for an empirical test of the hypothetically crucial role that municipal organization plays in integrating the diverse resources considered important for increasing the chance of an innovative combination.

The general and specified versions of the hypothesis on innovativeness both depend on several assumptions about the nature of programs. In both, new programs are regarded as interstitial developments that initially emerge as efforts by coalitions of power centers that forge a new programmatic emphasis out of their now combined interests, and ultimately locate this new program in some organized subsystem of the government similar to any other functional branch and center of power. Like other programs, the new one has some measurable output and both staff and line positions to get the job done. The new program may be more closely linked to its original organizational sponsors (who put up the initial coalition) than to other organized units of government, but it tends toward the same measure of semiautonomy that all such units have, or seek, in order to control its output function. These definitional assumptions about the nature of new programs are succinctly developed in full by Zald (1969) who adds, quite logically, that the proliferation of new programs increases the probability of new and novel coalitions and still other programs. The causal assumptions in Zald's theoretical discussion include both the general and government-specified versions noted previously. The issue here is whether the scope of government specifies crucial conditions of integrated diversity under which new program adoption occurs.

Hypothesis: In Comparison with Program Innovation in Narrow-scope Cities, such Innovation in Wide-scope Cities Will Be More Responsive to Situationally Unique Sets of Interests or Values, and Therefore Less "Accountable" with Respect to Universalistic Criteria for Programs

This proposition is a corollary of the basic Aiken and Alford thesis on program innovation, and contains some of the more interesting implications of that thesis. The thesis and its corollary together suggest that in wide-scope cities more innovative programs get implemented for a wider range of reasons, purposes, and valued outcomes. More specifically, if we take any formal definition of *need* for a program (e.g., the kind of definition that may be expected to appear in any request for funds), and if we consider this definition as a type of value having most universal applicability as a criterion for assessing program accountability, then the present argument implies that levels of formal need will have less effect on program implementation in wide-scope cities than in narrow-scope cities. Put another way, as scope widens, so do effective standards for program accountability. Let us consider the reasoning behind these statements, particularly in contrast to what may appear to be diametrically opposing statements derived by Turk (1973b).

There are two principal means by which wide-scope cities might arguably facilitate high levels of program innovation and, simultaneously, relative freedom from single-standard accountability. One of these alternatives involves what might be called "coalitions of the whole" and is associated with the concept of an unbounded system as the agent of action. The other alternative depends on "coalitions of parts" and is associated with the concept of bounded organizations, or organizational sets, as the acting agent. It is useful to take a moment to discuss both and to show the relevance of the latter for the present hypothesis on accountability.

First, consider the wholistic view. If we assume a general system's perspective on the coalitions behind new programs, then the following may be implied. Wide-scope governments may facilitate the convergence of a great many centers of power, drawing perhaps from each of the government's functional components and their clientele, or from a smaller set of overarching agents of the differentiated organizational structure, thereby producing a rather diffuse coalition of resources, each of which contributes some portion of the objectives and rationales for an innovative program. In this situation, certain values, such as reducing the proportion of dilapidated housing in the case of public housing programs, may ultimately play a very small role in the eventual initiative for innovation, with interests favoring various alternative objectives (e.g., collecting or dispersing the poor in new neighborhoods regardless of their prior housing conditions, or reallocating land-use patterns among the industrial and institutional, as well as housing, sectors) playing an additional role in the initiative for innovation.

This is one view of the principle of pluralist decision making in practice; it is the somewhat idealistic view (as critiqued by Connolly,

1969:3–34) that holds that all particular interests become diluted within a compromise package by way of the convergence of those interests within some coordinating instrumentality and consensus. No single beneficiary or center of power dominates, for many get a share of the action in defining a multipurpose program. The interests or needs for which the programs are formally defended are ordinarily "taken into account" but not given singular priority in the inclusive context for pluralist decision making. Although it is occasionally claimed that this process is approximated in some cities (Dahl, 1961), it is at least as often argued that there is a stronger tendency for new programs to become, in practice, captives of selected special interests (see, for example, Wilson 1966, Greer 1965, 1972).

In recent research, Turk (1973b) has, in effect, demonstrated a major flaw in this chain of deductions regarding the consequences of wholistic or diffuse-system coalition formation, and has offered an apparent opposing hypothesis of response to formal need. Turk notes that some community projects require, to function with legitimacy, a considerable measure of system-wide coordination and diffuse coalitions. Higher-level law, convergent consensus among national organizations, or the contingencies for receipt of external resources may require very broad local participation, or the formal manifestation of such participation may be the very function of the project. These projects may themselves be described as broad interorganizational networks. Examples of these networks include community-wide coordinating councils of various sorts, conduits of fiscal or technical assistance to other organizations, or other bodies whose principal functions are directly and broadly integrative rather than specifically programmatic.

For the establishment and activation of these networks in any formal way, Turk (1973b:3, 17, 42) suggests that strong tendencies toward agency autonomy and particularized coalitions must be overcome. Such tendencies are overcome, he further suggests, by the consensus and actions of a broader system, typically a national system that is the unifying headpiece for the vertical linkages arising out of communities, and which works through the horizontal linkages between local organizations to seek formal coordination of scattered local activities in accordance with universally applicable national standards and norms regarding need for such coordination. Turk's central hypothesis may, with some rephrasing, be stated as follows: New forms of local-system integration are more likely to emerge in cities already having the interorganizational linkages to receive the full message about national norms and resources, and these new forms of local-system integration will most likely meet and reflect the standards and norms of the corresponding national system in those very cities having the greatest interorganizational capacity. To measure interorganizational capacity, Turk uses the "scale" or size of the municipal government, which is similar to our measure of scope. Turk concludes with evidence to support his contention in the cases of coordinating networks for antipoverty projects, Model Cities, and health services. Among cities having large scale city governments, he finds strong positive relationships between "need" for these coordinating networks (e.g., poverty) and the "response" of developing the networks.

Turk's hypothesis on responsiveness to need appears to be the very opposite of the one proposed here, which contends that wide-scope governments are the *least* universally responsive to any particular standard, interest, or formal definition of need. This conflict is more apparent than real. It should be made clear that Turk's hypothesis applies to the formation and use of community-wide interorganizational networks, or more generally to what Warren *et al.* (1974) called some attempt at fulfilling, in the local context, the recent national, ideological prescription of reform through formally structured coordination. It may well be true, as Turk's work would imply, that wide-scope governments not only make such attempts more likely to succeed, but also are more sensitive to national definitions of need for coordination. From a perspective within governments that stand for something for everyone, formal coordinating instrumentalities may often be employed as mechanisms for reasserting the symbolic unity and consensual integration that is occasionally and seriously challenged by local unrest or national elites. This would indeed make broad-scope governments more responsive to evidence of *need for coordination* than narrow-scope governments.

But let us be clear about the nature of the response. Formal coordination of an inclusive set of diverse parts does not in itself necessarily alter the distribution of services and rewards in any consensually intended direction, or significantly reduce the autonomy of functioning programs, nor is there evidence to suppose that it does so in practice (Zald, 1969:562ff). As Alford (1974) has cogently argued in his study of health-service delivery, new formal coordination of the sort optimally attainable in the American context is often a symbolic response. Agreeing with Turk that formal coordination seems to arise where crises of unmet need also arise, Alford further observes that coordination is then feigned by its sponsors to be a satisfactory substantive response in and of itself, even without making any tangible changes in circumstances for anyone but the new cadre of coordinators. It is important to note that Turk (1973:59–60) accepts the interpretation that formal coordination may serve to reduce pressures for substantive change.

Further evidence of noncorrelation between formal coordination efforts and substantive program change is presented by Warren *et al.* (1974) in their study of Model Cities (see also Warren, 1970). In a study of heavily funded long-range coordinative planning for land-use policy, Brewer (1973) found that the planning cadre drifted away from its target program and policy units as its symbolic connotation of unified effort lost freshness, as the initial implied consensus failed to yield agreement on the details of programmatic options, and as events in each operational unit of government and in the community at large proceeded with reduced sense of crisis. A general review and theoretical treatment of the limits of action through coordination is presented by Zald (1969).

In short, formal coordination does not necessarily reduce the probability that enacted programs will represent selected or particularized interests. Indeed, that probability may, on occasion, be increased if formal coordination facilitates the discovery of latent, mutual program interests among specific factions of the cyclically appearing and abstract consensus-producing formal coordinating networks. As is implied in my original hypothesis on accountability to which we may now return, the integrative coordination provided by broad-scope governments (or, perhaps, by other and more formal mechanisms) offers a hospitable environment for bringing together unique and innovative coalitions and for legitimatizing their actions under a diffuse system-wide solidarity.

The present concern is, then, with specific new *programs* (e.g., the pre-Great Society programs for urban renewal and public housing), which might be fitted into the interstices between existing programs rather than placed over them as an umbrella, and which neither require nor necessarily supply any system-wide formal coordination. Unlike coordinating instrumentalities, the activation of specific programs does not in any way imply the activation of entire systems. In fact, this lack of system-wide activation was one very important reason why many of the early "piecemeal" federal programs were sharply criticized by recent advocates of structural reform.

This reasoning brings us to the "partial coalition" view of new program adoption and to its implications for accountability. The following is offered as a parsimonious (and, I believe, realistic) interpretation of how *new program* decision making in pluralist contexts takes place. Although a vast number of centers of power may potentially become involved, it is often suggested that, in practice, only a few do—and that this few may contain different types of organizations and actors in different cities. Aiken and Alford (1970b:662) describe the process this way:

> (I)t is precisely in the larger, more structurally differentiated communities that coalitions that can implement an innovation will be easiest to establish. If we assume that only a limited number of organizational units need to be mobilized to bring about a successful innovation, then it follows that in large, highly differentiated communities a lower proportion of the available organizations will participate in such decisions, and that there will be *wider latitude* in selecting organizations for these critical coalitions . . . . In one sense, this proposition is simply a spelling out of what is meant by "structural differentiation" or "functional specialization." The more highly differentiated or specialized a community system, the higher the proportion of decisions that are likely to be made by subsystems and the less likely the entire system will be activated on most issues [Emphasis added].

Disregarding for the moment the higher level of theoretical generality in this passage (e.g., the use of "large, highly differentiated communities" where we would use "wide-scope city governments"), the passage suggests that *each* pluralist context facilitates the emergence of a uniquely different small set of power centers in a critical coalition. The interests that these unique sets serve will, then, vary from city to city, thereby minimizing the extent to which any particular set of interests or values will shape the development of innovation in all such pluralist (or wide scope) contexts. In contrast, the narrow-scope city severely limits the number of possible unique power-center combinations or coalitions, and instead thrusts the burden of mobilizing for innovation upon an entire local-governmental system containing relatively few units. While this reduces the probability of innovation in the narrow-scope cities, it nonetheless means that such innovation that does occur will tend to serve (or "respond to") similar interests in all narrow-scope cities. Levels of formal need for an innovation may be particularly critical determinants of new program response in narrow-scope cities precisely because these city governments have few specialized subsystems that might give the programs more exotic or more complex objectives. This is what is meant by narrow-scope cities being more "accountable" for their actions, and wide-scope cities being more flexible and innovative with respect to both the likelihood of program adoption and the apparent rationales for adoption.

Hypothesis: The Broader the Scope of the Government, the Higher the Expenditures within Individual Functional Categories

This, too, is essentially a corollary of the first hypothesis. If broad-scope governments tend to be more innovative in new program areas, they may also be innovative in older and established ones. Municipal budgets for each function reflect not only on-going costs but also the costs of incremental innovation. Moreover, municipal budgets reflect the effects of demands placed upon the government for services. Just as broad-scope governments are likely to produce the capacities for innovation, so too are they likely to experience more extensive claims for a broadening and ramification of existing functions to service diverse, involved centers of power.

There is, however, one sense in which fiscal performance on on-going functions is considerably different from innovativeness. New program adoptions involve the creation of new organizational components or bureaucracies by combining resources from other governmental components or from outside organizations. Success in this innovative effort would seem to depend largely on the coalescence of certain critical boundary-spanning centers of power, which is presumably facilitated by a government having wide scope. In contrast, on-going programs are largely already in the province of a single and firmly established municipal agency, which may alone, and in self-interest, exert a considerable share of the effort necessary to increase budget allotments. Success in this expansionist drive may depend in part on which established bureaucracies can compete most effectively for the tax dollar, and, in larger part, on the aggregate weight of influence that all such government bureaucracies throughout the entire municipal enterprise jointly bring to bear as each pursues the same end of more funds. Wide scope is important here, as in innovativeness, for facilitating or recruiting extragovernmental influence. Scope is of additional and special significance with respect to performance on established functions, to the extent that scope determines the aggregate dimensions of internal bureaucratic demand during the familiar government-wide mobilization for annual budget increases.

Hypothesis: The Broader the Scope of the Government, the Higher the Level of Voter Participation in the Election of Officials

If a broad scope of functions provides multiple points of access for wider ranges of political actors, as suggested in the foregoing, then it seems likely that a greater share of the community would have enough at stake in such a municipal government to utilize the voting franchise. This hypothesis would be most tenable if we could assume that voting behavior involves essentially the same rational process as was assumed for centers of power forming interfaces. That is, if voters pursued their own ends in issue arenas in which they had some interest other than traditional and sentimental attachments, we could expect voting to be higher in municipalities where the government is involved in most public affairs of the city. This proposition has been widely discussed by scholars studying specific types of governments having narrow scope and traditionally low voter participation, such as independent school districts (Carter and Sutthoff, 1960; Iannaccone, 1967) or suburbs (Greer, 1962a, b).

Hypothesis: The Broader the Scope of the Government, the Higher the Probability That the Formal Leadership System Will Be Relatively Accessible and Politicized, That Is, "Nonreformed"

Nonreformed features of formal leadership systems, particularly mayors rather than city managers, councilmen elected by wards, and large city councils are often reputed to provide top-level power brokers for special interests and conflicting factions in the community (e.g., Lineberry and Fowler 1967). The thesis advanced earlier held that power brokerage and conflict resolution would devolve upon central political leaders more often in broad-scope cities where the diversity of agency and extragovernmental influentials is greatest. Such diversity would create pressures in these broad-scope cities sustaining nonreformed leadership systems.

Conversely, it was suggested that narrow-scope governments may so severely constrain the role of official leaders that it is reduced to perfunctory assignments and routine administrative bookkeeping. To the extent that this is true, narrow scope should create pressures to eliminate needless leadership involvement in community conflict and to establish the reformed practices of a city manager, at-large elections, and small council.

It is not likely that the causal direction of the hypothesized relationship between scope and leadership systems could be the reverse for most of the major functions included in the scope measure. The analysis in the previous chapter found that most of the identifiable forces behind change in municipal scope derive from extralocal factors such as increasing state centralization of functions and the emergence of interlocal elites favoring the specialization and standardization of the administration of functions. To the extent that such forces are strong, they weaken the impact on scope that purely local leadership might otherwise have. Moreover, it was also argued that scope is best understood as an "inherited" characteristic, or as the fulfillment of a kind of charter that remains relatively unchanged over time. Hence, the setting of parameters on scope would precede any *change* in the choice of formal leadership systems for any given city, and may even precede the initial choice made at the city's founding.

Yet, it does seem reasonable to presume that leadership systems have some effect on scope. Where a reformed or relatively inaccessible top leadership structure was established at some early point in time, pressures from constituents or from other centers of power may not have been received and acted upon by this government due to its leadership system. If these pressures include some demanding establishment of *new* functions within the jurisdiction of the government, reformist leadership could have a feedback effect that limits responsive *expansion* of the city's functional scope.

The thrust of these comments on feedback from leadership accessibility to scope is that such an effect may occur, but that it would be severely constrained by historically imposed definitions of functional jurisdiction (or potential scope). I therefore choose to emphasize the initially hypothesized causal effect of scope on leadership accessibility. That is, the incidence of municipal reform institutions may be a major consequence of the effacement of municipal functions, while contributing an additional but not major force behind that effacement by reducing the probability of adding on new functions. Specifically, narrow scope may bring about the acquisition of inaccessible leadership structures, and this reformed leadership may then lead to lower innovativeness in the adoption of new programs or functions.

This suggests a distinctive quality of formal leadership accessibility relative to the other indicators of political action. Given the definitional assumption that this accessibility is manifest in and measured by the presence or absence of municipal "reform," the concept refers to attributes that have generally emerged *prior to current* voting, innovation, and performance levels. City manager and other low-accessibility traits have characterized many cities' leadership systems for decades before current voters and innovators entered the present arenas of political action. As such, reformist institutions that reduce the political brokerage tasks of leaders may also (along with narrow scope) contribute to lower *current* levels of activation. For this reason, we may consider formal leadership accessibility a possible intervening variable between scope and the other measures of activation, partially or wholly mediating the effects of scope as well as contributing independently to activation levels.

THE ACTIVE SYSTEM: SIMILAR THEORETICAL MODELS

The model of political integration and action outlined in the preceding pages is comparable to three other models developed by Etzioni (1968), Hage and Aiken (1970), and Selznick (1969). Each of these models describes a system that is relatively more active with respect to innovation, output, leadership, and participation when conditions comparable to wide functional scope are present.

The Active Society

Etzioni (1968) analyzed the potential for the extralocal political integration of international communities. His concern with international units of analysis reflected, in large part, his belief that local communities no longer possess the power or resources to direct their own affairs. Throughout his lengthy discussion, he refers repeatedly to the upward expansion of fragmented power that leaves local areas with narrow options and a sense of alienation from their own decision-making contexts. Prime examples in the case of municipalities would be federally aided welfare programs, urban renewal, and even the much hallowed neighborhood school system. To the extent that Etzioni's hypothesis is correct on this score, he is indicating conditions affecting local municipal politics that cannot be measured with the use of purely city data. In this sense, the hypotheses listed previously may all have less force than the arguments for them suggest.

Despite this caveat, Etzioni's analysis of international community integration indicates that similar concepts and theory may apply to both contexts. His conception of an active society was one in which larger numbers of actors may successfully attain valued goals through commitment to a common political apparatus (p. 4). His three levels of politically integrative mechanisms were also similar to the ones listed here. The weakest mechanism, lacking collective focus of any kind, consists of "international exchanges of objects, symbols, and persons." This is the mechanism of the market without a specific marketplace. The social order that it yields is, to Etzioni, not sufficiently understood as an aggregated "social choice" of individual specialized units pursuing their own ends. He argues that this unguided order may very well arise from the separate rational strategies of each unit, but only at the demise of a society acting in the interests of many or all such units simultaneously. What concerned Etzioni, in this era when many global problems surpass specialized and local problems in their urgency, was that the elementary order of social choice offers little hope for broad sharing of the risks involved in undertaking extensive innovations in peace keeping and resource distribution and control.

A higher level of integration occurs when exchanges become patterned through what Etzioni called some common "functional organization." He refers here to the emerging international organization of a number of functions, of which finance, postal service, and aspects of scholarship and extractive industries might be examples. The final and highest level of integration occurs when many, if not all, of these functional organizations become "unified" by or within a supranational governing organ (pp. 558–566). It should be emphasized that Etzioni did not view this somewhat visionary proposition as "centralization" so much as "guided coordination" among actors sharing some common point of reference wherein consensus, compromise, coalitions, and legitimacy are constructed. Whether this is imminently likely at the international level is not at issue here.

The Dynamic Organization

With reference to a much smaller unit of analysis, Hage and Aiken (1970) developed two models characterizing polar types of complex organizations such as hospitals and police departments. Their term "complexity" is in some sense similar to the scope or functional differentiation of municipal governments. By complexity, they meant the number of occupational specialities in an organization; a variable not totally unrelated to the number of functional components in an institution like contemporary municipal governments.

Citing theorists from Durkheim through Parsons, Hage and Aiken asserted that complexity is "the single best measure of the development of an organization [p. 18]." That is, within an organization containing a wide range of specialized units, there is strong pressure toward the development of more such units through increasing specialization, recombination of resources (especially skills), and ultimately the adoption of "new programs" (pp. 13–15). This pressure was said to be generated partly by patterns of competition and problems of coordination among units seeking to expand the scope of their activities, and partly by the sheer quantity of different skills and interests that are both available and relevant to new problems (pp. 33–35).

Conversely, a simpler organization containing few specialized units would have neither the human resources nor the breadth of interunit competition that facilitates development and change. Moreover, for these same reasons the initiative and responsibility for decisions about change (or, more appropriately, about the management of routine) would tend to gravitate in this case to a few centralized positions in the organization (pp. 67–69). This is what Hage and Aiken called a "static style" as opposed to the "dynamic style" of the more complex organization.

If applied to the previous model of municipal political action, the term "interface" could be substituted for "competition" and the term "center of power" for "resources" or "skills." If wide-scope municipalities may be considered relatively more complex than narrow-scope municipalities, if organizational perspectives are indeed applicable to city government, and if we can disregard all organizations in a community other than city government, then the Hage and Aiken model would predict both innovativeness and "decentralization" (or nonreformed, accessible formal leadership systems) for wide-scope cities.

The Active Leadership

Selznick (1969) provides a third model of polar organizations differing in scope, and applies his comments directly to the issue of how politically active organizations are. His comments came in response to Wolin's (1960) charge that organization theorists ignore the political aspects of organizations, including those of governments. Wolin was particularly critical of the tendency to emphasize the unitary nature of bureaucratic organization at the expense of attention to the conflicts and coalitions that shape the policies of organizational management. This, in part, was Selznick's answer to Wolin:

> I do not believe that "all organizations are inevitably 'political' in character." Some are more so than others, and much depends on the narrowness or breadth of organizational ends. I have suggested that institutional leadership is dispensible when the organization's task is limited and closely defined, when technical criteria suffice for decision making. To the extent that

leadership can be dispensed with, by being reduced to routine management, the political perspective loses force and relevance.

On the other hand, many, and the most important, organizations have multiple goals and commitments. Those who run such organizations discover that the "purpose" of the enterprise is a complex and subtle product of external demands, internal needs, and capabilities; . . . they learn that the group structure of the organizations is a congeries of vested interests [p. 152].

In Selznick's view, the "politicalness" of a corporate group depends on—indeed, is largely defined in terms of—(1) whether the organization has broad enough sets of organizational ends to attract interest, (2) the expression of that interest through a combination of "meaningful participation" and visible leadership, and (3) the aggregate energy of potentially unifiable interests and influentials making diverse demands upon the group structure. Given relatively open organizations, as municipal governments are in contrast to private organizations, the second two conditions follow from the first. "Politicalness," then, depends on whether the organization or government does enough to attract the investment of interest.

Selznick's comments are particularly interesting and relevant in that they point to a distinction between "political action" and the more narrowly construed actions of the classical rational–legal bureaucracy. That is, action becomes less a matter of applying technical criteria and more of a political bartering process as the purposes of the organizational enterprise become more diffuse or complex. It is in this light that Selznick characterized the leadership of narrow-scope organizations as being reduced to routine management, for which he incidentally used the example of single-purpose special district governments to illustrate the point. It is but one small step beyond Selznick to hypothesize that the routine management of narrow-scope governments becomes housed within relatively "closed" or politically inaccessible formal leadership structures, and that a measure of routine in the management of such narrow-scope governments is an inclination toward minimum program innovation, tight-stringed fiscal performance, and maximum program accountability.

SUMMARY OF HYPOTHESES AND AN ALTERNATIVE VIEW

The theory of municipal political activation developed here and in the preceding chapters is depicted in Figure IV-1. Three basic sets of

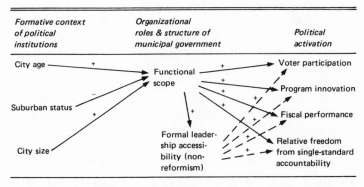

Figure IV-1. Causal model summarizing hypotheses. This model portrays the causal ordering and valence (+ or −) of hypothesized relationships, but implies nothing about the relative strength of these relationships. Solid lines distinguish relationships involving functional scope from other hypothesized relationships.

variables are ordered in causal sequence. *Political activation* is considered a consequence of *organizational roles* or functional scope, and scope a consequence of the government's *formative context* as discussed in Chapter III and as indexed by municipal age, city size, and suburban status. The only additional elaboration provided in Figure IV-1 is the placement of formal leadership accessibility in an intermediate position between scope and the other political-action variables, thereby reflecting the earlier presumption that the accessibility inhering in established nonreformed leadership arrangements may have an effect of its own on the more current types of activation or may partially mediate the effects of scope.

The central assumption in the depicted theory is that it posits a crucial role for functional scope as a factor mediating any pressures for or against activation emanating from the larger social and political environment of the government as denoted by the contextual variables. To help clarify this point, consider an alternative perspective to which we alluded earlier. One might argue that the three contextual variables denote forces giving rise to a host of structural arrangements in which diverse centers of power form interfaces, and that the functional scope of municipal government is but one manifestation of such arrangements.

That is, large, nonsuburban cities are generally understood to be more differentiated in a number of ways: in industry, in social composition and life styles, in civic organization, as well as within government. This diversity, even as it extends outside formal governing apparatuses, may be an important condition for active competition over governmental policy and outputs, and may facilitate the emergence of special coalitions prone to advance new government ventures and to bargain for the benefits of established functions. Stating this point another way, the less complex contexts of small cities and the specialized role of organized life in suburbs may engender considerable normative and interactive cohesion, but not the politically mobilizing dynamics of internal competition and coalition formation.

Similarly, the initial political culture formed in older cities may have assigned high value to broad-based networks of exchange through nongovernmental as well as governmental mechanisms, with all such networks in older cities gaining stability over time. Even within a government, there may be more ways of extending and unifying exchange networks than through expansion of functional scope, and nonreformed leadership arrangements may be a good example of one such possibility.

In other words, functional scope may be only one of many specific structural implications that the basic contextual factors have in a chain of effects leading from formative forces through organized structures of exchange to levels of activation. If this is true, little direct influence from scope to activation may be found upon simultaneously taking into account the *initial and more general* influences of the contextual indicators on activation. If, on the other hand, scope is a crucial intervening variable—if it is of singularly great significance as an indicator of integrated diversity—then it should have modest to strong direct effects on activation in the hypothesized directions despite simultaneous controls for effects of contextual factors. This is an empirical question to which much of the next two chapters is addressed, largely by use of path analytic techniques that distinguish between direct and indirect effects in a causal sequence such as the model developed here.

This issue illustrates once again that the model presented in Figure IV-1 is a specific form of a more general theory. This general theory may be termed the theory of activation by integrated, differentiated systems. Given a high degree of differentiation in any way, and given a high degree of integration of the differentiated parts within a system of exchanges, there will be correspondingly high level of activation, resource mobilization, or innovation, performance, and participation. As was noted earlier, Aiken and Alford (1968) advanced a general theory roughly similar to this in their initial studies of community adoption of federally assisted urban renewal, public housing, and poverty programs. The authors used the variables "city age," "city size," and "suburban status," as well as indicators of population heterogeneity and stability and governmental reformism, to denote the number of centers of power and number of interfaces between them in a city. Actually, some of these variables—in particular, the "contextual" ones—do not directly identify centers of power in interface, but instead refer to community attributes that create the conditions for the development of certain types, kinds, and qualities of organized exchange.

When Aiken and Alford specified this theory in subsequent published studies, they suggested that more direct measures of the critical independent variables should identify "the quality and stability of interorganizational ties, the accumulation of experience and information in a community system (continuity), and structural or organizational differentiation [1970a:863]." As an example of how at least the last of these three concepts might be measured, Aiken and Alford (1970a:859) suggested that researchers count "the number of organizations of various types which play some role in community life." The authors then employed data on the extensity of three types of organizations—manufacturing firms, banks, and trade unions—and found strong positive relationships between innovation in public housing and these measures of organizational differentiation. (Correlation coefficients ranged from .08 to .43.) In a similar study of poverty programs, Turk (1970) also used measures of industrial diversification to identify differentiation within an interorganizational system. Both the Aiken and Alford and the Turk studies suggested that these variables were still not entirely on target in that they refer to systems in the government's environment rather than to crucial characteristics of the government itself and its mode of organization. This brings us back to the scope variable.

We use functional scope to indicate differentiation within that interorganizational system for which the municipal government, through the functions and activities organized within it, is the focus. In one sense, then, the current study provides another opportunity to test the general theory using another indicator. Not only that, but the current study will also test the theory for several types of activation other than program innovation. More important, however, is the opportunity to assess just how important the governmental property of scope is, relative to environmental properties that also denote differentiating and integrating mechanisms.

It is in this last sense that we are dealing with competing theories. Are the inputs and outputs of relatively open organizational systems such as governments determined more by environmental attributes, or more by attributes of the organization of government? Even though scope may be shaped by broad national and regional influences, does not scope then become an internal organizational constraint on political-action processes? Do governments of varying structure and purpose effectively recruit and screen influence from the environment and, indeed, from their own paid staff, or are they subject willy nilly to whatever environmental pressures their host communities may happen to contain? The answers to these questions will help to assess whether the character of political action is truly affected by having limited rather than big government. It is to these questions that we now turn.

There is ample theory on both sides of these questions. This chapter has advanced a perspective once suggested by Lineberry and Fowler (1967), that governmental structure selectively integrates and mediates potential political forces located in the community. As elaborated earlier in terms of the scope variable, this thesis holds that the breadth of governmental activity is crucial for shaping the levels of political action it experiences and is a major condition for the exercise of influence by potential political actors in or associated with a community. Along with scope, another facet of governmental structure that might play the same role is the accessibility inhering in formal leadership arrangements, but even this may be a consequence of scope. The empirical analysis that follows focuses most sharply, then, on whether the fact of having broad rather than limited government is in itself substantial cause for greater and more diverse civic inputs and program outputs.

V.

The Activation of Voters and Leaders

Local politics became trivialized as the power and activities of state and national governments grew. The prestige of local public office underwent a considerable decline, and its former functions of public recognition and status allocation shifted to the private community service organizations. [From Rossi, P.H. and Rossi, A.S., An historical perspective on the functions of local politics; in *Social change and urban politics,* edited by D.N. Gordon. Copyright © 1973 by Prentice-Hall, Inc., Englewood Cliffs, N.J. p. 60].

The empirical analysis of the role of functional scope in municipal activation is sufficiently complex and lengthy to merit subdivision into two chapters. The present chapter deals with activation in the form of formal leadership accessibility and voter participation, both of which are chiefly concerned with aspects of civic involvement. Chapter VI takes up activation as government output in the form of fiscal performance, program innovativeness, and accountability.

For all but the accountability topic, the analysis begins in each case with a consideration of indicators and measurement problems, proceeds to an examination of simple bivariate or zero-order relationships between scope and activation, and concludes with a multiple regression analysis linking political activation variables in a causal sequence back to the environmental determinants of scope as indexed by municipal age, size, and suburban status. In several instances, these multivariate analyses are portrayed in path diagrams to facilitate interpretation. The remaining topic in the analysis, accountability, involves an interpretation of zero-order correlations between indicators of formal need and measures of program innovativeness, computed within categories of cities grouped by level of scope.

Discussion of the findings for each dependent variable suggests some modification of the scope-centered theory of what accounts for an active city. Environmental and organizational attributes have somewhat different effects, depending on the type of political activity involved. Scope never entirely proves to be without its predicted effect, while the city-age variable increasingly demands greater attention and interpretation. Conceptual and theoretical modifications of this nature are noted as the issues are raised by each set of findings. Some general implications of the overall findings, as well as some methodological and inferential limitations of the present study, are reviewed in the final chapter.

In focusing first on activation as civic involvement, the principal issue is the degree to which broad scope fosters the development of those leadership–participant linkages that provide a convergence of heterogeneous interests expressing various policy preferences. A convergence of this sort implies something quite different from consensus on substantive issues or centralization of decision making. The importance of broad civic involvement is that it extends a regime's basis for legitimacy to many quarters or to differing interests that may disagree on most policy matters but—because of involvement—are, in effect, expressing commitment to what Weber (1947: 126) called the "validity of an order." We want to know whether functional scope is an important part of the definition of that order.

Does broad scope extend leadership–participant linkages through such legitimacy-maintaining interactive patterns as the development of accessible or open leadership roles and a high level of voter turnout in a typical local election? Similarly, does limited scope sufficiently reduce the legitimate domain of government or, as Rossi and Rossi (1973:60) asked about the loss of local government functions, does it "trivialize" government for enough interests to result in little convergence of diverse interests, more narrowly defined leadership roles, and lower voter participation?

FORMAL LEADERSHIP ACCESSIBILITY

For roughly the last century, municipal governments have been the object of a multifaceted reform movement having as one objective the depoliticization of traditionally interest-group-based city governance. This movement has often rallied under the proposal that formal leadership roles should be derived more from the principles of managerial technique and efficiency and less from the political acts of power brokerage and negotiation, more from the representation of the community as a whole and less from the representation of a few specific interests (Stone et al. 1940). Reform measures that attain these ideological ends should have the practical effect of reducing the probability of advantage in efforts by interest groups to exercise influence, and should thereby reduce the accessibility of formal leaders. It is our hypothesis that this is more likely to occur in cities where narrow scope presumably limits the relevance of the government and of its leadership vis-a-vis many types of possible interests, and that wider-scope governments should correspondingly retain leadership systems that provide more diverse and open channels of access for the broader range of interests having something at stake in those governments.

Concepts and Indicators

Some important reforms that might limit accessibility have never been systematically reported or analyzed. For example, there is no comparative data on the relative fluidity of various bureaucratic procedures for transmitting influence attempts to leaders. Inferences regarding these procedures and the political process in nonbureaucratic contexts must be made from other data. The most widely recorded forms, and the ones considered here, pertain to gross "structural" changes in titles, recruitment procedures, and retention practices for leaders. These reforms include a city-manager form of chief executive, at-large election of councilmen, small city councils, nonpartisan elections, a short ballot or nonelective administrative officials, and civil service coverage of municipal employees. While all of these are "municipal reforms," some more clearly render government leaders inaccessible than do others if we consider some likely (but admittedly unsubstantiated) implications of each type of reform.

The *city manager* chief executive may be least ambiguous in this regard. City managers are usually trained in special schools of public administration, recruited through interviews with a city-council committee, charged with hiring municipal employees and with managing the municipal enterprise within general council policy, and they serve at the pleasure of as many successive city councils as deem their work acceptable. In contrast, the general public more directly monitors the development of mayors, for whom training is more diffuse in the sense of being rooted in the experience of competition for leadership, selection is normally by public election, responsibilities are founded in both constitutional and personal power-base obligations, and office holding is subject to periodically scheduled challenges decided by the voting electorate. By separating corporate management from public policymaking and influence, city-manager forms of chief executive most clearly constrain accessibility. An intermediate form of executive, the commission system, will be described later.

Although all cities normally elect their councilmen, the elections may constrain accessibility if they are conducted *at-large* and provide *small-city councils.* At-large elections make ward politics and the representation of residentially segregated interests relatively unlikely. Small city councils (e.g., those having six or fewer members) offer little heterogeneity of representation in policymaking, and would seem to increase the probability of unanimity or of dominance by an even smaller cohesive majority. In short, larger city councils and those elected by wards are more conducive to the elaboration of brokerage roles in service to more diverse centers of power, and therefore augment leadership accessibility.

The other three "reform" items on the previous list are more ambiguous with respect to accessibility. *Non partisan* elections may remove from citizen groups the leverage of coalescing behind competing parties, but they may also remove one of the most effective devices for centralizing power within tightly controlled political organizations. Nonpartisan elections may separate municipal leadership from the coattails of votes for the party of state and federal officials, thereby actually increasing the viability of purely local interests; although nonpartisanship may for the same reasons grant a cohesive, local power elite greater opportunities for behind-the-scenes manipulation or candidate and issue selection.

One important quality of the presence or absence of partisan local elections is the visibility of whatever exists in a particular city. Not all successful candidates are vocally loyal to the rules of their method of election, but the exceptions are probably not indifferent to them. The visibility of the partisanship variable is also evident in the major data compilations on city government and in the large-sample comparative studies of urban government. In studies covering this broad canvas, the partisanship of elections generally appears as an indicator of great electoral conflict, of multiple intraparty contending centers of power, and of extensive networks of party operatives providing access from constituent subgroups to party leaders and elected officials (e.g., Lineberry and Fowler, 1967; Aiken and Alford, 1970a; T. Clark, 1971; Turk, 1973b). Bucking this traditional definition is the professionalization of intraparty roles and the incomplete demise of those political machines that provided the lower-level access but little electoral conflict (e.g., Greenstein 1964). In nearly any type of city today, labeled civic groups other than parties often provide more critical sponsorship than does the party label. Given these developments, it is not at all unlikely that some partisan systems provide a maximum of two centers of power (or fail to identify any) while initiating many fleeting interfaces without exchanges. The growing proportion of "independent" voters is an indicator of this meaning of partisanship.

The empirical research on partisan versus nonpartisan elections has been extensive but tends to lead to conditional conclusions rather than general ones. For example, in his extensive literature review and original empirical study, W. Hawley (1973) reported concurring evidence that nonpartisan elections involve little competition or conflict, and that they enhance the electability of organizational dominants (of which the much-touted Republican bias of nonpartisanship is considered the prime example). Yet, Hawley demonstrates that this comparison with partisan cities holds only in some contexts and is conditional upon relative party strength, community class composition, and size of city. More generally, whether greater accessibility is found in partisan or nonpartisan elections would seem to depend on the character of both the two-party structure and the elite infrastructure.

The ambiguous political implications of the short ballot, or of *nonelected administrative officials,* concerns the degree of change in accessibility implied by this reform. Regardless of whether bureaucratic chiefs are elected, service agencies have direct constituencies comprised of affected or impacted interests, which have means of withholding legitimacy unless they are somehow involved or co-opted (Selznick, 1949). Frequency of succession seems more important in reducing oligarchic tendencies among chiefs than does the method of selection (Zald 1970:245ff, Michels 1949). More importantly, for new bureau chiefs to maintain control, they must ordinarily adapt to internal bureaucratic interests and to their standard operating procedures or, at most, attempt a further formalization of those procedures with the risk of noncompliance (Gouldner, 1954). Lower participants in bureaucracies have substantial control over information and other resources for power (Mechanic, 1962), may effectively resist policy-change attempts by elected officials (Lipset, 1950), and no doubt exercise disproportionate influence in the selection of either elected or appointed successors to the agency chief's role.

The forcefulness that a bureaucracy has in shaping its leadership roles may in the long run override and dissipate any autonomous channels of access inherent in the short-run election process. Although the deterioration of accessibility between elections is a classic problem affecting representatives holding any elective office, the countervailing pressures of persistent civic demands would seem to be far more plentiful in the case of legislators or other public-policy generalists than in the case of the man who heads a single bureau. As a result, there may be little actual difference in overall leadership accessibility in having several elected rather than appointed bureau or department heads.

Civil service reforms cut two ways in efforts to depoliticize government. On the one hand, civil-service coverage may sever many of the ties between bureaucracies and the constituencies to whom elected officials would otherwise give the spoils of victory. On the other hand, civil-service coverage increases the opportunity for governmental employees to develop constituencies autonomous from those of elected officials, although this autonomy may promote narrow bureaucratic self-interest more often than a more open ombudsman posture. It is not obvious whether the end result is greater or lesser overall accessibility.

Bivariate Analysis with Scope

Despite the ambiguities of some reform measures, all of them have been included in Tables V-1 and V-2 showing the relationship between functional scope and municipal reform. Table V-1 provides a full elaboration of the percentage of municipalities having each type of chief executive by functional scope. For the other measures, Table V-2 shows only the percent of municipalities having the "unreformed" features of formal leadership structure. Note that the categories of functional scope have been collapsed in three instances to facilitate comparison across cells having a small number of entries.

TABLE V-1

Percentage of Municipalities with Each Type of Chief Executive (Mayor, Commission, or Manager), for All Cities and by Levels of Functional Scope

Type of chief executive[a]	Functional scope (number of functions)						All cities
	0-1	2	3	4	5-6	7-9	
Mayor	23%	34%	32%	34%	54%	62%	38%
Commission	4	11	13	16	10	5	11
Manager	73	55	55	50	36	34	50
Totals	100%	100%	100%	100%	100%	101%	99%
	(71)	(91)	(158)	(174)	(109)	(65)	(668)

[a]Source for chief executive data: *The Municipal Year Book: 1963.* No missing data.

Table V-1 supports the hypothesis that inaccessible city managers are more likely in narrow-scope cities, and that the more accessible mayor system is more likely in wide-scope cities. The relationship is both strong and nearly monotonic across all cells, with the probability of a mayor chief executive rising from .23 to .62 as functional scope increases from 0–1 to 7–9 functions. The causal direction here, if there is one and if the relationship is not spurious, probably runs from scope to executive type. The mayor form has the earliest origins, deriving, I would suggest, from the diffuse executive and legislative responsibilities of early wide-scope cities. The city manager is a twentieth-century reform, made politically feasible and administratively desirable by more recent effacement of functions to a technically manageable few. Based on limited cross-sectional data, this explanation can, of course, be only highly tentative.

This same explanation is, however, greatly strengthened by findings on the functional scope of the commission form of government. Note that the commission type of combined executive–legislative– administrative leadership is disproportionately a middle-scope phenomenon. The commission system is essentially a topless city council, with each commissioner assuming administrative responsibility as chief of a department or functional branch. The reason for the clustering of this commission form among middle-scope cities may have to do in part with the mechanics of putting such a commission together. In narrow-scope cities, there may not be enough major functions for each of five to seven commissioners to have one. A single city manager is a more feasible alternative. On the other hand, wide-scope cities have so many functional components that management by an equally numerous set of commissioners may be unwieldy. Moreover, on the degree of accessibility, the commission system is neither low (due to the election of department heads

TABLE V-2

Percentage of Municipalities Possessing Various "Unreformed" Features of Formal Leadership Structure, for All Cities and by Levels of Functional Scope

Features of formal leadership structure[a]	Functional scope (number of functions)						All cities	N[a]
	0-1	2	3	4	5-6	7-9		
Election of council by wards[b]	17%	36%	31%	41%	54%	52%	38%	665
Large city council[b]	32	51	49	59	68	91	57	668
Partisan municipal elections[b]	17	33	30	31	28	23	28	668
Other elected officials[c]	54	47	37	39	24	59	41	644
Fewer than all city employees under civil service coverage[c]	48	52	63	64	61	59	60	633
No city employees under civil service[c]	20	15	19	12	21	13	17	633

[a] Coding procedures: Election of Council by Wards: Coded "by wards" if at least 67% of the council was elected by wards; three cities were deleted for lack of data. Large City Council: Coded "large" if the council consisted of seven or more members; no missing data. Partisan Municipal Elections: Coded as reported in the *Year Book*; no missing data. Other Elected Officials: Coded "others elected" if officials other than councilmen, commissioners, mayor, and/or city manager were elected to municipal posts; twenty-four cities with missing data were deleted. Civil Service Coverage: Coded as reported in the *Year Book*; thirty-five cities with missing data were deleted.

[b] Source: *The Municipal Year Book: 1963,* Table III.

[c] Source: *The Municipal Year Book: 1965,* Table V.

to general policy positions) nor necessarily very high (due to the inherent requirement of at-large elections). Finally, it should be noted that in time sequence, the commission form was invented intermediately between mayors and city managers, or at a time when middle-scope cities had come more to the fore than the still emerging narrow-scope cities.

Table V-2 presents additional support for the argument that reforms most clearly conducive to inaccessibility are least likely to occur in broad-scope cities. Most of the broadest-scope cities have councilmanic elections by ward and nearly all have large city councils (defined as seven or more members), while the opposite conditions of relative inaccessibility tend to hold for the narrowest-scope cities. Further inspection reveals that there is little or no relationship between functional scope and the more ambiguous types of reform pertaining to partisanship, election of administrative officials, and civil-service coverage.[1] The many facets of municipal reform include some aspects associated with functional scope and facilitating the accessibility of leaders, as well as other aspects having little to do with either scope or the question of accessibility.

In the interests of data reduction and for more accurate identification of the general concept of accessibility, a scale was developed from the three indicators of accessibility. Cities having nonmanager executives, elections by wards, and large city councils were assigned a high score of three on this "accessibility scale." Cities having only two of these traits were assigned a score of two, and so on through a low score of zero for cities having none. For the purposes of constructing this scale, commission cities were combined with mayor cities on the "accessibility" side of the scale. The alternative procedure, of placing commission cities with city-manager cities, was considered in experimental calculations and produced minor fluctuations from the findings reported here.[2]

---

[1] Civil-service coverage is reported in two ways due to data interpretation problems. The data source (see Table V-2) reported coverage for "all," "most," "some," "few," or "no" employees. If these categories are relative to the total number of employees in each individual city, then "all" for a narrow-scope city could be equivalent to "some" or "few" in a wide-scope city. If, however, the categories are relative to an absolute standard, then "few" in a narrow-scope city may actually mean "all" of those employed by that city. Given this, only the "no employees" category is clearly interpretable, while the "less than all" category *may* simply indicate whether civil-service coverage has gone as far as possible.

[2] This accessibility scale is very similar to Lineberry and Fowler's (1967) index of reformism. Both measures include items for the presence or absence of a city manager executive and of at-large councilmanic elections. In addition, my accessibility scale includes an item for the presence or absence of large city councils, while the Lineberry and Fowler

TABLE V-3

Matrix of Intercorrelations between Selected Measures of Formal Leadership Structure, the Formal Leadership Accessibility Scale, Functional Scope, and Contextual Variables (N = 668 Cities)

Variables	(1)	(2)	(3)	(4)	(5)	(6)	(7)	(8)
(1) Non-manager[a]	—							
(2) Elections by wards[a]	.37	—						
(3) Large city council[a]	.13	.46	—					
(4) Accessibility scale[b]	.68	.82	.72	—				
(5) Functional scope	.20	.19	.20	.27	—			
(6) Municipal age (High score = old)	.31	.17	.25	.33	.56	—		
(7) Suburban status[a]	-.08	-.05	-.05	-.08	-.37	-.45	—	
(8) City size (log n)	.11	.03	.21	.16	.34	.53	-.28	—

[a] Dichotomous (0, 1) variable with variable name indicating high score. See Tables V-1, V-2, and III-3 for data sources and for procedures by which variables were dichotomized. Missing data for political–structure variables were recoded with the mean for those variables.
[b] Computed by adding the scores on the Non-manager, Elections by wards, and Large city council variables. A high score of 3 indicates the presence of all three traits, and a low score of 0 indicates the absence of all three traits.

---

index instead included an item for the presence or absence of nonpartisan elections. For the 668 cities in the present study, the shared variance between the two measures is 68 % of the total. The two measures are nearly equally correlated with functional scope ($r = .27$ with accessibility, $r = -.26$ with reformism).

Experimental calculations using Lineberry and Fowler's reformism index produced no findings substantively different from those reported here for the accessibility scale. The principal difference was that the reformism index performed less well in that it generally provided slightly lower coefficients with all other variables than did the accessibility scale. I took that as evidence of greater consistency of meaning in the accessibility scale, as I have argued on other conceptual and empirical grounds in introducing the scale.

I am also motivated to discount the reformism index somewhat, in light of my earlier finding (1974a) that its substantive significance in helping Lineberry and Fowler (1967) to explain city government expenditures is spurious due to the great importance of functional inclusiveness in "determining" both total expenditures and certain aspects of reformism. The present study focuses explicitly on how scope and reform are in fact related, and how they in turn affect various political outcomes.

The correlations between each of the three indicators and the scale are all impressively high (Table V-3). In addition, functional scope is somewhat more strongly correlated with the scale ($r = .27$) than with any of the individual indicators ($r = .20, .19, .20$). If these latter coefficients seem smaller than might have been expected on the basis of the cross-tabular analysis, the difference between the two modes of analysis is more apparent than real. Modest correlations of $.20$ as represented in Table V-3 reflect strikingly variable conditional probabilities as presented in Tables V-1 and V-2.

Multivariate Analysis with Scope and Contextual Variables

Accessibility may now be treated as a single variable in more complex analyses. Specifically, we are concerned with multiple regression models that depict the independent contributions of functional scope on accessibility apart from effects due to the contextual variables of municipal age, size, and suburban status. The reasoning behind this procedure merits further elaboration.

Theory

Most relevant is the issue of competing explanations for the incidence of reformism in general and the components of the accessibility scale in particular. A number of different empirical studies (e.g., Schnore and Alford 1963, Alford and Scoble 1965, Wolfinger and Field 1966, Lineberry and Fowler 1967, Aiken and Alford 1968) have presented evidence that several types of reforms, especially the manager system, tend to occur in small, suburban, new cities.[3] Similar findings are shown in Table V-3 for the 668 cities in the present study. Explanations for these findings have typically been stated in terms of the low degree of social and organizational heterogeneity and the minimal political competitiveness indicated by these three contextual attributes. That is, reformed and inaccessible leadership arrangements may be in part a consequence of limited diversity and conflict in the environment of the government's host community. This perspective does not necessarily assume anything about the socioeconomic composition or normative ethos of com-

---

[3] Disregarded here are Wolfinger and Field's (1966) findings of a strong regional variation in the incidence of reformism. Municipal age is probably a viable substitute for whatever region "stands for."

munity contexts, other than that small, suburban, and newer cities are less differentiated along many lines and therefore generate fewer demands for multiple and autonomous points of access.

It is useful at this point to reiterate the conceptual interpretation of municipal age, size, and suburban status that was developed in the analysis of causes of scope. Municipal age is considered to denote, in the most general sense, the extensiveness of each organization or institutional network of organizations in a city, resulting partly from network expansion over time but largely from early community-like modes of organization. The extensiveness of these networks, whether assessed in terms of the number of social units that are formally federated, or less formally in terms of simple exchange patterns, is considered to be less in newer cities due to the absence of integrating organizational residues out of the past and to the greater structuring of community life by new forms of specialized organization. City size denotes differentiation among organizations or, more concretely, the number of different organizations, regardless of any networks that they may form. Suburban status denotes a particular type of specialization of community organizations: that which distinguishes suburbs as socially and politically specialized areas within the metropolitan context.

We are now faced with the proposition that communities having highly complex modes of organization on any or all of these measures (i.e., older, larger, nonsuburban communities) will also have such diversity of demand and such organizational weight behind demands that accessible formal leadership arrangements are maintained for multiple points of entry, and that the simpler structure of other communities generates pressures for a government that is essentially a bastion against the few remaining particularistic interests. This is what may be termed the "theory of environmental influence."

We have emphasized, partially opposed to this perspective, a scope-centered perspective, or what may be called the "theory of governmental intervention." In this latter view, the hypothesized effect of environmental influence is first on defining the proper functions of the government and then, through functional scope and as a result of an independent effect by scope, on delivering to the municipality its appropriate level of political activation. By this perspective, scope becomes a major, perhaps *the* major, constraint on the extent to which contextual pressures to activate (or to deactivate) are transmitted and received by decision makers. This mediating effect by scope may obtain even though there is an inseparably high covariance between scope and the contextual variables. Since the relationship between scope and the contextual variables is still far below unity (R^2 = .332; see Table V-4), there will be many cities having wider or narrower scope than their contextual status would predict. We would expect that for these deviant cases, scope is a better predictor of accessibility than are the contextual variables, and therefore a better predictor overall.

As a theoretical design, this approach is not unlike the causal models used in contemporary stratification research to analyze status attainment (and as summarized by Haller and Portes 1973). Contextual variables in the present instance are comparable in meaning and methodological usage to socioeconomic background variables in the stratification studies. The SES variables, like the contextual variables, have diffuse meanings with respect to formative processes, but they also have some relatively well known empirical relationships with the criterion variable (status attainment or activation). The intervening variables in these models are selected and inserted largely to decompose these relationships, to specify how they occur, or, to some extent, to explain additional variance in the criterion variable.

Methods

In causal models of this sort, the appropriate statistic for identifying effects is the standardized partial regression coefficient, also known as a *beta* and as a path coefficient depending on usage. The value that this coefficient takes is the number of standard units the dependent variable will change for every standard unit of change in the independent variable, holding constant other independent variables or regressors in the model. Using this as a definition of "effect," a coefficient of .40 would indicate an effect twice as great as one of .20. Another measure of effect, explained variance, is used here only with respect to the effect of all variables taken together and as indicated by the coefficient of determination (R^2).

Table V-4 presents the standardized partial regression coefficients in the regression of accessibility and of functional scope on the independent variables. The regression analysis for scope is a duplication of findings reported earlier in Table III-4, and shows the strong independent effects on scope by municipal age as well as the weaker independent effects of suburban status and city size. These findings are presented again here for inclusion in the path diagram depicted in Figure V-1.

Two regression models for explaining accessibility are presented in Table V-4. The first model includes as regressors all three contextual variables and functional scope. The second model deletes from the

TABLE V-4
Standardized Partial Regression Coefficients and R^2 in Multiple Regression Analyses
Explaining Accessibility and Functional Scope (Standard Error in Parenthenses;
N = 668 Cities)

Dependent variable	Independent variables				R and R^2
	Functional scope	Municipal age	Suburban status	City size	
Accessibility (Model 1)	.138 (.044)	.317 (.050)	.101 (.041)	-.030 (.043)	$R = .360$ $R^2 = .130$
Accessibility (Model 2)	.136 (.044)	.303 (.046)	.103 (.041)	–– ––	$R = .360$ $R^2 = .129$
Functional scope		.469 (.040)	-.141 (.036)	.052 (.037)	$R = .577$ $R^2 = .332$

regressors a contextual variable (city size) that, in the first model, had a standardized coefficient smaller than its standard error. Of course, all nonzero coefficients are "significant" in a study of a population such as this one. Some coefficients may nonetheless be considered to approximate zero, and therefore be of negligible substantive importance, if they are no greater than their standard error. Deletion of the corresponding regressors provides a simpler and more parsimonious model, with little or no loss of explained variance. Note that the coefficient of determination in Model 1 is $R^2 = .130$, and in Model 2 it is $R^2 = .129$. The path diagram in Figure V-1 is derived from the second or simpler regression model for accessibility.

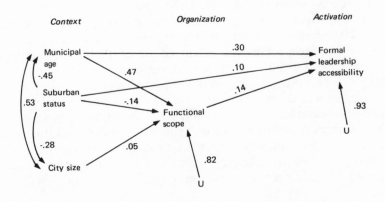

Figure V-1 Path diagram for accessibility and antecedent variables.

A final note on procedure is in order. Path diagrams facilitate interpretation of ordinary multiple regression models principally in two ways. First, path diagrams combine all stages of a causal sequence in a single and wholly deterministic representation. This identifies all analyzed variables in their assumed causal order and depicts their effects on subsequent variables controlling for prior variables. Secondly, path diagrams facilitate visual distinction of the direct effects of a variable from its indirect effects via intervening variables. A direct effect is equivalent to a standardized partial regression coefficient and is the value of a path coefficient in the diagram. An indirect effect pertains to any given chain of paths leading from an independent variable to an ultimate dependent variable. Each indirect effect may be calculated from data presented in the diagram by serially multiplying the path coefficients forming a chain.[4]

Findings

The first thing to note in the regression models and in the path diagram is that the coefficient indicating the link between scope and accessibility is reduced by about half from the zero-order correlation ($r = .27$) to the regression or path coefficient ($p = .14$). This reduction in the effect of scope is greater than the scope-centered hypothesis would lead us to expect. Yet, in support of this hypothesis, the effect does remain positive and of greater magnitude than the effects of two of the three contextual variables.

Having an even smaller effect than scope is suburban status, which unexpectedly has a *positive* coefficient of .10 on its direct path to accessibility. Controlling for scope, size, and age, suburban cities are *more* likely to have unreformed, accessible forms of leadership arrangements. This effect is not of sufficient magnitude to merit extensive comment, but we will return to it later because it is discrepant with the environmental perspective (which predicts a negative direct effect) and is not wholly in keeping with the scope-centered perspective (which predicts no direct effect). More in keeping with the latter is the negative *indirect* effect of suburban status on accessibility by way of scope (note the paths from suburban

---

[4] For discussions of path analysis in sociological research, see Duncan (1966), Land (1969), and Alwin and Hauser (1975).

status to scope and from scope to accessibility). This indirect effect is, however, very small indeed at only −.02.

The findings for city size are of even smaller magnitude, but they pose no problem of discrepancy from both environmental and scope-centered perspectives. Consistent with the latter, city size has essentially no direct effect at all on accessibility. Its indirect effect through scope provides very weak additional support to the same perspective, for although the scope-mediated effect of size is in the expected direction, it is also insubstantial at only .01.

As a matter of substantive importance, municipal age is far more significant than either scope or the other two contextual variables. The value of the direct path from age to accessibility is just over .30, compared with .14 for the path from scope to accessibility. This is contrary to what the scope-centered theory predicted, and gives greater support to the theory of environmental influence at least in this one very important instance. Note, however, that scope does have some mediating effect with respect to age, for the indirect effect of age on accessibility by way of scope is .06.

Discussion

What do these findings mean? First, it is instructive to recall that all of the independent variables in the analysis are considered ways of identifying the extent to which highly differentiated interorganizational systems are formed in the community. If the four independent variables are taken to comprise elements of this composite theoretical construct, then our measures of this construct jointly explain roughly 13 % of the variance in formal leadership accessibility. With the apparent exception of the direct contribution by suburban status, the relationship is always in the expected direction whether one is concerned with environmental or organizational (scope-determined) influences. In this sense, we have found relatively consistent support for the general thesis that cities with simple and limited networks of interrelated organizations tend to adopt reformed, non-politicized, and relatively inaccessible formal leadership arrangements. This generalization may be tentatively accepted, pending further research to assess whether greater variance can be explained by other general constructs or by more exact indicators of the construct considered here.

The major exception to this generalization concerns the independent role of suburban status. Suburbs may be socially, politically, and organizationally specialized vis-a-vis their metropolitan context, yet they have a slight tendency to adopt more open leadership arrangements when we take into account their newness, their small size, and their narrow scope. Some post hoc speculation may suggest an avenue for further research on this discrepancy. For example, suburban specialization may be found in many types of activity or organization and tends to form the basis for a distinctive life style on which the suburb's claim to autonomous existence or legitimacy often seems to rest. To protect and compete for special types of constituents and resources, to avoid blending with neighboring municipalities both socially and in legal fact, and ultimately to secure and reinforce the legitimacy of the suburban jurisdiction, the suburban polity may sometimes strengthen its own intramunicipal power base by keeping open many channels of access to the municipal leadership. Such a strategy would not so much increase the autonomous points of contact for dissimilar constituents as it would provide multiple points of entry for the same or similar constituents, especially if we control for size, age, and scope as factors affecting alternative strategies.

This line of reasoning has some support in the literature, particularly in Wood's (1964) study of the New York metropolitan area. Wood suggested that intermunicipal specialization and competition often give formal leaders more visibility and contact with their constituents than would be normal without the competition. The present data can hardly test this proposition in its full richness, and are only suggestive of an alternative line of inquiry. It also remains to be demonstrated whether this proposition offers any promise for explaining suburban activation in forms other than the accessibility of leadership roles.

On a methodological note, it should be kept in mind that suburbs do not label themselves as such. They must be identified through one of many possible classification schemes. For this study, cities have been classified as suburbs if they are within metropolitan areas, (i.e., 1960 Standard Metropolitan Statistical Areas or SMSA's), excluding the largest city in each of those areas. This classification serves the intended purpose of identifying the smaller communities surrounding central cities in highly urbanized settings. A different classification (e.g., including the "suburbs" of non-SMSA central cities, or excluding the smaller "twins" in twin-city SMSA's) might have yielded different findings in this instance and in others throughout this study.

The suburban question, and the broad generalization from which it is an exception, has important implications for a general theory of political activation by integrated systems of varying differentiation. The thrust of the inquiry here has, however, dealt with a more precise issue. Does this general theory reduce to a more specific one in which municipal functional scope plays a crucial role alone and as a mediator of the effects of contextual or environmental influences? Can we, in short, reduce our notion of relevant interorganizational networks to just one such network, which focuses on the organization of the municipality with its wide or narrow scope? With respect to explaining the likely accessibility of formal leaders, the answer must be a qualified "no" on the basis of the present data.

Municipalities seem to have acquired more or less accessible leadership arrangements largely as a result of environmental factors arising from age-cohort differences. The age-related differences that count may, in the simplest formulation, reflect the commitment by older cities to traditions of "nonreform" born of an earlier era, and the greater opportunity for newer cities to follow current reformist fads, regardless of scope. But what gives rise to such traditions and fads, if not historical changes in the parameters of governmental enterprise?

Following the environmental approach, it could be argued that, regardless of scope, older cities have long had more powerful or more extensively integrated blocs of interests demanding access than have organizationally amorphous new cities. Similarly, to the extent that newer cities are relatively unstructured in all institutional domains, their polity offers little foundation for pluralist-based leadership, the few who establish these new governments may more easily engineer restrictions on accessibility, and the state legislatures that charter them may face little local resistance in any effort to mandate restrictive local leadership roles. These are examples of ways in which leadership accessibility might be affected by a set of age-related environmental factors falling under the rubric of "institutional-domain integration."

Other environmental factors, pertaining to the differentiating implications of large city size and nonsuburban status, are far less important. More exact measures of diversity in the municipal community may prove the opposite, but within the limited framework of this study, diversity alone is of less significance in shaping accessibility than are certain integrative tendencies as indexed by municipal age and scope. Along this line, and still within the environmental perspective, we have suggested that some suburbs may actually adopt accessible leadership forms as a defensive or competitive strategy and as a means of reinforcing the integration of relatively undifferentiated constituent interests. Similarly, it seems that accessible leaderships are at least as compatible with the simple composition of small cities as they are with the more complex and fragmented composition of large cities.

Turning back to scope, the findings provide sufficient basis for further research on the scope-centered perspective. Consider the possibility that the initiative for many of the first accessibility-reducing reforms may have come from within municipalities newly experiencing the management of narrow-scope enterprises. The narrowing of scope may then have been a catalyst for these reforms and for fads that subsequently swept various types of cities regardless of their scope. This possibility may also be stated in interorganizational terms. Early reformers may have responded more to conditions and pressures generated internally by the organization of government, while later reformers may have responded more to contacts and knowledge provided by a growing national network of reformers. Unfortunately, the available data did not contain information on when cities adopted reform or nonreform features of leadership, let alone whether they have retained the system that they started with or have changed from one to the other. Historical research on this matter must await more extensive data collection.

Despite the evidence on municipal age, it seems that scope does have some independent effect on accessibility, and it does play some role in recruiting and screening environmental influences on the selection of leadership arrangements. Each of the environmental variables has some scope-mediated indirect effect on leadership accessibility. In comparison with indicators of environmental differentiation and specialization (size and suburban status), scope has the stronger direct effect in bringing pressures to bear for a more open leadership. Among all of the variables considered, a greater effect was caused only by the broad historical and formative experiences of different municipal-age cohorts. These observations provide sufficient basis for retaining the causal model depicted in Figure V-1, while calling attention to the mixed pattern of some effects arising from governmental attributes combined with persisting environmental effects on formal leadership arrangements.

VOTER PARTICIPATION

The analysis of voter participation and of the other types of activation will be abbreviated due to the introduction in the previous section of much of the relevant methodology. In particular, the general rationale and technical design of the multivariate analyses will not be reiterated, except where necessary to clarify new problems or to call attention to nuances of interpretation appropriate to each dependent variable.

Concepts and Indicators

Voter participation differs from other types of political activation in that it may be the only major political act for which individuals rather than organizations or their agents are the actors. In choosing to vote or not to vote, individuals are formally answerable to no one but themselves. Despite this fact, the nature of social ôrganization is quite relevant to studies of voting. Discussions of local voter participation (e.g., Pinard 1963, Alford and Lee 1968, Gordon 1970, and the literature review in Boskoff and Ziegler 1964) often take as their central hypothesis the proposition that voting is induced by "attachments" or forms of individual involvement or identification with reference groups of various sorts, including virtually anything from neighborhood groups through political parties to city hall itself. Since the probability that an individual does not have any attachments whatsoever may be close to zero, research has focused on the character of such attachments that may exist and on the group or groups with which they are made.

One seemingly important type of attachment that has been given little research attention is brought about by the government itself. To the extent that a government is involved in the various private, occupational, social, and public affairs of an eligible voter, that government establishes or fosters conduits of information to the voter regarding matters of mutual interest. Somehow, most voters learn how the government wants them to dispose of their garbage or where it wants them to send their children to school. If sanitation and education are functions of the municipal government, we would expect stronger citizen attachments directly with that government, or indirectly with it through civic groups, than if these and most other functions were performed by a different government. This statement would be true if, in addition, individual voters or their civic reference groups were generally aware of which government provides which function, and if they were generally interested in at least some of the public issues generated by governmental activity. Under these conditions, the functional scope of a government should be a major factor affecting voter participation.

This proposition can be elaborated further. High voter participation in wide-scope cities may, for some individuals, be an expression of concern with current issues or, for others, a diffuse reactive response to the traditionally pervasive role of the government. With respect to the latter, wide scope may be the condition facilitating long-term affiliations with some branch of the government and with interest groups concerned with some branch, or wide scope may simply obviate any confusion regarding the locus of governmental responsibility for any and all local public affairs. The common element in each of these examples is that the probability of individual voting, and therefore overall voter participation levels, depends on the breadth of governmental activity and on the presence of a focal municipal role in diverse issue arenas either currently or in the past.

To test this scope-centered proposition, two separate aspects of voter participation might be considered. First is the process of becoming qualified to vote by meeting standards of legal eligibility and by registering. Second is the actual act of voting by registrants. Either of these, or both taken together, may be used to define voter participation, although explanations for one may not be identical with explanations for the other. For example, local laws pertaining to eligibility may be highly restrictive in instances where the actual turnout of registrants is high. To avoid the peculiarities of de facto and *de juro* variations in state and local restrictions on voter eligibility, the present research follows a seminal study by Alford and Lee (1986) is using the *percent of registrants voting* as the defining indicator of voter participation.

The data for this indicator are also the same as those used by Alford and Lee, who provide a discussion of the 1961–62 survey in which the data was collected (see also Lee 1963). The sample will be restricted to the 282 cities over 25,000 in 1960 population for which this voter turnout data is available and in which municipal elections were *not* concurrent with federal, state, or other nonmunicipal local elections. This latter restriction minimizes the probability that voters went to the polls to vote for officials or policies other than those of the municipality. Because Alford and Lee restricted their sample to the same 282 cities for the bulk of their study, their findings regarding the effects on voting by reformist leadership and by environmental factors are in many respects directly comparable to findings reported here. The difference between that study and the present one lies chiefly in the use here of an additional variable, scope, to assess the importance of any "screening" and "recruiting" effects of this organizational property.

Bivariate Analysis with Scope and Control Variables

Some support for the scope-centered hypothesis is provided by an initial test presented in Table V-5. The table shows a zero-order correlation coefficient of .24 for the relationship between scope and registered voter turnout in the 282 cities reporting nonconcurrent municipal elections in 1961 or 1962. Considering the large number of possible unique situational factors that might increase the variance of voter turnout among all cities, the apparent zero-order effect of scope is substantial. If it were possible to statistically remove the variance in voter turnout that is due to situational differences in the personal appeal of candidates, to differences in weather conditions on election day, or to other unique or personalistic local events, and if scope is unrelated to such events, it would seem that scope is associated with a considerable share of the remaining variance in voter turnout.

The nonsituational or nonpersonalistic variance in voter turnout is presumably linked to the political and social structure of the community or, stated otherwise, is due to "attachments." There are, of course, types of attachments other than the scope-related type that arise from the breadth of governmental impingement on citizen affairs and in issue arenas. One other type of attachment pertains more narrowly to linkages between official leaders and constituents, arises from the greater receptiveness of formally accessible leaders to contact and influence, and may be denoted by the accessibility scale. Attachments of this sort may be conducive to voting regardless of the breadth of governmental activity, insofar as they reflect enduring civic liaisons with leaders rather than with any particular bureaucracy, program, or set of bureaucracies and programs. This was, in effect, Alford and Lee's interpretation of their findings that registered voter turnout is greater in cities having nonmanager ($r = .43$) and partisan ($r = .28$) political structures. In the present study, the correlation between voter turnout and the accessibility scale is .36 (see Table V-5). This rather strong correlation is somewhat greater than the correlation between scope and voting.

However, as Alford and Lee suggested, the relationship between voting and accessible formal leadership may be partially spurious in the sense that both variables may be caused by a third factor, such as contextual or organizational pressures to activate or to deactivate

TABLE V-5

Matrix of Intercorrelations between Registered Voter Turnout, Accessibility, Functional Scope, and Contextual Variables (N = 282 Cities)

	(1)	(2)	(3)	(4)	(5)	(6)
(1) Registered voter turnout[a]	—					
(2) Accessibility scale	.36	—				
(3) Functional scope	.24	.32	—			
(4) Municipal age	.29	.37	.58	—		
(5) Suburban status	-.06	-.13	-.47	-.48	—	
(6) City size	.02	.14	.28	.46	-.29	—

[a]Percentage of registered voters voting in 1962 municipal elections. Source: See Alford and Lee (1968); Lee (1963).

political forms and processes. Hence, the zero-order findings on accessibility are not yet evidence of a separate effect on voting by accessibility, nor do they yet suggest the extent to which accessibility plays an intervening role in transmitting the effect of scope or of contextual variables on voting.

There may be instances where the effects suggested here are the other way around, running from voter turnout to scope or to accessibility. That is, high voter turnout may sometimes convey a preference for a leadership styled to be more accessible or for a government that has more functions. Similarly, low turnout may sometimes cause atrophy of accessible leadership forms and of the development of functions. This line of reasoning, while perhaps valid on occasion, seems improbable in the main. Current levels of voting may not be at all similar to voting levels at the time when the institutions of government, including its scope and leadership arrangements, were established. These institutions were sometimes established prior to any elections. More important specific preferences are not necessarily indicated by turnout but by the decisions made by those who vote.

Aside from any effects on voting by the scope and leadership systems of the government itself, voting may also be induced by aspects of community social organization that are external to or in the environment of the government. The distinction here is between voting in response to the role of government and of its leaders, and voting in response to civic, social, or political attachments that exist regardless of governmental attributes. Although there is no way to draw this distinction with sharp empirical clarity by use of available comparative data, some tentatively useful distinctions can be made using municipal age, size, and suburban status as indicators of likely environmental impingements on the propensity to vote.[5]

One of these indicators, municipal age, was included as an important explanatory variable in the Alford and Lee study of voting (1968: 801). They argued that the *continuity* of local social and political life, as measured by municipal age, gives rise over time to solidly and traditionally maintained attachments with groups and institutions having a stake in the city's political and governmental system, and that this in turn results in high voter turnout. On the basis of the present study, we may add that continuity is most important in the sense that extensive networks of attachments are formed at or near the time of municipal birth in older cities, are reinforced and somewhat extended over time, but may *never* appear, or appear only in limited form, in newer cities as they age. By either view of age and continuity, the relevant attachments are, by imputation, presumed to invoke voting as a kind of traditional civic responsibility.

Initial empirical findings are consistent with this contention. Defining age as the elapsed time since the decennial census when the city first recorded a population of 25,000 or more, Alford and Lee (1968: 803) found a zero-order correlation between voter turnout and municipal age of .27. In the present study, using a population of 10,000 to mark municipal birth, the comparable correlation coefficient was .29 (see Table V-5). Of course, this is not yet evidence of a direct environmental effect as opposed to evidence of the covariance between age and the vote-inducing properties of scope and leadership accessibility.

[5] Disregarded here are certain "environmental" factors that may affect the propensity to vote, including the widely researched attributes of ethnicity, socioeconomic status, or party affiliation of potential voters. These have greater importance as characteristics of individuals than of the social systems under study here. Partly to develop the social-systems perspective, and partly to keep the study within manageable proportions, no attempt has been made to incorporate theories of voting that derive largely from interpretations of individual status, motivations, or self-concept. Such theories can, of couse, be adapted to a study of this nature and pitted against the more structuralist approach taken here.

We might also expect voter turnout to be high in a city that is rich in diversity and competing interests, and which has a political and social context offering a wide range of organized groups intermediate between government and citizens. If this pluralist principle is a foundation for activating an electorate, voter turnout should be relatively substantial in larger and nonsuburban cities. This proposition is fundamentally similar to the one that predicted greater leadership accessibility in larger and nonsuburban cities. It is restated here in terms of voter participation, in spite of the opposite contention, that less differentiated suburban and small-city contexts may heighten certain integrative attachments, which was suggested by the actual findings on accessibility. The tentative findings for voter participation, reported as zero-order correlations in Table V-5, give only the smallest shred of support to the original proposition. Registered voter turnout is a little higher in the more complex contexts, as indicated by correlations of −.06 with suburban status and .20 with city size. These findings are too small to be assigned any substantive significance at this point. Moreover, they once again may not indicate either the magnitude or even the direction of the direct effects of size and suburban status, due to covariance with other predictor variables.

Multivariate Analysis with Scope and Control Variables

Within the framework set forth here, the unresolved issues reduce to one focal question. Does the organizational property of scope alone, or scope together with government leadership arrangements, fully mediate and filter out environmental influences on voter participation? This and related questions may be answered for the present data by an interpretation of the multiple regressions in Table V-6 and the path diagram in Figure V-2.

The procedures for the multivariate analysis are the same as those employed in the analysis of accessibility, with three exceptions. Voter participation is now the ultimate criterion variable. The number of cities has been reduced from the original 668 to only 282 for which the necessary voting data was available. And one exception has been made from the practice of deleting paths having coefficients smaller than their standard error. The path from city size to scope was retained despite its near-zero value in this instance, for the same path was larger than its standard error in the calculations for the 668 cities. Deletion of this path would have had no effect on other

TABLE V-6

Standardized Regression Coefficients and R^2 in Multiple Regression Analyses Explaining Registered Voter Turnout, Accessibility, and Functional Scope (Standard Error in Parentheses: N = 282 Cities)

| Dependent variable | Independent variables | | | | | R and R^2 |
	Access- ibility	Functional scope	Municipal age	Suburban status	City size	
Registered voter turnout	.273 (.059)	.102 (.069)	.237 (.077	.104 (.065)	-.121 (.061)	R = .429 R^2 = .184
Accessibility (Model 1)		.186 (.070)	.331 (.075)	.106 (.065)	-.033 (.062)	R = .406 R^2 = .165
Accessibility (Model 2)		.186 (.070)	.318 (.070)	.108 (.065)	---- ----	R = .405 R^2 = .164
Functional scope			.462 (.058)	-.246 (.054)	-.003 (.053)	R = .617 R^2 = .381

reported coefficients, while its retention maintains a consistent diagrammatic representation of theory.

It might be noted in this regard that the restriction to 282 cities introduces some unknown bias or error in all findings on voting, relative to what might be found if data were available for all 668 cities, for some other general universe, or for a random sample of general universe. This does not negate the heuristic value of knowledge about voting in cities reporting turnout figures for nonconcurrent municipal elections. The data are properly interpreted if we are

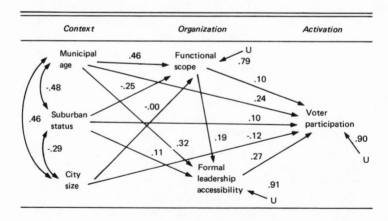

Figure V-2. Path diagram for voter participation and antecedent variables.

cautious in regarding any generalizations based on this unique set of cities as only suggestive, within unknown parameters, of what might be true of a more generally defined universe of cities.

Turning to the findings, attention focuses first on the role of functional scope. Although scope's zero-order correlation with voting was not insubstantial (r = .24), its direct effect on voting was the lowest of all five variables entered into the regression on voting (p = .102). The scope-centered proposition gets little support in this specific regard, other than the observation that scope's path to voting remains positive and, therefore, in the expected direction.

If, however, we look also at leadership arrangements, there is considerable support for the broader proposition that organizational traits of government directly affect voter participation and mediate environmental effects as well. Of all paths to voting, the one from accessibility is the largest (p = .27). Scope plays some role in this effect by accessibility, for separate calculations will show an *indirect* effect of .05 for scope on voting *by way of* scope's effect on accessibility.[6] Some of this indirect effect reflects, of course, scope's prior mediation of contextual variables. Accessibility also mediates the effects of two of the contextual variables. Whether through scope, through accessibility, or through both, municipal age and suburban status—but not city size—have some notable organiza-tionally mediated indirect effects on voting.

As with these indirect effects, most of the evidence on direct effects also supports the presumption of organizational mediation. Note that both municipal age and suburban status have stronger direct paths to scope (.45 for age, −.25 for suburb) and to accessi-bility (.32 for age, .11 for suburb) than to voting (.24 for age, .10 for suburb). Even scope has a stronger direct path to accessibility (.19) than to voting (.10). These observations on direct and indirect effects are suggestive that the chains of influence on voter turnout tend to converge by shaping leadership accessibility into the principal direct determinant of voting levels, with scope contributing an important link in these chains and having, as well, a small independent effect on voting.

Simultaneous with the important position that governmental role and accessibility plays in voter turnout, there are persisting and

---

[6] Indirect effects, it will be remembered, are calculated by serially multiplying path coefficients in each chain from an independent variable to a dependent variable. Indirect effects are defined as those effects of one variable upon another "which are transmitted via intervening variables [Alwin and Hauser 1975:45]."

rather interesting direct environmental effects. The greatest of these is indexed by municipal age and has a path to voting of .24, only a few points below the corresponding zero-order correlation coefficient of .29. It is possible that additional measures of governmental organization or role, if available, could reduce this age-related effect further. Or, it might be decomposed by exploring the contributions to voter turnout made by various community organizations. Tentatively, however, it is useful to follow through with the alternative interpretations that form the central issue in this multivariate analysis. It seems, then, that the direct effect of age derives much less from anything that the government does to generate attachments, than from the extensiveness of attachments to other traditionally community-minded organizations and from simple, traditional attachments to a government of whatever character and purpose. That this direct age-related effect is substantial, second only to accessibility's direct effect, strengthens the notion that age is a proxy indicator of extensive attachments or other forms of integration in various institutional domains, of which government is but one example.

The environmental effects on voting by suburban status and city size are not so substantial, but they are quite interesting because they are in the opposite direction from original predictions. The kind of opportunities for pluralist political competition and for variability about the mainstream that are found in larger and nonsuburban cities do not seem to have positive effects on voter turnout. Once we control for scope, leadership accessibility, and municipal age, the zero-order correlations are reversed *and* increased in magnitude, with the result that voter turnout is *higher* in suburbs ($p = .10$) and *lower* in large cities ($p = -.12$).

Discussion

These last findings, being unexpected, might be understood with an emerging post hoc interpretation. For example, as was suggested earlier for similar discordant findings on accessibility, there may be a kind of protective unity and involvement in suburban municipalities, and now it seems even in small cities. More specifically, one could stress here, and possibly for all independent variables, that what counts in getting out the vote in an electoral contest is the integration of *whatever* human and organizational resources happen to be in the city, regardless of whether they comprise differentiated centers of power, and that smaller and suburban cities are inherently given to this integration precisely because the potential base is not very broad. There is also the intriguing possibility that where differentiation is great, many potential voters have deviant or exotic interests which, in lieu of the integrative mechanisms denoted by accessibility, scope, and city age, entail attachments to groups having no real or perceived stake in elections.

Within this suggested revised framework, scope and city age remain as important indicators of the integration of diversified systems. More strongly evidenced in age than in scope, this manner of integration has significant effects in the predicted direction on extending the bases of regime legitimacy, as denoted by the accessibility in formal leadership roles and voter turnout levels. In addition, integration of another sort, arising from the lesser complexity of small and suburban community contexts, also seems to have some small positive (in one case, neutral) effects on extending civic involvement. Taking these two findings together, they would suggest that the breadth of active involvement in and legitimacy for a regime depend on the convergence of arenas of action, not only through the scope of government, but also through other integrating community institutions (age) and through simplicity of community social composition (size, suburb).

As for scope, itself, there is less than compelling evidence for the specific scope-centered theory that government screens and recruits its participants by way of the range of functions that it takes on. In support of the theory, it was found that leadership roles are more likely to be "reformed" in a manner that limits accessibility, and that the relative breadth of voter participation will be lower if a city has a narrow range of functions about which participants might express policy preferences. Also, there was evidence of the predicted chain of effects from contextual variables, converging through scope to accessibility and through both scope and accessibility to voting. To some extent, the scope of government mediates the claims on leadership that arise largely from historically rooted forms of community organization. Put another way, scope helps to specify the degree of organizational boundary spanning and integrated inclusiveness, as well as attendant definitions of the bases of regime legitimacy, which are more generally denoted by community age.

Reducing the force of the scope-centered theory were findings that scope was by no means an overwhelming determinant of either formal leadership accessibility or voter turnout, that scope did not totally mediate and explain contextual effects, and that community age was a stronger unmediated predictor of the civic-involvement indicators. The direct and scope-mediated effects of age were sufficiently strong to compel a concluding emphasis on age-cohort differences. If, as supposed, age identifies lasting or inherited organizational forms more than it does selectively achieved ones, then the present findings root the valid order and legitimacy of a government essentially in its founding constitution. Functional scope is one part of that constitution; other community institutions might also be identified as components. Over time, the order becomes natural and wholly valid as attachments to each component and among components take the form of traditionalized participation, and as any manifestly different interests more or less rationally compete for resources or influence within the traditional framework.

Older communities, it is suggested, have always had more inclusive frameworks for integrating this process. It is also inferred that new cities are constituted with fragmented and specialized organizational forms, and will likely retain the legitimacy of this order in the future. The most deviant cases would seem to be those few "administered, intentional, or designed" new communities of the type that planners rather fully develop. In a study of several of these recent planned communities, Gottschalk (1975) found that their deviant, formally constituted, communal integration is indeed a viable alternative, but at a cost to free choice, which he feels few will pay.

A vision might be appropriate at this point. Given the two "natural" alternatives, the trend for the future would seem to involve the emergence of more cities in which public functions, leadership, and civic participation are all increasingly limited as the legitimate role of city government shrinks. In contrast, there will remain a dwindling proportion of the oldest cities, which will become increasingly distinctive and command attention less for the size of their populations than for their extensive networks of public service bureaucracies and programs, for their embattled leadership seeking to maintain legitimacy for their regimes on many fronts, and for their traditions of citizen participation. To make this outlook explicit is, of course, to overstate it, for we should note once again that small suburban cities offer a third and less distinct pattern that mixes elements from both old and new city patterns in a manner that might be considered appropriate for preserving the simpler unity of these most "middle American" cities. With these patterns and prospects in mind, we turn now to explore public policy performances as possible consequences of the changing functions and founding constitutions of cities.

VI.

Program Outputs and Accountability

Although the capacity of a government to recruit and receive diverse participants is evidence of its openness to political influence, its production of public programs illustrates its capacity to influence, in turn, the destiny of social conditions. Political activation in an open society, therefore, has two sides, broad civic inputs and extensive program outputs. The following analysis of output extensity defines this property in terms of three basic attributes of a politically active government: (1) a strong tendency to generate new programs and to disseminate them internally; (2) a high commitment of fiscal resources to the on-going performance of established public programs; and (3) a practice of freely adopting programs for and by diverse interests rather than according to narrower standards of bureaucratic accountability.

With respect to innovativeness, public spending levels, and accountability, the central issue is again the extent to which each is affected
by the functional scope of the government. In a nutshell, is it true
that "big" government as defined by scope generates even bigger
more expansive, and more freely innovative government? Is small or
limited government less expansionist, more fiscally conservative and
more narrowly responsive to ascertainable needs for such new programs that it does adopt? Do governments effectively exercise some
control over their outputs as a result of varying resourcefulness
inhering in varying functional scope? The analysis of these questions
will generally follow the same methods and procedures used in the
last chapter.

INNOVATIVENESS

Concepts and Indicators

The term "innovation" has been used in a number of ways (see
reviews by E. Rogers 1962, Becker and Whisler 1967, Hage and
Dewar 1971), but generally it refers to changes resulting in new
tasks. **Innovativeness** is more specifically defined here as the recent
and continuing propensity of a government to take action adopting
and internally disseminating new programs or services. Governments
can be innovative in this sense whether or not they simultaneously
cut back old programs. Excluded from this definition are changes in
policy or organizational structure that do not entail program elaboration, as well as such changes as program termination or contractions.
Reorganization is only problematically innovative, depending on
consequences for program outputs. And while program cubacks may
be real changes, they are not innovative ones, for anything that
remains after a cutback is a portion of an old program rather than a
new one. Suffice it to say that we mean to generalize here to only
one type of change that could be termed innovative, and that
pertains to the implementation of new service programs.

To avoid confusing innovation with state-assigned or traditional
performance of a program, we are concerned only with programs
that have recently been "invented" and made available to city
governments for discretionary adoption or nonadoption. The two
examples of innovations that are used in this study are the federally
aided public housing and urban renewal programs. If, in many cases,
these programs are by now well beyond the experimental stage, they

are nonetheless of sufficient recency—having been implemented within the lifetime of most current political leaders—to be indicative of recent trends in community innovativeness. They are also two of the examples of innovation used by Aiken and Alford (1970a, b) in their studies, which facilitates comparison with their theory, procedures, and findings. The reader may refer to the Aiken and Alford studies for a brief description of the substance of these programs and of the various stages involved in the processes of municipal adoption and implementation.

For each of the two federally aided programs, two indicators of innovativeness will be used. The first refers to *adoption* per se, and indicates whether or not cities made formal decisions to participate in the programs during the period from federal enactment of public housing in 1933 to June 30, 1966, and during the period from federal enactment of urban renewal in 1949 to the same June 30, 1966 cutoff date for the available data. This is the same operational definition of adoption used by Aiken and Alford in their studies of these programs, and comes from the same original data sources that these authors used (U.S. Department of Housing and Urban Development 1966a,b).

A second pair of innovativeness indicators, also used by Aiken and Alford, refers to the extent of internal *dissemination* of the programs. The operational measures here are the per capita number of low-rent, federally assisted public-housing units constructed since 1933, and the per capita number of urban renewal dollars reserved since 1949, with June 30, 1966 as the cutoff date again. Although Aiken and Alford used the term "level of output" to characterize these variables, the term "internal dissemination" is preferred here in order to emphasize that one stage in the process of innovation is the cumulative penetration of new programs into an increasingly large share of community life. Not until after substantial penetration and general acceptance has been accomplished does a program make the transition from an innovation to a firmly established and deeply legitimated function. One other indicator of innovativeness, the speed of initial adoption, is also available in the data and was used by Aiken and Alford but, largely in the interests of some simplification, is not used here.

The cities in the analysis include all *innovation-eligible* cities having 25,000 residents or more in 1960, minus the eight cities for which sufficient data on scope was unavailable. The restriction to innovation-eligible cities was carried out according to procedures used by Aiken and Alford and summarized as follows. For the urban renewal analysis, 74 cities were omitted because their state governments had not passed enabling legislation by 1958, and another 20 were omitted because they did not exist in the 1950 census, the year after initial federal enactment of aid for urban renewal. All of the remaining 574 cities were eligible to participate by 1958, or earlier if they had gained the necessary cooperation of state-enabling legislation. For the public housing analysis, 30 cities that did not appear in the 1930 Census were excluded, leaving 638 cities that were known to exist when the first federal enactment of aid to public housing occurred in 1933. All of these cities had gained the authorization of state-enabling legislation by mid-1966, with a few exceptions in the states of Wyoming and Utah. Through an apparent oversight of negligible significance, these few unauthorized exceptions were not omitted from the Aiken and Alford study and were retained here as well.

Before turning to findings, attention should be drawn to the character of implementation procedures for these programs. Federal laws have required extensive intergovernmental cooperation, including not only state authorization and federal approval of local plans of action, but also some evidence of community support. These procedures are probably not as unusual in *de facto* aspects of innovation as they are in the more legalistic *de jure* aspects, for local and extralocal cooperation would seem to be a precondition for most innovations. Few contemporary innovations are probably of strictly local origin; most involve some boundary-crossing, interorganizational cooperation; and a theory of activation through interorganizational networks should, therefore, apply to many other program innovations as well as to urban renewal and public housing. Whether the findings reported here are more generally applicable remains, of course, to be determined.

Bivariate Analysis with Scope and Control Variables

The first set of findings, for simple zero-order relationships, provides considerable initial support to the hypothesis that governments are more innovative if their scope-determined networks of affiliations extend broadly. As reported in Table VI-1, scope has fairly strong correlations with the four measures of innovativeness and in the expected direction. Correlation coefficients of about .30 indicate that roughly 9 % of the variance in innovativeness is associated with scope and, so far as can be determined at this point, attributable to scope.

TABLE VI-1
Correlations between Measures of Innovativeness and Accessibility, Functional Scope, and Contextual Variables

Independent variables	Measures of innovativeness			
	Public housing[a]		Urban renewal[b]	
	Program adoption	Units per capita (natural log)	Program adoption	$ per capita (natural log)
Accessibility	.12	.09	.11	.11
Functional scope	.30	.29	.29	.30
Municipal age	.38	.38	.48	.49
Suburban status	-.30	-.29	-.28	-.28
City size	.32	.29	.34	.33
Dilapidated housing[c]	.31	.36	.20	.13
(Number of cities)	(638)	(638)	(574)	(574)

[a]Source: U.S. Department of Housing and Urban Development (1966a). *Program Adoption* is a binary (1, 0) variable with a score of 1 denoting any adoption of any federally aided public housing program between 1933 and June 30, 1966. *Units per capita* is the number of low-rent federally assisted public housing units constructed since 1933 per 100,000 population.

[b]Source: U.S. Department of Housing and Urban Development (1966b). *Program Adoption* is a binary (1, 0) variable with a score of 1 denoting any formal participation in the planning, execution, or completion stages of urban renewal programs since the federal urban renewal legislation of 1949. *Dollars Per Capita* is the number of urban renewal dollars reserved per capita as of June 30, 1966.

[c]Percentage of housing dilapidated in 1950. Source: *U.S. Census of Housing: 1950*, Volume I.

Although this is not an overwhelming relationship by most standards, it is greater than the correlations that Aiken and Alford found for the most of 20-odd independent variables used in their more comprehensive studies of urban renewal and public housing. These authors found consistently stronger relationships with innovativeness only for city size and municipal age, and for variables indicating housing conditions and low social status among community residents. The latter may, by some definitions, indicate *need* for these programs, and will therefore be discussed separately in the analysis of accountability.

The reasons for setting aside the issue of need are several. It was expected and will be reported that the relationships between innovativeness and certain measures of need are strongly interactive, depending on values of scope or on the overall structure of municipal decision-making processes. More theoretically, our interest in need focuses precisely on interactive effects or on the conditions under which some likely definitions of need are apparently given more or less weight by decision makers, rather than on any given notion of need as a cause, *sui generis,* of innovativeness. Additionally, we know from some experiences with urban renewal and public housing that the poor often have different ideas of need than do the actual decision makers who operate at higher levels of organized life where interests of greater weight often intersect, and where need can have many definitions.

Despite these concerns, one might argue that even if most operable definitions of need are tenuous and conditional, some assessment of community housing conditions is indispensible in the planning for public housing or urban renewal, if not in the actual criteria for adoption. For this reason, the level of dilapidated housing has been included in Table VI-1 as a possible control variable. It is moderately predictive of innovativeness in these program areas, but not more so than most of the other variables in the table.

Aiken and Alford's findings for the city size and age variables are of more immediate interest. As highly general indicators of diffuse organizational interests and of the probability that they intersect, these variables play a substantial role in the Aiken–Alford theory of greater innovativeness where such conditions prevail. The zero-order findings for the size and age variables are therefore included in Table VI-1, along with additional findings for our third and somewhat similar contextual variable, suburban status. Consistent with the Aiken and Alford thesis, these findings do show greater innovativeness in the more differentiated large-city and nonsuburban contexts (correlation coefficients range from .28 to .34 in absolute value), as well as in older-community contexts having greater continuity of interorganizational ties (correlations with age range from .38 to .49).

The remaining independent variable included in Table VI-1 is our measure of formal leadership structure on the accessibility dimension. Aiken and Alford used separate indicators of leadership reformism to denote political structure, while in the present case the separate indicators are combined and the valence is reversed to produce the accessibility variable. This variable is included here for the same reasons that it was included in the voting analysis. It indicates still another facet of system diffuseness, pertaining in this instance to the diversity of ties among formal leaders and between them and constituents. In Aiken and Alford's research, the separate indicators of reformism had correlations with innovativeness averaging around −.12, consistent with their general theoretical formulation. In the present research, the correlations between accessibility and innovativeness are of comparable magnitude (averaging about

.11) and also in the expected direction for our way of scoring leadership structure.

One of Aiken and Alford's indicators of "diffusion of community power," the percentage of registrants voting, might have been included as another independent and possible control variable in the present study. It had a zero-order correlation of around .17 with each of the innovativeness indicators, which is again in the expected direction if the theory of innovation in diffuse systems is extended to include voter turnout as a relevant measure of broad-based civic input. Use of the voting variable in this analysis would, however, have meant reducing the number of cases in the multiple regression analysis by nearly half in order to restrict them to cities of unknown representativeness for which the necessary voting data was available. We decided here to retain the full universe of innovation-eligible cities by disregarding the voter participation variable, and therefore to leave open the issue of voter turnout's unique role in innovativeness.

One overall conclusion is supported by all of the bivariate findings reported in Table VI-1. In Aiken and Alford's words, "The greater the number of centers of power in a community and the more pervasive and encompassing the interfaces, the high the probability of innovation in a given issue arena [1970b, p. 663]." Put another way, if community contexts and municipal government are sufficiently differentiated, there will be considerable choice among acting units as to which resources may be combined in coalitions favoring innovation, and if ties or interfaces among these acting units are sufficiently extensive and stable, the necessary coalition of diverse resources is also more probable. These generalizations set the issue for more complex analysis. What unique role, if any, does the organization of government, particularly in its functional scope but also in its leadership arrangements, play in shaping the course of municipal innovativeness? Are the innovation-inducing attributes of adopting organizations more or less important than those of the environment?

Multivariate Analysis with Scope and Control Variables

Table VI-2 presents the multiple regression analyses that answer these questions for the present data. The need variable, level of dilapidated housing, is omitted from these regressions for reasons stated earlier, although we will later consider the effects of intro-

TABLE VI-2
Standardized Regression Coefficients and R^2 in Multiple Regression Analyses Explaining Innovativeness (Standard Error in Parentheses)

Dependent variable[a]	Access-ibility	Independent variables Functional scope	Municipal age	Suburban status	City size	R and R^2	N
Public housing adoption (Model 1)	-.007 (.039)	.102 (.060)	.192 (.050)	-.154 (.040)	.143 (.043)	$R = .441$ $R^2 = .195$	638
Public housing adoption (Model 2)	——	.101 (.042)	.190 (.048)	-.155 (.039)	.143 (.042)	$R = .441$ $R^2 = .195$	638
Public housing units P/C (Model 1)	-.039 (.039)	.105 (.043)	.228 (.050)	-.148 (.040)	.097 (.043)	$R = .429$ $R^2 = .184$	638
Public housing units P/C (Model 2)	——	.099 (.043)	.215 (.048)	-.151 (.040)	.098 (.043)	$R = .428$ $R^2 = .183$	638
Urban renewal adoption (Model 1)	-.058 (.039)	.025 (.045)	.397 (.053)	-.061 (.042)	.111 (.044)	$R = .496$ $R^2 = .246$	574
Urban renewal adoption (Model 2)	-.055 (.039)	——	.408 (.049)	-.065 (.041)	.112 (.043)	$R = .496$ $R^2 = .246$	574
Urban renewal $ P/C (Model 1)	-.059 (.039)	.025 (.045)	.418 (.053)	-.058 (.042)	.087 (.043)	$R = .500$ $R^2 = .250$	574
Urban renewal $ P/C (Model 2)	-.056 (.039)	——	.429 (.049)	-.062 (.041)	.089 (.043)	$R = .499$ $R^2 = .249$	574

[a] For sources and definitions, see Table VI-1.

ducing it as an additional predictor variable. The principal findings are in the form of standardized regression coefficients in the simultaneous regression of innovativeness on four or five independent variables. Each of four pairs of regression models has one of the innovativeness indicators as the dependent variable. The second model in each pair differs from the first according to procedures discussed earlier, viz., variables having regression coefficients smaller than their standard error in the first model were deleted from the second in order to reduce explanations for innovativeness to the more parsimonious model. Note that both models in each pair have equal or nearly equal explanatory power, with multiple correlation coefficients of .43 or .44 for all public housing regression models and of .50 for all urban renewal models.

Table VI-2 presents only the last stage of a causal sequence, the stage indicating direct effects on innovativeness. A three-stage causal design is nonetheless assumed. The reader may wish to refer to Figure V-1 in the last chapter for illustrations of the first two stages, the stage indicating contextual effects on scope and the stage indicating the effects of context and scope on accessibility.[1] All three stages are not combined in path diagrams here partly because the last stage provides sufficiently conclusive answers to questions of theoretical interest.

Perhaps the most striking finding in Table VI-2 is that scope has virtually no direct influence on *urban renewal* innovativeness once controls for prior contextual determinants and for the role of accessibility are introduced. Scope's average zero-order correlation with urban renewal of .30 drops to a standardized partial of .025, which may be considered negligible. For *public housing* innovativeness, the same controls result in a small, but not negligible, standardized partial of about .10, down from a zero-order correlation of .30.

These unexpectedly low direct effects of scope cannot be due to the indirect mediation of scope's influence by accessibility, for accessibility itself not only has smaller direct effects on innovativeness, but these effects are also in the opposite direction from all predictions. In general, we can consider accessibility's influence to be negligible as well. Assuming accessibility as the only mediating variable for scope in the present framework, the indirect effect of scope is essentially zero.

---

[1] Note that Figure V-1 is based on all 668 cities in the study, and that small fractions of these cities were omitted from calculations for the innovation-eligible cities that are analyzed in Table VI-2.

From these findings, it is additionally clear that the governmental variables play little intervening role in mediating the effects of environmental variables. Overall, neither accessibility nor scope are of much substantive significance in explaining innovativeness. The strongest shreds of support for the scope-centered perspective concern the small direct effect from scope to public housing, and the fact that all of scope's effects in the multivariate analysis remain positive, even if relatively insubstantial.

The three contextual variables are, in all but a couple of instances, far stronger predictors of innovativeness. The relevant standardized partial coefficients are all in the expected direction, are by far highest for age, and are next highest for the effects of suburban status on public housing and for the effects of city size on urban renewal. Instances where contextual variables have a smaller direct effect on innovativeness than has scope are limited to the relationship between city size and public housing units per capita.

The findings center, then, on the interpretation of municipal age, size, and suburban status as indicators of causal factors. Again, one might argue that "need" is the true cause quite apart from the capacity to innovate arising from interorganizational networks, and that older, larger, nonsuburban cities simply have more run-down, out-or-date buildings that "need" renewal or replacement at public expense. All of the regressions in Table VI-2 were therefore rerun with the addition of another independent variable, the level of dilapidated housing. Introduction of this variable produced no changes greater than plus or minus .02 in any of the coefficients reported in Table VI-2, and added less than 1% to explained variance. We are left with essentially the same findings that were first reported by Aiken and Alford and were largely reiterated in the foregoing analysis. Our interpretation also parallels theirs.

Discussion

For reasons other than those indicated by housing conditions in a community, there is a higher probability of implementation of urban renewal and public housing programs in cities having, *in the nongovernmental sector,* the organizational capacity to do so. Tendencies to innovate in the establishment of new programs for government evidently do not principally depend on such governmental characteristics as the extent to which the scope of governmental enterprise or the accessibility of formal leaders specifically channel resources into the established governing apparatus. Instead, the evidence supports the inference that the larger community organizational system provides the necessary capacities for devising new programs and for implanting them within government. It is principally the age and differentiation of environmental organizational networks that determine opportunities for the formation of effective coalitions of implementers, while government plays only a minimal part as a kind of selectively mediating formal host for emerging programs. The accessibility of formal leadership roles is especially ineffective as a device for recruiting and facilitating participants in the innovative act.

Even with these findings, however, the importance of scope is nontrivial. Scope's direct effects on innovativeness may be weak, but they are in the predicted direction. In the case of urban renewal, which is generally a one-shot or self-terminating innovation, the effects of scope approach zero and should be considered negligible. In the case of the more lasting programs for public housing, where scope's effects are small but significant, we find that one standard-unit increase in innovativeness can be directly attributed to ten standard-unit increases in scope when environmental effects are separated out. The addition of fairly permanent new programs results, to some extent, from the prior existence of many regular programs. This consequence is certainly important from a policy perspective, since initial levels of scope are legislatively manipulable. The unification of functions within a single, local government might result in a small increment in permanent program innovative capacities. This implication will be discussed more fully in the concluding chapter, where we take up the possibilities and limitations of extrapolating into the future.

There is a second respect in which the small positive effect of scope on public housing adoption is nontrivial. It sustains the notion of a not insignificant feedback loop involving the accumulative expansion of scope, while suggesting an alternative strategy for further identifying and testing the nature of that loop in future research. Consider that a large set of major and generally essential or universal functions of some government, when unified within a single city government, increases the probability of adoption of what in this case is an optional minor new function. This results in a further expansion of scope to include the new minor function. The specialization, boundary spanning, and adaptive growth capacities entailed in this kind of optional, minor program accumulation may, in turn, have sizeable effects on increasing the probability of innovation within still other special program areas. If so, efforts to devise a measure of scope that more fully tap optional program accumulation should provide a much more effective explanation for the adoption of each additional new program than does the present measure of established major program functions.

The trail of evidence in support of the hypotheses on scope is, of course, insufficient to override a concluding emphasis on the environmental perspective. It has been presumed that the causative factors indicated by the contextual variables refer to the degree of differentiation of all aspects of community social structure and, in the case of community age, to the probability of extensive integrative networks of interaction among the diverse actors. The most direct and specific indicators of "integrated diversity" were the two governmental variables, which refer only to governmentally referenced networks; however, it was these relatively specific indicators that fared worst in the multivariate analysis. Until other specific indicators of diversity and/or integration among governmentally referenced or contextually located centers of power are found to more fully decompose the meaning of city size, suburban status, and especially age, we must retain the highly abstract theory of environmental determinants of governmental innovation in the adoption of new programs.

One leading candidate for an alternative to this theory might be *need* as, indeed, a cause *sui generis,* given any kind of leadership, government, or community organization. Although it is unconvincing in and of itself, one might take this argument so far as to suggest that older, larger, and nonsuburban cities are rich with need in many forms, and that there will, therefore, be a tendency to respond to some need—any need perhaps—in generally recognizing that the agenda of social problems is long and work must begin somewhere. This argument is not an uncommon plea that leaders in these cities both hear and make. In this vein, need alone could be a cause of innovation if all needs were known, or if we just had a count of them.

The reason for considering the existence of need in itself to be an implausible explanation is that it overlooks the social processes by which needs become defined as such. These processes would seem to involve exactly the same structural conditions that the contextual variables indicate in the abstract, for it is by no means novel in sociology to suggest that it is through structural differentiation that many social problems arise, and, further, that it is through inter-action among the differentiated units that these problems become noted and defined as needs. For example, inner cities deteriorate in many ways, not just in housing, whenever some rather influential interests pick up and locate elsewhere or yield territorially linked resources to less productive tenants (differentiation); and if these interests, their competitors, or coalitions of them later have the right connections (interfaces, interactions) they may well return to dis-place the poor, the vacant warehouses, or whatever, all in the name of "renewal." The details of whose "needs" are being met may vary widely, but this is in general the process that we are suggesting best applies to the environmentalist perspective.

It may well be, then, that a count of needs (as defined by all potential participants) would suffice as a statistically powerful pre-dictor of innovativeness. But such a count would only be an imper-fect proxy for the differentiating and interfacing processes through which organized interests not only give recognition to certain needs, but also produce a response to them. The response may only occa-sionally have much to do with any particular kind of need, such as that pertaining to housing conditions of the poor. The innovative social system is too complex to have any universally applicable or conventional definition of need. This assumption brings up the question of accountability.

ACCOUNTABILITY

Concepts and Indicators

The term "accountability" has had extensive recent use in most areas of public affairs, particularly with respect to the relationship between administrative officials and the policymaking bodies to whom officials must somehow answer for their use of resources. One observer (Wynne 1972), writing on accountability in schools, defined the concept as involving first, an explicit determination of specific program objectives on which administrators and policymakers agree and, second, some demonstrative evidence that the program attained those objectives. In the present case, we are interested in accountability as it pertains to the correspondence between program innovativeness (in public housing and urban renewal) and some standard or conventional indicators of need for new programs (in this case, poor housing and poverty). We are further interested in the hypothesis that this correspondence is greater, and that accountability is therefore greater, where the acting social system is relatively undifferentiated. The other side to this hypothesis is that more complex systems may act on so many different needs that none, not even the most "basic" or universally appreciated, has much importance alone.

This hypothesis was originally stated in terms of "scope" being the variable on which complexity of the system would be controlled. This procedure is still appropriate, even though we found little or no independent effect of scope on the probability of innovation. Scope may still, to some extent, condition the match between innovation and standard notions of need. For example, narrow scope may result—as was originally suggested in theory—in greater government concern over matters of technical proficiency, standardized procedures, and standard program emphasis, even if environmentally located influentials are not very innovation prone. If this were so, a given level of scope may help to determine which cities innovate ("needy" or "nonneedy"), even though comparisons across levels of scope show no independent effect by scope on the probability of innovation.

Conversely, of course, scope may simply be an imperfect proxy for more important, but environmental, aspects of system complexity, as might be inferred from the previous analyses. If so, then we are using scope as one of four possible control variables that would denote the same general concept. Indeed, this is true, to some extent, whatever the independent contribution of scope to accountability. Since independent effects cannot be sorted out by the procedures used to analyze accountability, it is advisable to stick with one control and to treat it as an indicator of both environmental and governmental system complexity. This variable will be scope.

Four ways of identifying "need" were used. These are the percentage of families with incomes under $3000 in 1960, the percentage of residents who were nonwhite in 1960, median education of adults in 1960, and the previously noted variable, percentage of dilapidated housing in 1950, using the U.S. Bureau of the Census of Housing definition of "dilapidated." The last of these is most obviously appropriate as a measure of need for urban renewal or public housing, for it identifies conditions that these programs were congressionally authorized to alleviate. Since some adopting cities may have succeeded to some extent, this variable is taken from 1950 Census data.

The other three indicators are more indirect measures of conventionally defined need for these programs, for while the programs may not alter income, race, or education, those who score low in the status hierarchies with respect to these variables have long been considered legitimate targets of public housing and urban renewal ventures. The percentage of families below a $3000 poverty income level denotes the probability that self-help family resources are insufficient to upgrade housing or to renew neighborhoods. Larger minority racial populations and lower education levels denote the likelihood that affected neighborhoods lack the political and social, as well as economic, resources either to change their own conditions without intervention or to resist intervention. Taken together, the four "need" indicators deal with four types of data that might well appear in proposals for these ventures. It would certainly be inappropriate to ignore all of them, or something nominally similar, in a proposal to the federal government.

Analysis and Discussion

The findings, as reported in Table VI-3, are fully consistent with expectations. In cities having relatively little complexity of government (or of social context), the correlation between need and innovativeness rises to over .50 in many instances, and to no less than .28. In contrast, cities of greatest organizational complexity, in government or out, sometimes innovate with no noticeable regard to some types of need, and always have a tendency to do so with less regard to need than do the less differentiated cities. In short, the relationship between need and innovativeness, and therefore, the degree of accountability, is always lower among cities of wider scope and greater complexity than among other cities.[2] The sole exception, the percentage of nonwhite (Black) relative to urban renewal dollars per capita, is not great enough to affect the generalization.

There are some interesting differences between the four indicators of need with respect to their importance or relevance to program responses. Measures of the extent of dilapidated housing and of poverty provide the greatest discrimination on accountability between wide- and narrow-scope cities. Among the more complex wide-scope cities, low levels of these capital-resource needs have

[2] An examination of unstandardized slopes revealed that they are nearly parallel to the standardized slopes reported here. That is, the unstandardized slopes are distinctively and consistently steepest for narrow-scope cities and flattest for broad-scope cities.

TABLE VI-3

Accountability: Correlations between Measures of Innovativeness and Indicators of Need, within Levels of Functional Scope

Innovation[a] (Dependent variable)	Scope[b] (Control variable)	Need[c] (Independent variable)				
		Pover	Dilap	Black	Educ	N
Public housing	Wide	.24	.20	.36	-.29	173
adoption	Medium	.38	.28	.44	-.39	327
	Narrow	.50	.54	.54	-.51	138
Public housing	Wide	.31	.26	.40	-.36	173
units P/C	Medium	.42	.33	.47	-.41	328
	Narrow	.55	.59	.58	-.55	138
Urban renewal	Wide	.02	.00	.34	-.20	169
adoption	Medium	.15	.07	.35	-.29	272
	Narrow	.34	.29	.40	-.39	133
Urban renewal	Wide	.02	.00	.38	-.20	169
dollars P/C	Medium	.16	.07	.35	-.31	272
	Narrow	.34	.28	.40	-.40	133

[a] Sources and definitions: See Table VI-2.

[b] Wide scope = 5-9 functions; medium scope = 3-4 functions; narrow scope = 0-2 functions.

[c] Definitions: *Pover* = Percentage of families with incomes under $3000 (1960); *Dilap* = Percentage of dilapidated housing (1950); *Black* = Natural log of percentage of nonwhite (1960); *Educ* = Median school years completed among persons over 24 years (1960). Sources: For *Dilap*, *U.S. Census of Housing: 1950*, Volume I; for all others, *U.S. Census of the Population: 1960*.

little, if any, inhibiting influence on the development of public housing or urban renewal programs. Among the simpler narrow-scope cities, these same capital-resource needs are far more important predictors of innovative program response. This highly differential correspondence between response effort and the strongest indicators of need for capital aid applies both to effort as a mere program adoption and to effort as the cumulative magnitude of the programs. The previously reported high frequency of program innovations in complex wide-scope cities results in a distribution (among those cities) of both program occurrence and scale of programs that has minimal dependency, if any, on relative capital-aid needs. The less frequent narrow-scope adoptions are, in both occurrence and scale, distributed to fit much more closely with capital-aid needs.

In contrast, minority racial composition and median educational level do not discriminate as effectively between wide- and narrow-scope cities. The predicted pattern is evident, but it is weaker. Even within wide-scope contexts, it is at least moderately predictive of innovation to have available relatively large subpopulations having minimal social and political resources. It would seem that the non-white and poorly educated sectors provide the most insistent needs or most irresistible targets in all contexts, perhaps because of their more general poverty of resources and the consequent ease of their relocation. Viewed from the other side, a well educated and sub-stantially white population would seem to place a ceiling on the probability of public housing and urban renewal. Yet, even with the constraints that racial and educational composition may impose on these types of innovation, the expected pattern of greater account-ability in simpler, narrow-scope cities does in fact clearly occur.

It should be noted that none of the correlations in Table VI-3 shows greater innovativeness where need is low. As need is defined here, i.e., referring to community attributes that might most ap-propriately justify urban renewal or public housing, it is never negatively associated with innovativeness. This fact still leaves sub-stantial discretion among potentially innovating cities. The more complex cities use this discretion to considerable advantage, innovat-ing not only quite often but also for reasons that are not readily discernible in comparative analysis of their needs. The less complex cities seem to behave with less discretion, innovating less often and only where the most obvious types of needs are relatively great. With so much variability in the relevance of need, it is erroneous to consider any type of need to be a "cause" of innotativeness apart from the conditions that seem to make it more or less so.

The exercise of a "wide latitude of discretion" is another way of looking at relative "freedom from accountability." Neither of these terms is meant to imply a reified calculating consciousness within all innovating groups. Quite the contrary, for many concrete interests are assumed to be involved. The point is that in the case of complex systems, so many interests may be involved, or such specialized and unique ones, that the central tendency of the innovative act is somewhat unpredictable. The variability of program emphasis is a far more important characteristic. Here is where politics becomes very diffuse and, as a result, relatively unanalyzable with respect to program objectives, even while being quite analyzable with respect to the probability of innovation and change.

The notion of a reified consciousness may be somewhat more appropriate to the less complex contexts, where innovation is pre-sumably achieved by less differentiated interests among whom a central tendency toward "objectives" or "need satisfaction" is more probable. Here is where politics is sufficiently simple, conflict free, and consensual, if not also routine and predictably bureaucratic, to permit analysis of outcomes in terms of the efficiency of matching means with conventional goal orientations. Actors in the less complex cities apparently relate to simple and basic needs of the sort analyzed here. Even if this relationship does not reflect a consciously enacted strategy, it is strong enough to suggest that conventional definitions of need do not escape influence on the outlook and response of the potential innovators in the less complex cities. In the absence of resourcefulness, convention is the rule.

The accountability findings may be more fully interpreted by focusing on those agencies of policymakers to which program innovators are formally accountable. In the present case, federal bureaucracies are the principal relevant agencies to which aspiring innovators must account for their efforts and intentions. To the extent that these federal bureaucracies devise abstract definitions of need, they no doubt rely principally on conventional and formal definitions of the sort used here (Turk, 1973b). Nearly all cities could make a case that they have such needs as these in some sector of their communities, so that the real problem is why only some take action on any needs and how they come to define needs in relation to conventional federal standards.

The more active cities—that is, the highly innovative complex ones—seem to respond to internally generated and outwardly extended appeals having more basis in the varying interests of the coalitions involved than in whether a particular need is relatively great, moderate, or small. In a sense, they have the capacity to make sufficient importance out of whatever conventional needs they do have precisely because they have additional interests involved. Conversely, urban renewal, public housing, and perhaps most other available public program "inventions" of national sponsorship may present to the more lethargic cities (i.e., to the newer narrow-scope ones) certain *external* pushes or inducements having greater force where externally assessable needs are also great. These cities are evidently not likely to "reinvent" these programs in locally suitable forms nor to compromise the formal or customary uses of the programs, perhaps because these simpler-structured cities more readily exhaust the varieties of power bases that could provide local alternatives for program definition. It is in this sense that the accountability of local officials to superordinate policymakers is a special mark of distinctive action for city governments that would otherwise have unimpressive records of inaction.

As a concluding qualification, it is important once again to distinguish between the processes of adopting *substantive programs* of the type that we have just considered, and the opposing process of adopting *formal coordinating mechanisms* (see Chapter IV, pp. 78–84). The latter, as analyzed by Turk (1973b), involves the establishment of councils or commissions to bring together representatives from most, if not all, of the organizations or interests concerned with some issue, service, or set of issues or services. The new entity has no program function apart from its service to affiliated groups. The formal objective of these unifying mechanisms is to "coordinate" by sharing information, resources, or perceptions of need. Their symbolic objectives, which Alford (1974) holds to be of primary importance, is to demonstrate a show of unity and shared fate whenever crises arise threatening or testing the legitimacy of a regime.

These efforts at *formal coordination* are, in Turk's analysis, much more responsive to conventional evidence of need (or of crisis) within the contexts of integrated diversity than within the simpler-structured cities. My interpretation of this in the earlier discussion of it (Chapter IV) follows Alford's emphasis on the symbolic significance of coordinating mechanisms. For cities in which the legitimacy of leadership rests on extensive attachments throughout an inclusively integrated system, as was evidenced in the case of older and broader-scope cities (Chapter V), formal coordination attempts would symbolically reaffirm the communal commitment of service for all that is periodically threatened by alarm over unsatisfied expectations. Newer narrow-scope cities are quite legitimately fragmented, so that the crisis-provoked call to coordinate might well receive its more eager response in the opposing context of integrated diversity. Conversely, as we have just found, specific new *programs* are less closely related to conventionally defined need in this latter context because of the capacity of the system to differentiate within its extensive interactional network. Some implications of these two different types of responses will be considered again in the concluding chapter.

FISCAL PERFORMANCE

Concepts and Indicators

Within the general notion of output levels, fiscal performance may be usefully distinguished from innovativeness. Fiscal performance refers to the budgetary commitments made by a city government to maintain a certain level of performance in established public functions. This performance is distinguished from the more irregularly occurring processes of innovation by which governments take on additional nonmandated programs. There is, of course, no doubt that an annual budget for an on-going function may include some increments for wholly new enterprises within the service-function package, as well as other and possibly decreasing sums for later phases of previously adopted innovations. But it is assumed that the balance in any given annual budget, taken together with funds for traditional, unphased, or recurring activities, reflects a certain established local norm for the commitment of community resources to the performance of all activities within a functional or programmatic area. In principle, then, fiscal performance differs from innovativeness as a general policy differs from a discrete decision.

Consistent with this distinction, the hypothesized positive effect of the scope of government on fiscal performance rested on rationales that included, but went beyond, the theory on innovativeness. Decisions to have government implement new programs, as well as fiscal-performance policy, were theoretically said to depend on two aspects of scope: the extent to which scope increases civic involvement and service demands, and especially scope's impact on the probability of an innovative combination of interests and resources. It was found that, in fact, the government-based networks denoted by scope are less than crucial for either civic involvement or innovativeness, and that new programs seem to arise largely by the action of boundary spanners who are best identified with indicators of the nongovernmental organization of cities.

It is especially important, then, to emphasize the additional distinctive aspect of scope that is particularly relevant for fiscal-performance policy. It was noted that once programs become well established as on-going governmental bureaucracies, the momentum for maintaining or expanding performance levels would shift from innovators (who may have largely extragovernmental roles) to government, itself. The range of resources that government organizes and controls would then become more important for determining output. In short, environmental volunteers may propel government into new ventures, but established bureaucracies will then grow from interagency competition to control and commit the great resources of wide scope.

The expenditures data necessary to test this hypothesis pose some irresolvable problems of comparability (see Liebert, 1974a,b). Government expenditures are reported in aggregate, without distinguishing the proportion for each function that comes from transfers, grants, or aid provided by other governments. Aid of this sort may sometimes result from local effort or commitment, but it may also come without effort locally. City governments also differ in the amount of activity each of several superior governments *directly* perform in cities, and the amount left to local initiative. City governments differ, in ways not noted in budgets, in the extent to which their planning and budgeting operations must follow directives, agreements, or guidelines set by or with other governments. There is no way to control for all of these "disturbances" on the meaning of expenditures as an index of local effort and commitment. We progress only one step beyond many previous studies of expenditures by having some knowledge of whether or not city governments exercise any responsibility for various funtions. If they exercise no responsibility for a given function, the question of fiscal performance is irrelevant, for some other government or private agency may have totally preempted the field or, alternatively, the city government may not yet have innovated in an area where it legitimately could do so.

With these problems in mind, we will report the expenditures data separately for each major function, and then *only for the cities exercising some responsibility for the function* as determined by the procedures used to code functional scope. This will avoid the misleadingly circular finding that wide-scope governments spend more in total. The unanswered question is whether two governments having the same function differ in spending on that function because they differ in scope.

Disaggregation into expenditures by functional category also permits useful comparison of different types of functions. This procedure is most useful, methodologically speaking, because some functions are performed by so few cities as to make statistics unstable and inferences unwise. Moreover, the little that we know about nonlocal disturbances on expenditures suggests that some functions, such as education or welfare, are more extensively "disturbed" in unknown ways than are others, such as police or fire protection and a host of minor optimal functions. In short, we are on safer ground in placing greater emphasis on findings for functions performed by all cities, or performed with minimal likely external disturbance.

The disaggregation of total expenditures was accomplished within ten functional categories. These are listed in Table VI-4. The source

TABLE VI-4
Correlations between Functional Scope and Fiscal Performance within Ten Functional
Categories, for Only Those Municipalities Having Responsibility for Each Category

Functional category	Correlations between scope and: Expenditures per capita[a]	Expenditures per dollar income[b]	Number of cities[c]
(1) Police	.30**	.41**	663
(2) Fire	.42**	.50**	663
(3) Highways	.09*	.16**	663
(4) Education	-.16	.01	145
(5) Welfare, Gen. Asst.	.40*	.41*	101
(6) Welfare, both kinds	.06	.04	57
(7) Hospitals	.05	-.01	12
(8) Health	.09	.09	389
(9) Sanitation & Sewers	.00	.01	315
(10) "Other, unclassified"	.32**	.41**	663

[a] Source: *County and City Data Book: 1962,* Table 6. This is 1960 expenditures data standardized on 1960 population.
[b] Source: *County and City Data Book: 1962,* Table 6. This is 1960 expenditures data standardized on 1959 aggregate personal income.
[c] The number of cities for each category is the number having responsibility for the functional category. E.g., only 145 cities have responsibility for education. A few cities (five in the cases of police, fire, highways, and "other") were deleted due to missing data on expenditures. "Welfare, both kinds" is constrained to cities having both general assistance and federally aided welfare responsibilities. "Welfare, Gen. Asst." is constrained to cities having responsibility for general–assistance welfare but not for federally aided welfare. "Hospitals" and "Health" are each constrained to cities having responsibility for one of these functions but not the other. "Sanitation and Sewers" is constrained to cities having responsibility for both sanitation and sewers.
$*p < .05.$
$**p < .01.$

for the 1960 expenditures data (U.S. Bureau of the Census, *County and City Data Book, 1962*), had separately itemized listings for police, fire, highways, education, a few others, and "total." Subtraction of the itemized functions from the total provided an "other, unclassified" item containing expenditures on general administration, parks, and a wide set of residual functions not included in the scope variable. The data source did not disaggregate the two types of welfare; it combined hospitals with health; and it listed sanitation together with sewers. Some further disaggregation of these groupings was deemed desirable to make comparisons across more categories, which was accomplished by procedures described in Table footnote *c* below Table VI-4, and further elaborated as follows.

Any cities responsible for federally aided welfare also maintained locally funded general assistance, even though the reverse was not true. The only feasible disaggregation of welfare was, therefore, to isolate "general assistance only" from responsibility for both types. Health and hospitals were disaggregated because, in practice, they have little in common. Sanitation and sewers were retained as a single category partly because very few cities have one and not the other, and partly because they are alike in one important sense: Both are concerned with waste-disposal problems. The result of these procedures was the production of ten functional categories, varying in numbers of cities within each category from 12 for hospitals to 663 for police, fire, highways, and other. Five cities were deleted from the universe of 668 cities for lack of expenditures data. Finally, expenditures on each function were standardized in two ways for the two types of performance indicators: expenditures per capita and expenditures per dollar of aggregate personal income.

Bivariate Analysis with Scope

The findings in Table VI-4 are generally consistent with the hypothesis that wide scope generates high fiscal performance. The zero-order correlations between scope and expenditures are in the expected direction in all but a few of the relationships. Only two coefficients are negative and one is zero. Seven others, ranging from .01 to .09, give very modest support to the hypothesis. Far stronger support is found in the 10 coefficients ranging from .09 to .50 and having statistical significance at the .05 level.

Statistical tests are, of course, no more formally appropriate here than elsewhere in this study, for the cities in each functional category are never a random sample. They comprise a universe of all cities or of some purposively selected subset. Statistical tests are, nonetheless, used in this instance to help judge differences in the reliability of statistics arising from the effects of widely different universe sizes on net measurement error and the normality and variability of distributions. We find that, in actuality, all of the "nonsignificant" findings pertain to low correlation coefficients that are based on smaller numbers of cities. We may consider these coefficients to be a little more unstable than the others.

There are some other peculiar qualities in the low coefficients, besides the fact that they apply to smaller numbers of cities. They also pertain to the types of functions that invite speculation over how they are financed. Consider education. It is financed in many cities with more state and federal money than with local funds, and the formulas that are used to determine this aid to schools are hardly uniform across the nation, or even within states. These formulas may redistribute wealth in the sense of altering what would be true if local effort were the sole determinant of educational budgets. If so, broad scope could increase effort even without necessarily increasing educational expenditures on the local school system, or narrow scope could decrease effort, but not the total federal, state, and local income for expenditures.

Note also that most of the municipally dependent school districts are located in the Northeast where, in the domain of religious, ethnic, and cultural institutions, many groups maintain traditional and functionally diffuse integrative patterns partly through the socialization of their children in an unusually large number of parochial and private schools. The public school function is an instance where community effort may be high but overall public funds low because of the nongovernmental complements of broad municipal scope, or because of what we have called (Chapter III, pp. 62–64) the broad integration and development of institutional domains other than government. Combined with complex state and federal financing arrangements, this historic co-development of public and private control over education in the older locales of the Northeast could alone account for Table VI-4's anomalous negative correlation between per capita educational expenditures and municipal scope.

Diverse financing arrangements may also significantly alter municipal funding levels for hospitals and for the types of welfare over which states and the federal government set standards and cost-sharing arrangements. For the type of welfare that more fully reflects a local monopoly of decision-making power—general assistance—we find a strong positive correlation between expenditures and scope. In this latter instance, there is support for the scope-centered hypothesis that output or costs for a function will rise with the growth of local bureaucratic power in broad-scope governments. The generality of this inference is, unfortunately, limited, for the findings on general-assistance welfare apply to the set of only 101 municipalities having that function and not having the federally aided welfare function. As a local organizational dynamic, broad scope's hypothesized effect on raising the level of on-going program performance is certainly supported by the evidence on the locally sensitive and responsive general-assistance welfare function, but with the stricture that the evidence pertains to a selected subsample.

The financing of sanitation, sewers, hospitals, and health functions generally entails some direct user charges, a procedure that may broaden the resistance to higher charges, even if it should increase demand for higher performance. It would be useful, if data were available in sufficient detail, to isolate types of fiscal input to determine whether scope or other variables have differing effects for different income sources and for corresponding expenditure assignment. This prerequisite for the elaboration of expenditures research would apply to most functions in our complex federal system. Not even city streets are financed solely through municipal budget making, for cities do not maintain the highly variable proportions of municipal street mileage belonging to county, state, and federal road systems (Liebert, 1974a). About the only functions uniformly financed directly out of the general municipal budget are police and fire and some of the smaller discretionary activities undertaken under the classification of "other." Even these are increasingly subject to intergovernmental fiscal exchanges, which are now arising partly to subsidize the tremendous growth of these functions in some cities. Broad scope appears, from the zero-order findings, to account for some of this growth.

The "other, unclassified" category of expenditures deserves additional comment. Of all output measures in this study, it may be the most pertinent to a general theory of activation of program outputs. The category includes costs for general administration, any judicial functions, recreation, libraries, urban renewal and public housing, public markets, subsidized transportation systems, some port facilities, and numerous other possible programs. As such, it is at once a kind of residual measure of functional scope, innovativeness, *and* fiscal performance. It combines some aspects of all three concepts and should, for this reason alone, correlate with autonomous measures of the same concepts. It is included here as a performance variable on the assumption that annual expenditures on "other" functions are most strongly indicative of municipal commitment to levels of performance within established program areas. This assumption would apply even to any urban renewal or public housing component of "other," for federal aid in these areas is not granted without request, these programs had often become well established by 1960, and we are concerned here with *annual* expenditures on maintaining a performance level rather than with the total capital that was historically invested in bringing these programs beyond innovative experimentation. We should, nonetheless, bear in mind one distinctive aspect of "other," namely that many expenditures items in this category will depend *directly* on prior innovativeness and on unmeasured components of functional scope, and will, in this sense, be partly tautologous with these concepts.

All of these qualifications come down to two points. For the purpose of indicating local effort in municipal fiscal performance, the best measures are for police and fire protection. For the same purpose and for its conceptual overlap with scope and innovation, expenditures on "other" command similar emphasis. These are the indicators of performance that will be carried over into multivariate analyses where control variables are added. Although the risks of generalization with this selective emphasis are acknowledged, these indicators will be regarded as suggestive of the local fiscal-effort component in general program performance.

Multivariate Analysis with Scope and Control Variables

In setting up the multivariate analysis, expenditures on police and fire protection were combined in a single variable. Not only are they very much alike in financing and in some substantive aspects, but they also behaved very similarly in tentative experimental calculations. The single variable is, therefore, a more efficient procedure. "Other" was kept apart as a second performance indicator for reasons of distinctiveness noted previously. Both of these expenditures variables were standardized only on the per capita basis, in keeping with the most common convention in fiscal research, and again to reduce duplication. Finally, the five cities for which 1960 expenditures data were missing were included by assigning them means on expenditures, in order to have all 668 cities represented in the multivariate analysis.

Table VI-5 presents zero-order findings for the relationship between scope and the control variables and per capita expenditures on police and fire protection and on the residual "other" category. The four control variables—accessibility, municipal age, size, and suburban status—are used here for the same reasons that they were considered relevant to the innovativeness analysis. In reiteration, it should be sufficient to say that these variables are expected to provide evidence, at least among zero-order relationships, of higher performance levels in political contexts having greater differentiation and more extensive interfacing among differentiated centers of power.

The evidence in Table VI-5 is generally as expected. Larger and older cities spend more on police and fire protection and on residual

TABLE VI-5
Zero-Order Correlations between Selected Measures of Fiscal Performance
and Accessibility, Functional Scope, and Contextual Variables.
(N = 668 Cities)

Independent variables	Measures of performance[a]	
	Expenditures per capita on police and fire protection	Expenditures per capita on "other unclassified" functions
Accessibility	.16	-.02
Functional scope	.39	.32
Municipal age	.41	.28
Suburban status	.01	-.07
City size	.34	.32

[a]For sources, see Table VI-4. Expenditures on police and on fire
were added to get expenditures on both. Five cities with missing
data on expenditures were assigned the mean and retained in the
analysis.

functions. The relevant correlation coefficients are similar in magnitude to those between scope and expenditures on these functions, except that age and police–fire expenditures provide the strongest reported correlation. In light of this, it is particularly surprising that suburban status has weak correlations with both types of expenditures. Suburbs are not distinguishable for higher *or* lower fiscal performance in police and fire functions, but tend to have slightly lower expenditures within the set of residual functions. Lastly, while accessibility and "other" expenditures are barely associated in the negative direction, there is some tendency for cities having more accessible formal leaderships also to have higher fiscal performance on police and fire protection. Although these findings are somewhat mixed, on balance they support the contention that government costs go up where points of contact between government and constituent centers of power are most structurally diverse, and where the constituent power centers are, themselves, diverse.

Turning immediately to the multivariate analysis in Table VI-6, our interest centers again on whether the independent contributions of the five variables form a pattern, and whether any such pattern

TABLE VI-6

Standardized Regression Coefficient and R^2 in Multiple Regression Analyses Explaining Fiscal Performance (Standard Error in Parentheses)

Dependent variable[a]	Independent variables					R and R^2	N
	Access-ibility	Functional scope	Municipal age	Suburban status	City size		
P/C expense on "other"	-.154 (.038)	.259 (.043)	.139 (.050)	.140 (.040)	.217 (.042)	$R = .428$ $R^2 = .183$	668
P/C expense on fire & police (Model 1)	-.028 (.035)	.277 (.040)	.302 (.047)	.299 (.037)	.178 (.039)	$R = .542$ $R^2 = .294$	668
P/C expense on fire & police (Model 2)	—— ——	.274 (.040)	.295 (.046)	.297 (.037)	.178 (.039)	$R = .542$ $R^2 = .293$	668

[a] For sources and definitions, see Tables VI-4 and VI-5. The symbol, P/C, means per capita. Five cities with missing data on expenditures were assigned the mean and retained in the analysis.

152

favors an explanatory emphasis on direct environmental influences or whether it favors a scope-centered or government-centered perspective. It turns out that all five independent variables have at least modest independent effects on per capita expenditures on the residual functions. None of the regression coefficients in the equation predicting "other" expenditures falls below its standard error, and all fall within the range of .14–.26 in absolute value. In the case of predicting expenditures on police and fire, four of the regressors have coefficients in roughly the same range, with only accessibility having a very low coefficient—lower than even its standard error. These initial observations assure us that the findings remain somewhat mixed with respect to the government versus environment issue, and that a distinctive pattern may again be decipherable only with closer inspection.

The Multivariate Findings in Detail

In weighing the evidence in Table VI-6, it should first be noted that the scope of government has relatively strong influence on increasing the expenditures levels indicated by both the performance variables. Scope's coefficient in the regression on police–fire is just slightly below the largest ones in this regression (.27 for scope versus .30 for age and for suburban status); is somewhat greater than the city-size coefficient (.18); and is considerably larger than the negligible coefficient for accessibility. Scope's independent direct effect on "other" expenditures is somewhat larger than that of any other regressor, providing even stronger evidence of the significance of scope as a determinant of governmental growth. These observations help sustain the thesis that the extensity of governmental bureaucracy and its capabilities for controlling and committing resources, as indexed by scope, have strong effects on setting on-going performance levels, even while having the previously reported weaker effects on the probability of innovation.

It should be stressed that scope's greater effect on performance, as measured by fiscal policy, is presumed to result most directly from intragovernmental competition for massive available resources and from an attendant bargaining process by which all agencies share in the drive for larger budgets. This process may be most characteristic of the classic battle between policemen and firemen for the favor of higher salaries and greater public recognition, which usually resolves into what has become identified as a "parity" arrangement providing to each profession the manpower, salary scale, or equipment sufficient to satisfy, for the moment, claims of greater relative occupational risks and civic significance. The same competitive process probably occurs with less publicly visible drama among bureaucrats and professionals within other agencies having some reference groups in the system that municipal government budgets and payrolls. Teachers and welfare workers readily come to mind; as might garbage collectors and street maintenance crews; judges and school superintendents or hospital administrators; and assorted planners, program evaluators, bookkeepers, and speciality office personnel having all kinds of programmatic affiliations. They compare for priorities, and the priorities of all rise as their scope of competitors widens.

Quite distinct from the effects of scope are the effects of the other governmental variable, formal leadership accessibility. The independent effects of accessibility on both the performance variables are not only among the smallest in the regression analyses, but they are also unexpectedly negative. Hence, it cannot be said that the two governmental variables operate in the same way, stimulating growth of governmental budgets where points of contact between agencies, or leaders and constituent power centers, are most diverse. In particular, greater civic involvement, which is indicated by both government variables, is clearly not the aspect of governmental organization that accounts for higher expenditures. Instead, it was suggested that scope, alone, may bring about higher expenditures, due largely to intramunicipal competition and bargaining among government agencies and the constituent interests that they can mobilize.

To the extent that greater leadership accessibility brings nonemployees and other outside parties into negotiations, the effect seems to bring pressures on central executive and legislative leaders to keep the taxpayer's costs down. That this negative effect on expenditures is not substantial invites further qualification. It may be that outsiders behave in this situation as they do in relation to many service organizations, demanding costly services but at low cost. If outsiders lack access to make these demands, we find that the reformed leadership of this governing arrangement does indeed put forward the services, but without the check on its costs.

The expenditure-inhibiting role of formal leadership accessibility is not at all what we would expect on the basis of the rhetoric and theory of municipal reform. Advocates of reformed or inaccessible governments (e.g., see Nolting 1969, Stone *et al.* 1940) have suggested that reform would reduce expenditures through greater efficiency and professional management. Lineberry and Fowler (1967) found empirical support for this theory in their often cited and frequently reprinted analysis of expenditures and reformism. They observed that the reformers seemed to be right about the lower costs of their type of government. However, Lineberry and Fowler did not control for differences in the assignment of functions to cities, for scope, or for any of the other variables used in the present theoretical model.

It was demonstrated in a more recent study (Liebert, 1974a) that controls for functional assignment effectively eliminate any patterned effects of reformism on expenditure levels. In the theoretical framework of the present study, and with additional control variables, we find that reformist attributes ironically seem to result in slightly higher costs per function than do the old-fashioned unreformed leadership arrangements. Perhaps, as was suggested previously, the relative absence of constituent inputs into reformed governments removes certain external checks on the performance policy costs (or, more in keeping with reformist principles, on the "quality" of performance) of their more politically insulated administration and professionally managed service package. Recall that expenditures on "other," on which accessibility has its significant negative effect, include costs for general administration and for various minor specialized functions. The principal sense in which it can be said that reformed cities spend less is that they are assigned fewer functions. In particular, they rarely have the costly welfare and public schools functions, but have instead acquired a sizeable residual expenditure commitment, which is independent from the effects of scope, community age, suburban status, and city size.

Finally, there is a question of the role of the contextual variables. All three have strong enough effects to require rejection of the notion that governmental attributes of the sort discussed here fully mediate or amply decompose environmental influences on expenditures. Of course, scope does have some mediating role, and additional data on other governmental attributes—such as more direct measures of intraagency interaction—could well decompose or partial out some of the apparent effects of the contextual variables. In the absence of that data, the emphasis should be on interpretation of the effects of contextual variables from an environmentalist perspective.

The independent effects of municipal age and city size are fully in keeping with that perspective, although they are not particularly large, except in comparison with a few of the other effects reported in Table VI-6. Like the zero-order findings, this table shows higher performance levels by municipal governments of older cities, where there is presumed to be substantial continuity in the interweaving and interfacing of diverse organized community interests. This integration may give outsiders more direct penetrating influence on government agencies. Or, to be more in keeping with the implications of scope while remaining in the environmentalist perspective, the same integration could provide government agencies with more partners in the quest for funds. Irrespective of whether this is a matter of unilateral influence or of coalition formation, the ties that are formed are not like the relatively individualized attachments to policy generalists, as denoted by leadership accessibility. Rather, we speak of age and continuity as denoting ties among well organized groups, typically organizations with specific missions of their own and a stake in maintaining government support or protection in those missions. In this view, the evidence suggests that these organized interests lend support to higher government fiscal performance. The differentiation of these interests in larger cities seems to provide additional support for high expenditures, by providing additional potential partners for this quest.

While all of this is consistent with the general theory of activation presented earlier, the findings for the independent effect of suburban status are wholly discrepant with expectations. Suburbs spend *more* on police and fire protection, and on the miscellaneous "other" category, than do nonsuburbs, controlling for size, age, and governmental attributes. How can this be true if, at the same time, suburbs have less differentiated interests of any type from which support for higher expenditures could be provided? Once again, we may have to turn to an emphasis on the intermetropolitan specialization that distinguishes suburbs in the conceptualization developed earlier. Acting protectively in this broader context, and apart from influences associated with other variables, the suburban community may emerge as a relatively unified interest of a single type, competing not internally as much as with neighbors in its metropolitan context, and in the process strengthening the legitimacy, the distinctive quality, and the overall performance of its namesake municipal government. Greater wealth in some suburbs may be an additional factor, although wealth in its various forms may be attracted by high-performing suburbs rather than the cause running the other way.

This brief portrait of suburban performance policymaking is essentially similar to the one more extensively documented by Williams *et al.* (1965). Their study of metropolitan Philadelphia was in large part an attempt to instruct us that there is a persisting discrepancy between the image of floundering no-account suburban government and the reality of effective vehicles for political action. They demonstrated also that the distinctive interests and resources in each suburb provide varying bases for the high performance of suburbs, with some selective emphasis of certain functions over others. The present study confirms this conclusion with the findings of very high suburban commitment to the protective functions of police and fire, and of lower, but still substantial, suburban commitment to the residual set of general administrative and minor functions.

Discussion

The preceding analysis has made little attempt to distinguish between the two measures of performance in terms of patterns of influence. In fact, the patterns are different only in lesser details. In commenting on the overall structure of the findings, the substantive significance of the slightly different models for the two performance indicators will first be briefly noted. A broader view of fiscal performance, in general, then follows.

With regard to expenditures on police and fire protection, most of the explained variance is associated with the scope of government, age of community, and suburban status. If these three variables have anything in common relative to the other two independent variables, it is that they pertain more to the lasting integrative properties of a community than do the municipality's sheer size and type of leadership roles. In this sense, high performance on the protective functions of police and fire would seem to result from some of the more continuously maintained patterns of organization, whether it is the integrated diversity of the old, wide-scope city or the specialized role of the suburb in its metropolitan context. A performance policy to maintain high commitments of resources depends on the persistence of organized demand.

More specifically, the police and fire functions may be especially well suited (1) to service what Sennett (1970) called the culturally prized disorder of the rich and diversified organizational life of older cities, (2) to service as well suburban commitments ot security in a distinctive and simpler social order, and (3), as bureaucracies engaged in ostensibly essential work, to compete effectively for no less than their claimed share of resources and recognition within those broad-scope governmental systems that are comprised of many such competing units. Functions other than police and fire may, to varying degrees, serve the same organizational ends. To recount these organizational determinants is, once again, not wholly to discount such "needs" as official crime or arson rates, but only to set the latter aside as factors partly subsumed by the organizational determinants and largely outside the present theoretical framework and available data.

Turning to expenditures on the residual category of "other," it was found that the explained variance is more evenly spread out over all five independent variables. Here is where formal leadership accessibility, or nonreformism, had its interesting negative effect on the costs of government, after separating out the effects of other variables in the model. This suggested the post hoc inference that, at least with regard to central administrative and legislative costs and the costs of optional minor programs, citizen access to leaders imposes a kind of external grassroots constraint on the inner organizational dynamics of fiscal growth.

This assertion might be generally true of all aspects of expenditure policy and program development, given that we also found a tiny negative effect from accessibility to police—fire functions as well as comparable or stronger negative effects in the earlier analysis of innovativeness. The check on performance decision making, which seems attributable to broad accessibility of formal leaders, corresponds to what Crain *et al.* (1969) found to be a barrier to water fluoridation adoption decisions wherever broad community involvement in the issue was manifest. This should lead us to observe once again that the potent decision makers for governmental growth are more typically organizations or their agents rather than the ordinary citizens or neighborhood groups who gain access from nonreformism.

Among all of the determinants of expenditures on "other," the influence of the scope of government is more pronounced. In fact, nowhere in this entire study does scope provide a stronger direct effect on activation than in this instance. It is important to repeat in this context that the "other" category is in part an indicator of that *accumulated portion* of the scope of government which is not included in our measure of largely *inherited* scope. We have here further confirming evidence that cities wide in scope on some functions will be wide in scope on all. More meaningfully, broad scope appears to contribute to a further broadening of scope. There was a little evidence of this effect when we looked at the determinants of innovativeness in the creation of new program functions. Scope's substantial effect on enlargening the residual program category appears to support this inference further.

In addition, given the entire set of findings on scope's generally positive relationship with expenditures, there may be a more involved feedback effect of scope on itself. This would occur if scope's effects on increasing the size of established programs ever resulted in due course in differentiation into more specialized programs, some of which may presently fall under "miscellaneous" in the budget. Any of these various feedback routes would complete one circle in the spiraling process of organizational change implicit in many theories of development, including the interorganizational variants of those theories as used throughout this research.

In the end, however, it is not the scope of government that takes command over the processes of activating a community's political resources. Scope is, in fact, part of the output of the commanding agents of development, although it is an output with predictable and empirically supported expansionist consequences for all the examined aspects of political action—including the further broadening of scope, itself. Behind scope, largely determining it and generally more significantly affecting all modes of governmental action, is the unfolding of historical trends in the founding organizational constitution of community life, as denoted by municipal age.

The age of cities was once again found to be of clear importance, this time in determining police–fire and "other" expenditures. Its indirect effects through scope ($p \simeq .13$), when combined with its strong direct effects, leaves age rather than scope with the greatest total analyzed influence on expenditures. Scope effectively decomposes and explains much of the meaning of community age for expenditures, but it does not dispense with the task of attending to the effects of age on its own terms. It is important to emphasize, here and in the concluding chapter that follows, that the intercity polarities in community and governmental organization, in civic involvement, and in program expansion and fiscal policy are deeply rooted. They are rooted initially in the persistence of older and more communally integrated local systems of high action density, and subsequently in the more recent and foreseeably continuing creation of increasingly specialized and manageable local organization systems of much lower action density.

VII.

Patterns and Prospects
for the Role and Scope of City Governments

The scope of government and the particular sets of public norms which have developed historically in each community will represent a selection from those available in the repertoire of ideological components and perspectives comprising American political culture . . . . Gradually embedded in the political structures and patterns of legitimate influence of the community, these norms become—in a degree which may differ sharply from community to community—accepted as the proper procedures and substance of political processes [From Alford, R. R., *Bureaucracy and participation:* Political cultures in four Wisconsin cities. Copyright © 1967 by Rand McNally, Chicago. p. 203.].

Since its appearance in America as one of the European settler's first corporate entities, the institution of municipal government has been greatly transformed in how it is constituted. Early forms were given the general functions of the principal community superstructure, while more recent forms are founded as specialized organizations in a milieu of such organizations. The old and the new forms both survive today, at least with respect to one of the more pronounced ways in which general and limited governments in America differ—their functional scope.

This enduring, if not growing, difference in scope raised the issues, just considered, of whether there might be corresponding differences in how municipal governments relate to their communities, in their level and character of political action, and in their roles as vehicles of community participation and service performance. Governments structured along broader lines in the old-fashioned way were expected to mobilize wide civic involvement and extensive program outputs. Functionally limited governments were expected to be correspondingly limited in both civic inputs and outputs.

This question seemed especially relevant today when, by one view, governments at all levels may overcome the inertia of inaction and aloofness only by the consolidated exercise of broad powers, and when, by another view, the proper time and social technology have arrived for halting or even reversing the expansion of the role of government in order to secure the supposed rational restraint and economy of limited government. The present analysis supports the more encompassing view that, among city governments, both of these patterns of political-action preferences can be found. The differing patterns seem indeed to be partly due to differences in the scope of government, but they seem to be more generally due to the age of a city's institutional life and culture.

In the following pages, the separate elements of the previous analysis are first drawn together in a general synopsis. The major patterns in the findings are highlighted in this context, as are limitations on their empirical and theoretical adequacy. Topics needing further research are also noted. This is followed by a more elaborate discussion of the prospects for change in the scope of municipal governments. To complete this volume, and to raise some of the broader tentative implications of the present work, a final section focuses on the age variable and on the probability of a widening gap between polar forms of civic organization and culture in local American political systems.

A SYNOPSIS OF THE FINDINGS

It has been one intent of this research to devise a measure of municipal government scope suitable for the questions analyzed here. This involved developing a measure of role responsibilities that would not be directly dependent on performance levels, and yet would be more empirically estimable than a legal or social charter would be. The devised "count of major functions" estimate of scope had some nominal face validity, correlated high with performance-based estimates of scope, and, in the subsequent analyses, behaved in a theoretically consistent way. The fact that it was a crude estimate of a role-defined concept of scope should lead other researchers to try other measurement procedures. Its exclusion of certain components of a looser or broader meaning of scope (e.g., minor optional functions, performance, intraagency task differentiation, and aspects of legal and social charters) means that there is room for a more thorough treatment of the scope of governmental activity than that presented here.

It was a second objective of this research to trace the origins or causes of variability in municipal functional scope. Beginning with a long look back to the earliest patterns of settlement in each region of the eventual transcontinental states, there were found to be strong time-ordered changes in the prevailing organizational constitution of city governments. These changes were attributed chiefly to trends toward organizational specialization and centralization in newly developing areas. These trends were initially strongest and are presently best documented for the social-justice functions of judicial, education, and welfare activities. Other functions, also increasingly attracting the attention of interlocal organizational elites, have more recently begun to follow the same trend. The result has been a kind of regionally based generational cohort effect, where cities growing up in the same period tend to adopt similar organizational forms. With recency of formation, the adopted forms are increasingly more specialized and less general, inclusive, or communal.

Drawing partly from Stinchcombe's (1965) analysis of similar cohort effects in the organization of work and voluntary organizations in general, it was inferred that city age is a useful indicator of the degree of long lasting interactional linkages within and among many institutional domains of social organization. Age was considered a measure of organizational density and interrelatedness. On this score, there is some validation in Turk's (1970) findings of high correlations between age and number of national association headquarters, banking activity, diversification of "export" establishments, and level of industrial development. Yet, the correspondence of the city-age measure with the conceptualization of its general meaning depends on assumptions that clearly merit further empirical testing and validation. Within the present study, as organizational integration, age is strongly demonstrable in the specific case of municipal functional scope, and lends theoretically meaningful interpretation to the observed consequences of age for all aspects of political organization and action.

It was a final intent of this study to assess the implications of differing scope, and of its antecedent causes, for levels of political action by and through municipal government. The findings on this question are both complex and not always in accord with predictions. In general, wide or narrow scope had its predicted activating effect, but was less than crucial to the character of political-action processes in cities. The dynamic types of action, involving both wide participation and extensive outputs, seem more fully to be shaped by the larger social contexts in which city governments are located, and only secondarily by their scope. Before exploring the ramifications of these conclusions, it is useful to briefly review and synthesize the evidence.

There are broader implications in the findings that turn the question of analyzing political dynamics back to a more historical perspective. In particular, one must be impressed with the persistence of municipal age as a predictor not only of scope, but also of nonreformed leadership or accessibility, of high voter turnout, of innovativeness, and of high levels of expenditures for program performance. No other variable was a better predictor overall, and none was as consistently positive and substantively significant.

If there was a second-best predictor overall, it was, in fact, scope; for while its independent effects were generally rather weak, it always had the expected positive relationships with political-action variables. Scope's zero-order effects were always larger than its direct effects in multiple regression. This indicates two things. Descriptively, much higher civic inputs and program outputs are indeed found in wider-scope governments than in narrow-scope ones. However, as an explanatory variable, some of scope's effects are spurious (due largely to antecedent effects of city age), so that scope only partially mediates, selects, or screens contextual determinants of governmental activity. Broad-scope governments are more open to activating influences than are narrow-scope governments, but governments of any scope are even more activated if they serve the older organizationally dense communities. Scope, then, provides one way in which interrelated social organization generates active and expansive government roles, and serves as a proxy for less concretely measurable ways.

In contrast to age and scope, there was little consistency in how well, or even in what direction, population size and suburban status predicted political-action processes. The implications of these latter findings are fragmentary at best, so we have simply noted in discussing them that they suggest conjecture along alternative lines of inquiry. For example, it was found from the full regression analyses that larger cities had somewhat higher innovative and budgetary outputs, but had slightly lower voter participation and were not distinguished from smaller cities in terms of formal leadership accessibility. Sheer size would seem to place little if any independent demands on government by way of input, while nonetheless providing a depth and range of contextual resources that centers of power may reach and use through governmental programming.

Suburban status had more interesting effects in the full regression models. Independent of other analyzed factors, suburbs unexpectedly had slightly greater formal leadership accessibility, higher voter participation, and larger local budgetary commitments, but they also had the expected lower innovativeness on urban renewal and public housing. The latter finding on suburban disinterest in these rehabilitative innovations might be viewed as understandable on the rather particular grounds that, regardless of age or size, suburbs tend to be self-maintaining systems of continuing capacity, solvency, and good repute. If they innovate, it is not to rehabilitate. The other findings show suburban status giving rise to political activation of all other types, including output on the innovation-contaminated category of "other, unassigned" functions. These findings may still be somewhat surprising, but they do lend additional support to the increasingly established evidence that suburban viability for political action may be more accurate than are simpler images of low suburban involvement and commitment.

Finally, we should note the marginal importance of formal leadership accessibility as a factor affecting other types of activation. The kind of "nonreformism" that this variable denotes did have a strong positive effect on voter turnout, both directly and indirectly through scope. Where formal leaders are more accessible and their government wider in scope, they receive their legitimate authority through broader voter participation. On innovativeness and fiscal performance, however, this same accessibility of leaders tends to place small negative constraints on outputs, holding other factors constant. This feature of accessibility was viewed as a minor check on governmental expansion, which importantly occurs more often in just the types of government (older, broad scope) that are otherwise given to expansion. We will return to this point later.

Overall, any issues about city size, suburban status, and formal leadership accessibility prove not to be central here. Within the concerns of this study, far greater emphasis must be given first to issues about the strong and consistent role of municipal age vis-a-vis political action, and secondly to the weaker but still consistent role of functional scope. It is in this framework that some further summary observations are in order before proceeding to a discussion of prospects for changes in scope and of trends in age-related civic culture.

The importance of age as an attribute of social systems has not been very widely recognized in American social science, perhaps because America has, since its birth, been more widely characterized as "new." Some students of the metropolitan mosaic have, however, taken a different view. Puzzled about why urban residents seem to resist reorganization of school districts and other metropolitan-area jurisdictions, Zimmer and Hawley (1968) conducted an inquiry into the roots of this contentedness. The first sentence in their reported research posed their perspective on the problem this way: "There is a marked tendency, in any society, for established behavioral patterns as well as organizational structures to persist in their present form long after social and economic conditions have reached the point where change is necessary for the system to function effectively [p. 19]."

I agree with most, but not all, of the burden of this sentence. The age of a social system, of a municipality, and of the larger community it encompasses, seems indeed to establish organizational structures along lines dictated by prevailing social and economic circumstances, and these structures tend to persist despite changing circumstances. The analysis of causes of scope illustrated this point and suggested its general applicability to all areas of social organization. Zimmer and Hawley suggest, in addition, that behavioral patterns are also forged early in the life of social systems, and persist contentedly through time as they become, well, traditional. They found evidence of this in the sentiments of metropolitan-area residents. Not inconsistent is the evidence here of age-related patterns of political action. This raises the prospect that most forms of political action and policy options, including those that were studied here and many that were not, have been traditional behavioral patterns that are recurringly manifest in the same cities.

If so, present social and economic conditions may in themselves make only small differences in many political processes of cities. Even the advancement of structural differentiation through growth in size may well take place *within* established organizational superstructures or along established patterns of exchange among those structures. As a consequence, size of cities would be unimportant in itself, or of small importance. It is in this perspective that scope, too, may have little contemporary meaning apart from the broader civic culture in which governments operate. That we found some consistently positive effects of scope on political action suggests that this variable taps current interorganizational networks having some significance in activating governmental processes, but not as much significance as the more diffuse *Gemeinschaft* civic culture that implicitly seems to linger among older city-age cohorts.

Unfortunately, the data that can be assembled on modest budgets are not the kind necessary for testing whether political-action processes are indeed traditionalized expressions of established ways of life. The contemporary data used here lead us back to age as an important determinant, but leave us speculating whether our best interpretation of its meaning applies as intended to much of the past as well. In short, if this matter is to be explored further, it seems necessary to assemble historical data that will permit longitudinal comparisons of changes, if any, in the determinants of political action over time. Some questions for this future work to address are more explicitly proposed in the final sections of this chapter.

On theoretical matters, there is considerable need for more specification of the whole framework of interorganizational analysis. The presumption that organized units are the important political actors and that their interactions are the key to the outcomes of their actions seems to be still quite appropriate, but also still quite elementary. The problem is one of clearly defining boundaries of organized units, and of developing direct, reliable measures of exchanges across those boundaries. It was thought that the measure of scope used here drew a boundary around municipal government, while indicating the probable extent of its internal and external exchanges. Perhaps this is true of a more elaborate measure of boundaries on scope, but the present findings are not supportive enough to be fully convincing that our measure of scope identifies the important effective bounds of a system of integrated exchanges. There are substantial inputs and outputs that are regulated by other units of community organization, or which depend in only modest ways on how many functions are part of the same formal system of government.

Despite these qualifications, there is one point that can be made with some assurance and in contention with part of Zimmer and Hawley's fears about old, established social systems. The old municipalities may be unable to "function effectively" if effectiveness is efficient matching of resources with conventional notions of need, but they do function more innovatively, with higher voter participation, with more accessible formal leaders, and with higher commitments of capital to on-going programs. This is effectiveness if, in an open society, we value wide civic involvement and if, in a community of diverse needs, we value any attempt to deal with at least some of those needs, even if at the risk of overcommitment to which at least one old, wide-scope city (New York) seems especially prone. Cities work out different solutions to the problems of being effective in governing. As we have seen it here, it is the old organizational arrangements that have the action; the new ones have efficiency.

Insofar as these differences result from the scope of government, they are relevant in a very special sense to controversies over whether to reorganize local government. These controversies are played out with big stakes by partisans of all types of effectiveness. One should not be cautious in noting the relevance of the present study for the reorganization issues. First, there are limits to what can be said. Nothing in this study speaks to issues of central-city–suburban consolidation (although we will briefly touch on this question a few pages later). The study speaks instead to *functional* consolidation, and then only to the variation in functional consolidation that, at present, exists among city governments. Lacking evidence on what happens when existing arrangements are in fact changed, we can make only the most tentative statements about what to expect *if* our simple causal model is reasonably valid and *if* it should also happen to remain so.

In this limited framework, the evidence in this study would suggest several consequences of conversion to full functional consolidation within present city governments, other things being equal: There would be a general rise in citizen participation in the local electoral process as the legitimacy of each regime took broader roots; the official leaders in most cities would have greater difficulty remaining in unpoliticized roles or in the aloof administrative echelons of earlier reforms; innovativeness would probably increase, and for more inventive and unconventional reasons; and local budgetary commitments and costs would rise. In short, the action-type of effectiveness would increase, and efficiency would fall. This is, of course, not a forecast, for no such reorganizational reform is imminent, other things being equal.

Moreover, it should be clear that the behavioral outcome differences between broad- and narrow-scope governments do not invite characterization as "strong" ones, precisely because other causal factors cannot be equally brought in line with change in scope. Age, in particular, and all that it denotes about aspects of organizational life that are beyond the range of viable public policy, can hardly be as easily changed as might scope. Traditions of political culture might change very little regardless of great changes in scope. One might, nonetheless, reasonably argue it to be otherwise for, in the fairly unprecedented instance of interventions that greatly change scope, there could be a sufficiently strong break with tradition to significantly reconstitute the rest of the political order. Knowledge of what would happen awaits, of course, more elaborate research on changing settings.

Finally, there is no way in which the political-action differences between broad- and narrow-scope cities demonstrate in themselves a compelling need for policy intervention to eliminate the differences. Objectively, these differences do not alone provide a sufficient basis for metropolitan governmental reorganization either by consolidation of functions or by the radical surgery of thoroughgoing fragmentation. What is missing is a premise as to what is valued. One must first put to the test of public policy choices whether the potential increments in capacities for political action are worth the possible loss of economy and control by limited governments. So far, the answer has clearly been no, for, if anything, the drift of social choice is toward more of the limited types of government.

PROSPECTS FOR CHANGE IN THE SCOPE OF CITY GOVERNMENTS

While there has been little public policy commitment to making wholesale changes in the scope of municipal governments, there are various prospects for change that merit our attention. Several quite different prospects are discussed here, based largely on projections from portions of the previous analysis. Program expansion within existing governments, consolidation of different governments, and fragmentation of functions will be considered, together with possible parameters on each of these prospects. Currently existing cities provide the principal focus for this discussion. Prospects for still-to-emerge cities are taken up in the final section on age cohorts.

It must be emphasized that what is intended here is, once again, not a forecast, but only a brief review of possible alternative implications of the earlier analysis. It is convenient to review such implications in the language of what might be anticipated. The limitations on such an exercise are obvious. It is hoped that the gain in perspective on research and policy options for the future are nearly as obvious.

Consider first the nature of governmental growth through program expansion as analyzed previously. The findings on program outputs indicated greater growth in older wide-scope contexts than in newer narrow-scope ones, due to the dynamics of organizational development. Two types of growth were involved: relative size of on-going programs or per capita expenditures, and the adoption of new programs. Insofar as either of these further expand functional scope, they have a feedback effect. In the long run, *and without constraints,* the net result would seem to be continuous expansion of the total program package in the older and broader-scope cities at rates exceeding the expansion in newer narrow-scope cities. Clearly, there must be constraints, or we would surely have found far stronger effects of scope and age on output levels.

The example of New York City is useful here. Apart from its unsurpassed population, it is a prototype of the very old and thoroughly wide-scope city. In 1969–70, New York City had per capita general expenditures of $754, more than any other city included in the present study and at least twice as much as all but 13 others (all of which, incidentally, were also fairly old and broad scope, except for Highland Park, Michigan). Within the next 5 years, New York City's per capita expenditures nearly doubled, at a pace that was also kept by Baltimore and a number of other major cities for which data have been published in the press (*New York Times,* August 10, 1975, Sec. 4, p. 1). In the eye of the reading public, this expansion was additional evidence that New York City was the clear budget leader in a rising procession of cities. Its leadership in this regard has been long standing, but the mid-1970s had become a time of belt tightening throughout most of the rest of a recessionary economy.

There can be no doubt that unique expenditure-raising qualities of New York City can be identified. Not the least of these is the fact that it has been among the nation's most functionally and fiscally inclusive major cities (Campbell and Sacks 1967:115). If it were stripped of all functions that most narrow- or even medium-scope cities lack, it would no longer be the leading spender. This point is of some symbolic significance to those who look at gross figures. More importantly, perhaps, New York is one of the relatively few cities in which there are so many agencies competing for resources as to compel all to be sufficiently organized to push claims to the limit. It is one of the few city governments that has enough functions to inspire an intricate procedure for paying for one of them now by borrowing on the future income of another (Weisman 1975).

The example of New York City is cited to help illustrate one source of constraint on program expansion, not only for New York but for all cities. Specifically, by the mid-1970s, New York's growth had exceeded the capacity of its available resources and funders to sustain it. Growth of federal aid for new programs had been slowed and largely given over to general revenue sharing; recession and inflation had reduced the extent to which available dollars would reach; growing local tax rates in the shrinking economies of the major cities were viewed with increasing alarm; credit was hard to come by; and New York best symbolized a problem of government's unresponsiveness to the seeming need for cutbacks everywhere. The crunch came when municipal bondsmen could no longer find confidence in New York's capacity for stability among the nation's investors. The investors in early 1975 produced demands for retrenchment that were the first within a generation to be effective in producing massive employee layoffs in New York City (Weisman 1975; note, however, that the layoffs may only be temporary in the longer run). The city and many others began to find ways to cut back.

These events help to mark a major departure from the period of enthusiasm for governmental action. No longer were growing urban programs considered to be as much a source of stability and governmental effectiveness as they were during the New Deal, the New Frontier, or the Great Society days. The data analyzed previously were from this earlier period, when the currently evident checks on governmental growth were less operative. It would be interesting to find out whether the present (i.e., late 1975) moment of heightened interest in efficiency and of tightened controls on governmental action will ever eliminate the output differences between broad- and narrow-scope governments, or whether there will be little change or only a degree of change that will keep the differences within a constrained range. This, too, is an issue for longitudinal research.

The kind of limits of growth noted here have been characterized in more general terms elsewhere. For example, Blau (1970) has suggested that there is a built-in check on organizational growth dynamics such that resources allocated to expansion begin to cut into and reduce resources available for maintenance of that which is already expanded. Blau's specific hypotheses on how this happens might be adapted to a study of municipal performance over time.

Some checks on growth of the sort suggested by Blau were evident in the present study. Where citizens have greater access to formal leaders, which is the case for older and wider-scope cities, the independent effect on outputs is to depress them slightly, perhaps again reflecting a kind of funder's constraint on expansion over maintenance.

This constraint should not be taken to imply that the limits of legitimate support will not be exceeded. Indeed, many cities have recently tested those limits, with the greatest public attention going to those cities still having some social-justice functions and a perceived ever-growing need for them. The only implications suggested here are that older and broader-scope cities may reach the limits of legitimate support sooner or more often than others, and that there seem to be undercurrents of periodically arising constraints on program growth. Whether this brinksmanship continues apace depends in large part on other prospects for change in the scope of municipal governments.

One such prospect may be seen in continuing signs of the fragmentation of functions. Prospects for interfunctional consolidation or coordination are also important and will also be considered. But because consolidation issues arise from fragmentation trends, we will consider fragmentation first.

Involved here is the structural separation of specialized functions from local general-purpose government, together with the coincidental centralization of those functions within an areally wider and administratively longer chain of authority. Heightened state or federal participation is often the occasion for this structural separation. This, in general, was the process of fragmentation that tended to lodge the major social-justice functions within more specialized or state-created governmental units rather than in multipurpose community governments in the more recently developing areas of the nation.

Underlying all of my hypotheses on the significance of scope was the assumption here that this trend has had far greater effect on newer organizational development than on older, established patterns. That is, formal functional consolidation was taken to imply strong interactional integration as well, while formal functional fragmentation in the newer areas was taken to imply weak interactional integration of functions housed in different governments. Maybe so, but this should not be affirmed too strongly.

Particularly in light of the findings on the effects of scope, it should be clear that functional scope identifies only a weakly bounded local system. The fragmented portion of specialized narrow-scope systems behave differently, but not overwhelmingly differently, from the integrated whole of diffuse broad-scope systems. In practice, of course, the personnel of public schools, welfare agencies, and certain other local public service groups attend to the functionally relevant policymaking affairs of their state and national governments or associations to a considerable degree, regardless of whether these functions are formally a part of a general-purpose municipal government. This amounts to reduced meaning for any local government boundaries, to a lessening of local organizational autonomy, and to a narrowing of city government scope of responsibilities in ways not captured by our measure. To the degree that this interlocal administrative interdependence of specialized functions continues, scope as measured here probably loses some relevance and impact in any analysis of its effects. In short, there may be sufficiently increasing interfunctional fragmentation in all contexts to result in decreasing effects from formal consolidation of functions.

Current trends seem to promise a continuing weakening of each function's integration with city government. There is an enduring conflict between specialization and community government that the former has generally won with the aid of extralocal centralization. Not wholly improbable is a formal separation of some functions from the city governments now responsible for them. Public schools and welfare are perhaps the prime candidates, although most other local functions are in some contention in some quarters.

The situation with public schools is particularly interesting, for it has long been a model of the search for functional autonomy from community conditions. The whole purpose of schooling, we have increasingly come to understand as a matter of public policy, is to undo community conditions and to give all children equal developmental opportunities. The chief vehicle for this policy has become the judiciary, which alone exceeds schools in gaining early functional autonomy, national centralization, and standardization. Whereas the judiciary protects national rights, it has therefore properly sought to protect those of school children. With sufficient backing from other policymaking sectors, the courts have sought to standardize two types of school resource inputs—funding and racial composition.

In doing so, the courts have run up against local governmental boundaries in a number of settings. School districts, whether municipally dependent or not, differ in wealth and racial composition. To redistribute either or both more equitably, special metropolitan or intercity school districts may have to be formed in some locales.

Current public policy commitments do not always extend this far, but there is a prospect that they will. If so, municipally dependent school systems will become more rapidly antiquated and more fully eliminated than they are now. Formulas for equitable resource distribution may, in any event, make current distinctions between local governing systems less meaningful.

Similarly well developed as a local function commanding national attention is welfare. In recent times, welfare has actually been divisible into several structurally separate subfunctions, the principal groupings being three. First, and not directly relevant here, are those activities of nonlocal significance, mainly state or federal unemployment compensation and retirement or disability social security. More relevant are the local government (or state agency) administered but federally aided welfare programs such as aid to financially dependent children. The data used in this study came from a time (in the mid-1960s) when aid to the blind and old age assistance were part of this second and locally administered group of welfare programs, but they have since been incorporated within the federal social security program. This transfer narrowed the functional scope of some city governments, and was generally urged and welcomed by them as a way of reducing local costs. A third type of welfare of particular local importance are those programs providing general aid to the needy and falling under "general assistance" in local budgets.

Every type of government that is involved in welfare experiences great conflicting pressures either to widen or to contract welfare programs. On one point, however, there seems to be substantial consensus, i.e., that welfare programs should be streamlined "to cut out waste and duplication." The moment seems to draw nearer when a specific proposal for national reorganization of welfare functions at last gains sufficient support from Congress, backing by the president, or attention by the judiciary to be put into effect. Such a proposal, if it comes, has a high probability of resulting in the unification of various types of local and nonlocal welfare programming, and in the establishment of special administrative jurisdictions or federally staffed and locally autonomous regional agencies to oversee the unified function. New York City's long-standing request to be entirely relieved of its welfare functions would be satisfied by this type of reorganization.

To a much lesser degree than welfare, the public health and hospitals functions are also prospects for reorganization. The rubric of efficient health care delivery provides a banner for administrative reform activists (on this, see Alford 1974). They pursue a degree of interfunctional consolidation of public health and hospitals, but they also pursue administrative autonomy to control the unified public health care delivery function. Considering the different levels and types of government that are currently involved, full unification may be possible only through separation under federal or state sponsorship.

Functions concerned with the physical environment arouse much less urgent pressures for overall reorganization. Instead, certain selected portions of these functions (e.g., water supplies, drainage, waste disposal, parks and greenbelts, mosquito control) seem to become intergovernmental problems in some cities but not others (Bollens 1957). The tendency is to establish metropolitan-area councils to coordinate the problematic activities, or to establish largely independent special districts. This, too, would generally narrow the functional scope of existing city governments.

Last, but not to be ignored, are prospects for reorganization of police and fire functions. At present, these functions often, if not ordinarily, entail some interlocal agreements about service exchanges. Problems of coordination arise as these agreements become more complex. Moreover, as cities reach the limits of local fiscal capacity in various times and places, they may increasingly turn to federal and state governments for administrative and fiscal aid. The prospect of more special districts for these functions seems to be slight, but not wholly out of the question.

The fragmentation trends are real from the perspective of existing city governments. These trends are also partly illusory from the perspective of other governments. This is because of two related types of interfunctional consolidation, which may occur at one level of government even as fragmentation at another level proceeds. One interfunctional consolidating process involves direct overnight reorganization in the form of city–county consolidation or metropolitan government. The other process involves an incremental expansion of interlocal or intergovernmental coordinating authority, and may have similar long-range effects as formal consolidation.

The rate of formal consolidation of local governments, especially of city–county consolidation, increased substantially during the 1960s (Winter 1969:220ff, U.S. Bureau of the Census, *County and City Data Book*, 1972:xxiii). Actually, there are many different types of formal consolidation. They include the establishment of what the U.S. Census Bureau terms "county equivalents," which "serve as primary subdivisions of their States," as best illustrated by the growing number of independent cities in Virginia. Because these are functionally consolidated single cities that are often surrounded by more conventional suburbs and counties, these county equivalents are subject to some of the previously noted pressures toward the separation of functions to serve a larger urban area (Bain 1967). This was evident, for example, in the short-lived court ruling for Richmond, Virginia, and its suburbs to form, in effect, a shared school district.

Other types of city–county consolidation include the merger of cities with their areally larger counties in such a way that either city government or county government fully absorbs and replaces the other. An example is the consolidation of South Norfolk City and Norfolk County into the new Chesapeake City, Virginia, which may be a unit of sufficient size to assure somewhat more lasting functional consolidation. As a fully consolidated unit, it differs somewhat from the model of Nashville–Davidson County, Jacksonville–Duval County, or Miami–Dade County consolidations. In the latter cases, a partly consolidated general government retains internal municipal units as legal entities for separate service and taxing purposes. Not all internal municipal units receive the same services, or control what they receive in the same way. This achieves some interfunctional integration and intercity coordination, even while retaining relatively narrow-scope city governments. This partly consolidated form may be the principal model of superordinate metropolitan government which we now have.

In a sense, this model is not entirely different from those places where counties are, in fact, the major general-purpose local governments, and where functionally specialized municipalities have elaborate ad hoc agreements or formal coordinating linkages with counties. The county of Los Angeles may best illustrate this, as would hundreds of other counties and metropolitan areas to one degree or another. Even in their most fully developed forms, however, intergovernmental linkages do not as thoroughly consolidate functions as do the broadest-scope cities.

Yet, it is along lines of incremental elaboration of county, metropolitan, or district-wide coordinating activity in which we might find the most widespread pattern of interfunctional reintegration. If this is a trend leading to formal, umbrella local governments, it is certainly a long-range trend. Given this study's findings and interpretation of the roots of political action in traditional institutions, there will be much to overcome before each community's commitments become somehow consolidated with those of another. Increasing incidents and mechanisms of interlocal cooperation are clearly evident in metropolitan-area research. But as one such study concludes (Williams *et al.* 1965), the emerging linkages among formally and culturally differentiated communities are insufficient for inferring that consolidated metropolitan government has much foreseeable chance as an incremental development.

Federal or state action might accelerate the pace of change, although it would do so against predictable local resistance. These higher governments have well established competency and legitimacy for establishing or reconstituting local governments, as is evident in their propensity to create special districts. More special districts may come with the kind of functional fragmentation and centralization noted earlier. Viewed from above more so than from below, federal as well as state programs exhibit an increasing need for local and regional coordinating offices. Here, too, is a prospect for incremental functional consolidation within local administrative districts as they are built into or over existing local governments.

On balance, several rather cautious judgments may be entertained regarding prospects for change in the scope of city governments. We might expect greater program and functional expansion in older and already broad-scope city governments, subject to less than total checks and constraints. One constraint of major importance, where and when it occurs, involves the loss of functions via special district fragmentation and/or state or federal takeover. Perhaps in the longer run, we might also anticipate an increasing reintegration of local functions within a more consolidated and higher-level government than cities themselves now provide.

What kind of political action this rather visionary prospective system would produce is surely an open question. Such action may well correspond to the very active mode of current broad-scope cities. It may, like some city–county consolidations, provide a mix of higher-level, broad-scope integration with lower-level, narrow-scope administrative and political units. There is also always the prospect that little higher-level integration will be achieved, as specialization proceeds apace with its promise of efficiency, less politics, or lower costs. Better models of these alternatives might be found by looking not at single city governments but at entire local systems of governance. They deserve comparative study.

There is also a very open question of whether any major reorganization of existing local governments can reasonably be expected in at least the near future. The leading prospect may be for little change, for traditional forms of organization have great staying power. New forms emerge easiest where they least disturb older ones, and then they too persist in their own tradition. Patterns of political action derive from these differing traditions, and both together express a commitment of a civic culture to a proper role and scope of government. We have seen the differences between the old and the new in the earlier data. We can be more sure of those differences than we can be about the prospects for local governmental reorganization. Community age-cohort differences, then, are most appropriate for the focus of a brief closing comment.

COHORTS OF CIVIC CULTURE: DIVERGING POLARITIES?

In analyzing a variable, there is often a tendency to interpret meaning in terms couched around only one end of the distribution. So it was with the age variable in the present study. Older cities were more often the point of reference than were newer ones. The following discussion gives more balance to this treatment of age by focusing largely on what happens as we move toward the new-city end of the age continuum. This raises questions about possible future trends to which the present study provides no answer. The objective here is to draw out some important emergent implications of the present study for future research and policy consideration. In particular, a case is made for diverging age-based polarities in local civic culture, and for further examination of those polarities as possible bases of interlocal political conflict and accommodation.

The greatest difference that was found between old and new city governments was in the scope of their major functions. The relationship between age and scope was not only very strong, it was also monotonic. That is, the narrowing of scope for younger cities continues even through the most recent cohorts. This relationship was independent of such other age-related developments as growth in city size or the spread of suburbs. It is a trend that is important enough at the moment, but may be even more important if it continues.

Differences in age-determined scope concretely express contemporary options for specialized and limited rather than for general and large new community governments. They may ordinarily be forced options, due to the preemption of functions by superior governments or existing organizations. They may also be ideologically preferred options. In either event, they denote a change in the nature of community as it is experienced.

The older broad-scope cities attempt to maintain community as a functionally inclusive system contained within a formally organized framework. Aside from such attempts, the functionally inclusive context has, in practice, become societal, regional, or metropolitan in areal dimensions, rather than local and communal. It is as wide ranging as increasingly are extended family networks and work organization hierarchies, markets, associations, and other groups to which one may be affiliated. Local "communities" tend to form as functionally specialized retreats from the broader context, rather than as miniature reproductions of all that the broader context offers. As Dorfman (1970) notes in his discussion of the functions of the modern city, there have emerged strong social predilections to break ties with firms, markets, and other economic and political organizations at the end of the work day and to attend to only a few during the day. This is partly accomplished by simple specialization of work, but largely by the separation of residentially based communal ties from the demands of complex formal organization. The preferred community is a retreat from which one might selectively relate to some, if any, of the various organized units of American life. The idea is to let the experts in each specialty decide things, and to be left alone by them.

Newer cities best reflect this option in terms of governmental organization, more so than even suburbs or small cities. The government that gives a newer city its name and formal identity is hardly obtrusive, and other governments are more distant and, in any event, fairly unavoidable. It has also been assumed that newer cities, as social systems, are similarly lacking in substantial formal organizational integration in institutional domains other than government. This integration may exist for a much larger system of action, but it would seem to have little bearing on the civic culture of new cities.

We may think of these newer cities as sometimes suburbs and sometimes central cities in rapidly developing areas, as well as growing settlements of formerly ex-urban enclaves. The newer cities particularly abound in the urbanizing areas of what political commentators now call the Sun Belt: the American South and Southwest. The newer cities are, of course, the major factor in the nation's continuing urban growth, so that the civic culture of the new is the growing type of the future.

This newer civic culture takes shape as a coherently meaningful orientation in ways observed in the earlier empirical analysis. It is rather strongly distinguished from older systems by several political attributes other than having a narrower functional scope of government. These distinctions between old and new are partly due to, or mediated by, the scope of government, but they are also largely independent of scope.

Role relations between city government formal leaders and their constituents are very different between the new city and the old. With the recency of city birth, there is an increasing probability that the government will be installed with less broadly accessible leadership. The reformed role patterns of new city officials involve little expectation of exchange relationships with constituents, and little variability in leadership resources or bases for power. Newer cities ostensibly promise themselves a leadership that will reduce politics to efficient trouble-free administration. There may be aspects to this retreat from politics other than those identified here, such as the disinterest, recruiting problems, and high turnover in city councils, which Eulau and Prewitt (1973) found in many San Francisco Bay area city governments (which, incidentally, tend to be relatively new and narrow in scope).

The newer cities politically defuse and isolate their formal leaders to a greater extent than can be attributed to the mediating effects of their narrower scope. In their rejection of political brokerage roles and embracement of smoother administration, newer cities are even quite unlike small cities (no independent effect on accessibility) or suburbs (which, independent of age and scope, tend to take on the more accessible arrangements). Hence, we can speak of the newer civic culture as being distinctly hospitable to the recessive leadership roles of management experts. This may be increasingly true of currently emerging cities, some of which merely contract for services from outside agencies (Cion 1971) or are at least initially managed by the firms that developed them.

Voter turnout also tends to recede with recency of city birth, and to a degree not attributable to other analyzed variables. Theories of electoral participation would suggest that this low turnout indicates a relative lack of traditional "attachments" to community institutions of various sorts. One might hypothesize that, with time, those attachments would develop as organized community life becomes more fully developed. This theory assumes that little or no "cohort" effect in organizational development would occur, for each system would develop into the same form as its next oldest cohort.

There are good reasons to doubt that this assumption is fully valid, and to hold instead that there is at least some distinct cohort effect involving the persistence of organizational forms. By this alternative assumption, a cohort effect on electoral participation could be expected on the grounds that the organizational life that contends for attachments is and will tend to remain quite unrelated to the proper roles of newer city governments. The relative validity of either assumption awaits longitudinal research. For now, it is sufficient to note that there are clear differences in voter involvement, according to city age. These differences will probably not vanish, and may even increase, as long as new cities continue to emerge in forms consistent with trends.

On innovativeness, the very newest cities were obviously not even candidates for being adopters of public housing or urban renewal. They were eliminated from the analysis, along with cities in states that had not authorized the necessary legal machinery for the federally aided programs. The cities that were eliminated from the analysis of urban renewal included all municipalities not appearing in the 1950 Census; for public housing, the cutoff Census year was 1930. Among the remaining older cohorts, the younger cities might well have made a policy choice for public housing, if not for urban renewal. They were significantly less likely to do so for either program than were the older cities, which arguably reflects mere differences in wear and tear due to varying degrees of aging.

Perhaps in time some newer cities will have their turn at these types of programs, for reasons not much different from those that would lead one to expect voter turnout to rise with aging. Increasing organizational richness over time, a corresponding ecological succession and elaboration of territorial rights, and a growing differentiation into target and control groups would mean little cohort effect that sheer aging would not alone explain. And such an explanation is not inconsistent with the earlier analysis of the structural determinants of program innovation in American cities.

Even so, it should not be readily assumed that today's new cities will as routinely produce tomorrow's slums and ghettos as was true of older cities in the past. Our set of older cities were, after all, uniquely fated for their "melting pot" roles. They were, from the beginning, the only cities around for taking on the function of servicing the initial dismal, raucous stages of urban ecological succession, incorporating marginal immigrants into the city's dense organizational networks, and transferring the more successful out to less dense and slower-paced enclaves. Today, with reduced immigration, with population growth approaching zero, and with differentiation increasingly of the formally ordered type that seeks no melting pot, the current stock of strategically located older cities may be largely sufficient for fulfilling the city's classic unofficial function of urbanizing immigrants, which has perhaps been their greatest function of all.

Some newer cities may yet approximate the classic developmental pattern, but one might reasonably expect the imitation rate to decline. The nation has developed sufficiently differentiated community systems to permit long-lasting functional specialization of many of them. If all cities need no longer take on the early, urbanizing functions of broad social integration, then many newer ones may find stability with organizational life already in the hands of experts, with quality control, and without the challenge to rehabilitate. In short, the diffuse complexity of organization, which is the mother of social invention, may never develop as thoroughly in aging, newer cities as in already older ones.

Innovativeness per se is one aspect of program adoption. The other aspect that was analyzed pertains to the bases of innovative policy in collective decision making, and to the question of accountability. With levels of scope used as a control variable, it was found that the cities with less diffuse decision-making organs innovate more strictly in response to conventionally defined needs than do other cities. This program response pattern seemed to be no simple artifact of the distribution of these needs among cities of differing complexity, for Turk (1973a) found opposing response patterns for similar city groupings and similar measures of need in his studies of why cities establish formal coordination mechanisms. More will be said about formal coordination in a moment.

With respect to collective decisions for new programs of tangible impact, we found support for the assumption that there are relatively few interorganizationally produced interests or needs in the more specialized or organizationally fragmented systems of action. Criteria of need are not very likely to emerge from an interplay of diverse interests where there is little such interplay. Need is instead experienced and defined in simpler ways; much of the puzzling red tape and political compromises of organizationally denser systems is avoided. The result seems to be a kind of rationality that conforms with models of bureaucracy as a goal-specific form of organization (Weber 1947: 328–334) having analyzable tasks (Perrow, 1967) and low, but methodically controlled, innovativeness (Burns and Stalker 1961). To the extent that the trend is toward emergence of functionally specialized new communities, there should be an enlarging set of similarly rationalized city governments.

The apparently more free-wheeling (the term is from Gottschalk 1975) innovative propensities of other, diffuse-goal cities have less conventional rationales. They do, of course, have varying levels of need in a formally objective sense, and on average have more need than new-style cities. More important, the existence of defensible needs sufficient for new program action is fairly well assured somewhere in the complex interactional networks of old style cities, regardless of differences in externally observable types of need.

Are these qualities equally predictable in the future for aging newer cities? The answer should be negative if we give increasing weight, as we should, to intercity differentiating trends and to tradition rather than to the notion of diverse systems of civic culture all evolving in the same pattern. Are all types of innovations equally relevant here? Certainly not, for we have focused only on innovations as new lines or types of public works, using examples of unknown representativeness. Distinct from new public works are purely administrative innovations (e.g., "reformism" of leadership roles or formal coordination instrumentalities), which appear to be entirely different matters.

The fragmentation of governmental systems in newer contexts is itself an administrative innovation. From an uninvolved observer's perspective, this fragmentation might seem to pose problems of coordination requiring solutions via formal integrative mechanisms. But from the perspective of civic partisans, the newer fragmentation may be fully proper and legitimate, with any incidence of formal coordination being a more idiosyncratically than organizationally determined choice. The latter view is supported by Turk's (1973b) findings that the less organizationally interlinked city systems are unlikely to adopt formal coordinative mechanisms, and that the few that do have no greater city-based need for them than do the many that do not adopt such mechanisms. In contrast, Turk also found that the more organizationally interlinked city systems are much more prone to adopt formal coordination mechanisms, and to do so in response to such city-based needs as a large number of clients or service centers. It is an extension of Turk's analysis to suggest that the older-style cities are, in effect, augmenting their existing integrative capacities, tightening the unity that broad scope and other civic traditions in part symbolize, and doing so where that unity is most threatened by intramunicipal diversification of service delivery or by incipient client demand and discontent.

This discussion points to a dilemma about formal coordination and program innovativeness, and to another aspect of the distinction between older and newer cities. We can only suggest these issues here. More certain evidence awaits research dealing simultaneously with both formal coordination and program innovativeness.

There is at present enough evidence at least to suggest that coordination and innovativeness each responds in a different way to conventional needs in older-style contexts as well as in newer-style contexts, and are in this sense unrelated policy options in each context. Research is needed to determine more definitively whether newer-style cities sometimes innovate with a formal rationality and effectiveness that has no relationship to their lesser involvement in formal coordination, and whether older-style cities often attempt formal coordination with a predictable responsiveness that has little bearing on their more randomly generated program innovations. We may have here a dilemma that may be added to the ones that Gottschalk (1975) addresses in his study of the limits of planning: Within either of the polar extremes of an inclusive interorganizational context or an organizationally specilized or fragmented one, is it possible for there to be a concerted relationship between inclusive planning and specialized programming? Or do these tend to be unrelated policy options in each context? It seems likely that they are unrelated, both for reasons noted here in comparing Turk's findings with ours and because of the kind of tensions and divergencies between planning and programming that Alford (1974) made the focus of his case study of health delivery in New York City. The question deserves comparative study.

More generally, the apparent patterns of responsiveness for planning and programming point to important differences in what might be called the overall roles of newer and older city systems of city government. The same role differences appear in the analysis of other political-action variables. In essence, the newer types seem to be more task oriented in the sense of meeting specific goals with stark efficiency and with little concern for building community-wide unifying linkages of involvement. The older types seem to be more process oriented, both in fostering inventive expression of program needs and encouraging symbolically unifying participatory linkages throughout the community. These differences correspond roughly to Hillery's (1968) principal distinctions between formal and communal organizations. It is the major emerging contention of the present research that these two age-determined polar roles identify alternative and perhaps increasingly divergent patterns of internally consistent civic cultures among American cities.

Intercohort differences may be most important in the area of fiscal performance levels. Overall spending levels capture everyone's attention in ways that no single incremental decision can. So it is of special concern that the old have much higher expenditure rates than do the new. This difference is evident not only in the respect that the old have huge general budgets covering many more program functions than the new, but also in greater old-city than new-city budget allotments for functions that all cities have. Many individual factors account for the differences, including the one sense in which the adoption of formal coordination mechanisms and of new programs appear to be related—the lower overall incidence of both (and of costs for both) in the newer style cities.

Clearly, the most prominent reason for a difference in the overall costs of older and newer city governments is the difference in number of performed functions. When we look at older cities, attention is too easily and misleadingly drawn to their general per capita municipal budgets, which are often many times larger than what is ordinarily found in middle or newer America. We may also see great exorbitance contrasted with splendid thrift, until we realize that the *principal* reason for this difference is that the apparent big spenders simply perform and budget for all or nearly all of the functions that are elsewhere largely distributed among special districts, counties, and other state administrative units, or are directly assumed by the state itself. Very early in this study, it was noted that over 50% of the variance in general per capita expenditures for American cities were accounted for by variance in the functional scope of city governments. Because the functions in the measure of scope are fairly permanent in their assignment, much of general expenditure levels is due to lasting age-cohort differences in mere governmental assignment patterns rather than to recent or ahistorically emergent issues of public policy. In short, the overall cost differential between older and newer cities is easily overrated if deemed to be a new problem, and probably even overrated as a problem.

Despite this, there are important policy issues about costs of government arising from differences in the extent of functional and budgetary consolidation. One issue to which no one yet has a definite answer concerns the degree of redistribution of gross revenues from one political jurisdiction to another under various functional assignment arrangements. It is an important issue because one would like to know whether City A would receive a greater net subsidy from revenue collected outside the city if its Function X were transferred to a different, areally larger government. The problem in answering this question for any large sample of cities involves trying to identify the gross revenues collected and total expenditures made within each local jurisdiction by all other jurisdictions having functions within it. Published records do not break governmental data down this way. For one attempt to deal with some aspects of this issue under these severe limitations, see Campbell and Sacks (1967). They are convinced that current jurisdictional and redistributional patterns are sufficiently complex to warrant more disaggregated data before final judgments may be made.

What may, in practice, be a more important set of policy issues bearing on general city budgets has a more symbolic quality. I noted earlier that New York City would certainly be far from the leading per capita spender were it a city of average functional scope. Under this hypothetical circumstance, some other city might be the example of municipal profligacy. Where to assign credit or blame is much more apparent where all costs and benefits of local government bear the same label. A government in such a situation has more fronts to cover and takes on a certain flamboyancy in the process. A government in a functionally fragmented context will always be smaller and attract less attention than any formally inclusive governmental system.

To the extent that newer city governments have eluded the appearance of budgetary excess due to narrow scope, they are likely to elude such an appearance long into the future. They have fortuitously escaped responsibility for a number of major functions that add greatly to older city budgets, notably public welfare, education, and a community-based judicial system, but extending often to health, hospitals, and lesser functions. The residents of newer cities are doubtlessly paying something for these functions, and may increasingly be called upon to subsidize those in other jurisdictions, but not through their own city governments. Newer cities have emerged in contexts where most resources destined for the local public domain are already preempted, even if not always equitably, by other governments and quasi-public organizations. The newer cities relate to their citizens largely by servicing the physical environment and by providing police and fire protection. Increasingly with age, cities relate to their citizens by doing as little as possible. Barring unforeseen changes in long-range trends, newer cities will long continue to be lean operations, a largely illusory virtue that may have attractiveness far beyond its fiscal significance.

There is much greater substantive significance to another fiscal performance issue that was analyzed here. On functions that all cities do perform or optionally might perform, newer cities have lower budgetary commitments than do older cities. In large part, this finding seems to be due to side effects of differences in functional scope. That is, newer city governments have very few agencies reaching for recognition, rewards, and resources; their level of interagency competition is therefore low, perhaps nonexistent; and their rate of governmental growth is consequently tempered. For these reasons, the narrow scope of newer cities is a major factor in their lower costs on police, fire, general administrative, and miscellaneous minor functions. An additional factor is newness itself. Unlike older cities where the government keeps a fairly strong presence within organized community life and along its assimilating edges, newer cities have in each sector an order that functions with little servicing or maintenance by its little government.

It might be true that over time the low fiscal commitment of newer cities will rise to the level of older cities. This question is like all of the parallel questions in this discussion of possible implications for future consideration—it merits longitudinal study. The present study invites the contention that aging does not make the new like the old in many respects. At least insofar as organizational forms persist, successive generations of city residents must work within structures that help to select their options and to limit their commitments.

There is a certain legend in American culture to the effect that older cities lost a youthful simplicity and acquired their expansive and politicized governmental style from waves of non-WASP immigrants coming into New England, New York, Baltimore, St. Louis, San Francisco, etc. It was as much a legend a century ago as it is today, and for the same cities but for different types of immigrants. Despite the legend, there are historical grounds (discussed previously in Chapter III) for believing that the organizational machinery of city government over which each wave of immigrants assumed some control was generally found by them to be already a functionally inclusive vehicle for community action. Even outside of government, it is rather unlikely that new immigrants routinely invented wholly new patterns of secular organizational life.

Rather than to infer that immigrants reshape civic culture, consider the probability of the process running the other way. The communal commitments of old style cities would seem to have a special attractiveness for most new immigrants to American urban and organizational life. The older type of community has had little legitimate basis for disclaiming relevance to the problems of the marginal, has provided opportunity for integration into a diffuse organizational system, and has offered symbolic and substantive support en route. Simultaneously with providing opportunity for the marginal, older communities also give roots to the organized. That is, older communities have also exported a certain amount of the highly developed social roles and technology that they produce, involving outwardly expanding networks of affiliations among the more established organizations and individuals.

Largely because of this outward extension of development from older cities, newer cities are not the first organizations to arrive in the external milieu of the old. A host of other governments and organizations increasingly arrive there first. This leaves to the legitimate functional domain of the new city a degree of specialization that is only partially revealed by the narrow scope of the government. Other aspects of the social life of the new city are likely to be oriented toward selected organizations that are above and beyond the community, toward the agencies of larger and superior governments, and toward the markets and work organizations that are often extensions from older cities. We have understood the meaning of city age to imply that newer cities are, and will likely continue to be, communities of limited commitment in most aspects of local civic culture, including not only the functional scope of government, but also formal leadership arrangements, voter participation, innovativeness, and fiscal performance levels.

America has long had deep cultural conflicts testing the compatibility of the older areas of the nation with the newly developed ones. On the one hand are persisting communal civic traditions of liberal political action, and on the other the once "progressive," then "reformist," and now "new conservative" fondness for the social technology of harnessed bureaucracy. There have been times when the expansive energies of the one have been widely encouraged, and times when campaigns for municipal reform along lines of the other have drawn greater overall national encouragement. The foundations for the two competing orientations are present in differing community traditions. What we have observed in the data here was contemporary evidence of the likely bases for this conflict in age-differentiated modes of community organization, political processes, and governmental outcomes.

If the differences between polar prototypes persist or grow, the nation's tolerance for diversity will be tested further. The older prototypes involve costs and a flamboyancy of leadership and participation that may often (as in the present) be very disconcerting for champions of the restraint of the newer prototypes. Adaptations may have to be made, including the current possibilities of further local governmental fragmentation and the assumption of some of the public costs and functions of the older communities by the newer ones through more centralized fiscal and administrative arrangements. These types of accommodation seem to be favored by the long-range trends toward reduced local commitments to a community government. At the same time, and perhaps more so at times other than the present, there are somewhat opposing pressures to adapt to the problems of diversity by consolidating and making the newer fragmented political systems more like the older, inclusive ones. Such adaptation involves making explicit and rather difficult policy choices to merge dissimilar existing community service institutions.

Yet, it seems rather unlikely that we will soon wholly dismantle our communal monuments to the past, or reconstruct and consolidate the streamlined organizational machinery of the modern trend. Both have their champions, with one having traditions deep enough to be taken for granted and the other having modernity on its side. The great bulk of cities in the middle range (of which Chicago may be the illustrative prototype) also provides some balance on net prospects for nationwide change and probably help to temper diverging ideologies. Moreover, there would be much more to the wholesale accommodation of one polar type to the other than mere administrative reform, for deeper patterns of civic culture would also have to change. At the core of community political action is not simply the scope of government, but also conceptions of the proper role of each available government and organization as a vehicle for satisfying wants.

Appendix

Code Sheets for Indicating the Presence or Absence
of Municipal Government Functions

The following is a duplicate of the coded raw data which was used to measure functional scope. The reader should refer to Chapter II, for a discussion of the procedures used to make judgements regarding the presence or absence of functions, and for a brief descriptive definition of each function.

The functions coded on these sheets and their abbreviations are as follows: Edu = education; Wfa = welfare; federally aided; Wga = welfare, general assistance; Hos = hospitals; Hea = health; San = sanitation; Par = parks and recreation; Sew = sewers; Jud = judicial. The codes are: 1 = present, 0 = absent.

Code number	City name	Function								
		Edu	Wfa	Wga	Hos	Hea	San	Par	Sew	Jud
110100	Bangor, ME	1	0	1	1	1	1	1	0	1
110200	Lewiston	1	0	1	0	1	0	0	1	1
110300	Portland	1	0	1	1	1	1	1	0	1
120100	Concord, NH	0	0	1	0	1	1	1	1	1
120200	Manchester	1	0	1	0	1	0	1	1	1
120300	Nashua	1	0	1	0	1	0	1	1	1
120400	Portsmouth	1	0	1	0	1	1	1	1	1
130100	Burlington, VT	1	0	1	0	1	0	1	1	1
140100	Attleboro, MA	1	1	1	0	1	0	1	1	1
140200	Beverly	1	1	1	0	1	1	1	1	1
140300	Boston	1	1	1	1	1	1	1	1	1
140400	Brockton	1	1	1	0	1	1	1	1	1
140500	Cambridge	1	1	1	1	1	0	1	1	1
140600	Chelsea	1	1	1	0	1	1	1	1	1
140700	Chicopee	1	1	1	0	1	1	1	1	1
140800	Everett	1	1	1	0	1	0	1	1	1
140900	Fall River	1	1	1	1	1	0	1	1	1
141000	Fitchburg	1	1	1	1	1	0	1	1	1
141100	Gloucester	1	1	1	0	1	1	1	0	1
141200	Haverhill	1	1	1	1	1	0	1	1	1
141300	Holyoke	1	1	1	0	1	1	1	1	1
141400	Lawrence	1	1	1	1	1	1	1	1	1
141500	Leominster	1	1	1	0	1	0	1	1	1
141600	Lowell	1	1	1	0	1	0	1	1	1
141700	Lynn	1	1	1	0	1	1	1	1	1
141800	Malden	1	1	1	0	1	1	1	1	1
141900	Medford	1	1	1	0	1	0	1	1	1
142000	Melrose	1	1	1	0	1	1	1	1	1
142100	New Bedford	1	1	1	0	1	1	1	1	1
142200	Newton	1	1	1	0	1	0	1	1	1
142300	Northampton	1	1	1	0	1	0	0	1	1
142400	Peabody	1	1	1	1	1	0	1	0	1
142500	Pittsfield	1	1	1	0	1	1	1	1	1
142600	Quincy	1	1	1	1	1	0	1	1	1
142700	Revere	1	1	1	0	1	0	0	1	1
142800	Salem	1	1	1	1	1	0	1	1	1
142900	Somerville	1	1	1	0	1	1	1	1	1

Code number	City name	Edu	Wfa	Wga	Hos	Hea	San	Par	Sew	Jud
						Function				
143000	Springfield	1	1	1	1	1	1	1	1	1
143100	Taunton	1	1	1	0	1	0	1	1	1
143200	Waltham	1	1	1	0	1	0	1	1	1
143300	Westfield	1	1	1	0	1	0	0	1	1
143400	Woburn	1	1	1	0	1	1	1	1	1
143500	Worcester	1	1	1	1	1	1	1	1	1
150100	Bridgeport, CT	1	0	1	1	1	1	1	1	1
150200	Bristol	1	0	1	0	1	1	1	1	1
150300	Hartford	1	0	1	1	1	1	1	1	1
150400	Meriden	1	0	1	1	1	0	1	1	1
150500	Middletown	1	0	1	0	1	1	1	1	1
150600	Milford	1	0	1	0	1	1	1	0	1
150700	New Britain	1	0	1	0	1	1	1	0	1
150800	New Haven	1	0	1	0	1	1	1	1	1
150900	New London	1	0	1	0	1	1	1	0	1
151000	Norwalk	1	0	1	0	1	1	1	0	1
151100	Norwich	1	0	1	0	1	1	1	0	1
151200	Stamford	1	0	1	0	1	0	1	0	1
151300	Torrington	1	0	1	0	1	1	1	1	1
151400	Waterbury	1	0	1	0	1	1	1	1	1
160100	Cranston, RI	1	0	1	0	0	0	1	0	1
160200	East Providence	1	0	1	0	1	0	1	1	1
160300	Newport	1	0	1	0	1	0	1	0	1
160400	Pawtucket	1	0	1	0	1	1	1	1	1
160500	Providence	1	0	1	0	1	1	1	0	1
160600	Warwick	1	0	1	0	1	1	0	0	1
160700	Woonsocket	1	0	1	0	0	0	1	1	1
210100	Albany, NY	1	0	0	0	1	1	1	1	0
210200	Amsterdam	0	0	0	0	1	1	1	0	0
210300	Auburn	0	1	1	0	1	1	1	0	0
210400	Binghamton	0	1	1	1	0	1	1	1	0
210500	Buffalo	1	0	0	0	1	1	1	0	0
210600	Elmira	0	0	0	0	1	1	1	0	0
210700	Freeport	0	0	0	0	0	1	1	0	0
210800	Hempstead	0	0	0	0	1	0	1	0	0
210900	Ithaca	0	0	0	0	1	0	1	0	0
211000	Jamestown	1	1	1	1	1	0	1	0	0
211100	Kingston	0	0	0	0	1	1	1	0	0
211200	Lackawanna	0	0	0	0	1	1	1	0	0
211300	Lockport	0	0	0	1	0	1	1	0	0
211400	Long Beach	0	0	0	0	0	1	1	0	0
211500	Mount Vernon	0	0	0	0	1	1	1	1	0
211600	Newburgh	0	1	1	0	1	0	1	0	0
211700	New Rochelle	0	0	0	0	1	1	1	1	0
211800	New York City	1	1	1	1	1	1	1	1	1
211900	Niagara Falls	0	0	0	0	1	1	1	1	0
212000	North Tonawanda	0	0	0	0	1	1	1	0	0
212100	Poughkeepsie	0	1	1	0	1	1	1	1	0

Code	City	Function								
number	name	Edu	Wfa	Wga	Hos	Hea	San	Par	Sew	Jud
212200	Rochester	1	0	0	0	1	1	1	1	0
212300	Rockville Centre	0	0	0	0	0	1	1	0	0
212400	Rome	0	0	0	1	1	0	1	0	0
212500	Schenectady	0	0	0	0	1	1	1	0	0
212600	Syracuse	1	0	0	1	1	1	1	1	0
212700	Troy	0	0	0	0	1	1	1	0	0
212800	Utica	0	0	0	0	1	1	1	1	0
212900	Valley Stream	0	0	0	0	0	1	1	1	0
213000	Watertown	0	0	0	0	1	1	1	1	0
213100	White Plains	0	0	0	0	0	1	1	1	0
213200	Yonkers	1	0	0	0	1	1	1	1	0
220100	Atlantic City, NJ	1	0	1	0	1	1	1	1	0
220200	Bayonne	1	0	1	0	1	1	1	1	0
220300	Belleville	NO DATA								
220400	Bergenfield	NO DATA								
220500	Bloomfield	1	0	1	0	1	0	1	1	0
220600	Camden	0	0	1	0	1	1	1	1	0
220700	Clifton	1	0	1	0	1	0	1	1	0
220800	East Orange	1	0	1	0	1	1	1	1	0
220900	Elizabeth	1	0	1	0	1	1	1	1	0
221000	Englewood	1	0	1	0	1	1	1	1	0
221100	Fairlawn	0	0	1	0	1	0	1	1	0
221200	Garfield	1	0	1	0	1	0	0	1	0
221300	Hackensack	1	0	1	0	1	1	1	1	0
221400	Hoboken	1	0	1	0	1	0	1	1	0
221500	Irvington	1	0	1	1	1	1	1	1	0
221600	Jersey City	1	0	1	1	1	1	1	1	0
221700	Kearny	1	0	1	0	1	1	1	1	0
221800	Linden	1	0	1	0	1	1	1	1	0
221900	Long Branch	1	0	1	0	1	0	1	1	0
222000	Montclair	1	0	1	0	0	1	1	1	0
222100	Newark	1	0	1	1	1	1	1	1	0
222200	New Brunswick	1	0	1	0	1	1	1	1	0
222300	Nutley	0	0	1	0	1	1	1	0	0
222400	Orange	1	0	1	0	1	0	1	1	0
222500	Passaic	1	0	1	0	1	1	1	0	0
222600	Patterson	1	0	1	0	1	1	1	1	0
222700	Perth Amboy	1	0	1	0	1	1	1	1	0
222800	Plainfield	1	0	1	0	1	0	1	1	0
222900	Rahway	0	0	1	0	1	1	1	1	0
223000	Ridgewood	0	0	1	0	1	0	1	0	0
223100	Trenton	1	0	1	0	1	1	1	1	0
223200	Union City	1	0	1	0	1	1	1	1	0
223300	Vineland	1	0	1	0	1	1	1	1	0
223400	Westfield	0	0	1	0	1	0	1	1	0
223500	West New York	1	0	1	0	1	1	1	1	0
223600	West Orange	0	0	1	0	1	1	1	0	0
230100	Aliquippa, PA	0	0	0	0	0	1	0	0	0
230200	Allentown	0	0	0	0	1	1	1	0	0

Code number	City name	Function								
		Edu	Wfa	Wga	Hos	Hea	San	Par	Sew	Jud
230300	Altoona	0	0	0	0	1	1	1	0	0
230400	Bethlehem	0	0	0	0	1	1	1	1	0
230500	Chester	0	0	0	0	1	1	1	0	0
230600	Easton	0	0	0	0	1	1	1	0	0
230700	Erie	0	0	0	0	1	1	1	0	0
230800	Harrisburg	0	0	0	0	1	1	1	0	0
230900	Hazelton	0	0	0	0	1	0	1	1	0
231000	Johnstown	0	0	0	0	1	1	1	0	0
231100	Lancaster	0	0	0	0	1	1	1	0	0
231200	Lebanon	0	0	0	0	0	0	0	0	0
231300	McKeesport	0	0	0	0	0	1	1	0	0
231400	New Castle	0	0	0	0	0	1	1	0	0
231500	Norristown	0	0	0	0	1	0	1	0	0
231600	Philadelphia	0	0	1	1	1	1	1	1	1
231700	Pittsburgh	0	0	0	0	1	1	1	1	0
231800	Pottstown	0	0	0	0	1	0	0	0	0
231900	Reading	0	0	0	0	1	1	1	1	0
232000	Scranton	0	0	0	0	1	1	1	1	0
232100	Sharon	0	0	0	0	0	1	0	0	0
232200	West Mifflin	0	0	0	0	0	1	0	0	0
232300	Wilkes-Barre	0	0	0	0	1	1	1	0	0
232400	Wilkinsburg	0	0	0	0	0	1	0	1	0
232500	Williamsport	0	0	0	0	1	0	1	0	0
232600	York	0	0	0	0	1	1	1	0	0
240100	Baltimore, MD	1	1	1	1	1	1	1	1	0
240200	Cumberland	0	0	0	1	0	0	0	0	0
240300	Hagerstown	0	0	0	0	0	0	1	0	0
240400	Rockville	0	0	0	0	0	0	1	0	0
250100	Wilmington, DE	1	0	0	0	1	1	1	0	0
260100	Washington, D.C.	NO DATA								
310100	Akron, OH	1	0	0	0	1	1	1	0	0
310200	Alliance	0	0	0	0	1	0	0	0	0
310300	Barberton	0	0	0	0	1	1	1	0	0
310400	Canton	0	0	0	0	1	1	1	0	0
310500	Cincinnati	1	0	0	1	1	1	1	0	0
310600	Cleveland	0	0	0	0	1	1	1	0	0
310700	Cleveland Heights	0	0	0	0	1	1	1	0	0
310800	Columbus	0	0	0	0	1	1	1	0	0
310900	Cuyahoga Falls	0	0	0	0	1	1	1	0	0
311000	Dayton	0	0	0	0	1	1	1	0	0
311100	East Cleveland	0	0	0	0	1	1	1	0	0
311200	Elyria	NO DATA								
311300	Euclid	0	0	0	0	1	1	1	0	0
311400	Findlay	0	0	0	0	1	0	1	0	0
311500	Garfield Heights	0	0	0	0	1	1	0	0	0
311600	Hamilton	0	0	0	0	1	1	1	0	0
311700	Kettering	0	0	0	0	1	0	0	0	0
311800	Lakewood	0	0	0	1	1	1	1	0	0

Code number	City name	Edu	Wfa	Wga	Hos	Hea	San	Par	Sew	Jud
311900	Lancaster	0	0	0	0	1	1	1	0	0
312000	Lima	0	0	0	0	1	0	1	0	0
312100	Lorain	0	0	0	0	1	1	1	0	0
312200	Mansfield	0	0	0	0	1	1	1	0	0
312300	Maple Heights	0	0	0	0	1	1	1	0	0
312400	Marion	0	0	0	1	1	1	0	0	0
312500	Massillon	0	0	0	0	1	1	1	0	0
312600	Middletown	0	0	0	0	1	1	1	1	0
312700	Newark	0	0	0	0	1	0	1	0	0
312800	Norwood	0	0	0	0	1	1	0	0	0
312900	Parma	0	0	0	0	1	1	1	0	0
313000	Portsmouth	0	0	0	0	1	1	1	0	0
313100	Sandusky	0	0	0	0	1	0	1	0	0
313200	Shaker Heights	0	0	0	0	1	1	1	0	0
313300	South Euclid	0	0	0	0	1	1	0	0	0
313400	Springfield	0	0	0	0	1	1	1	0	0
313500	Steubenville	0	0	0	0	1	1	1	0	0
313600	Toledo	1	0	0	0	1	1	1	0	0
313700	Upper Arlington	0	0	0	0	0	1	1	0	0
313800	Warren	0	0	0	0	1	0	1	0	0
313900	Youngstown	0	0	0	0	1	1	1	0	0
314000	Zanesville	0	0	0	0	1	1	1	0	0
320100	Anderson, IN	0	0	0	0	1	0	1	0	0
320200	Bloomington	0	0	0	0	0	0	1	0	0
320300	East Chicago	0	0	0	0	1	1	1	0	0
320400	Elkhart	0	0	0	0	0	1	1	0	0
320500	Evansville	0	0	0	0	1	1	1	0	0
320600	Fort Wayne	0	0	0	0	1	1	1	0	0
320700	Gary	0	0	0	0	1	1	1	0	0
320800	Hammond	0	0	0	0	1	1	1	0	0
320900	Indianapolis	0	0	0	0	1	1	1	0	0
321000	Kokomo	0	0	0	0	0	1	1	0	0
321100	Lafayette	0	0	0	0	1	1	1	0	0
321200	Marion	0	0	0	0	1	1	1	0	0
321300	Michigan City	0	0	0	0	1	1	1	0	0
321400	Mishawaka	0	0	0	0	0	0	1	0	0
321500	Muncie	0	0	0	0	1	1	1	0	0
321600	New Albany	0	0	0	0	1	1	1	0	0
321700	Richmond	0	0	0	0	1	1	1	0	0
321800	South Bend	0	0	0	0	0	1	1	0	0
321900	Terre Haute	0	0	0	0	0	0	1	0	0
330100	Alton, IL	0	0	0	0	1	1	1	1	0
330200	Arlington Heights	0	0	0	0	1	0	0	1	0
330300	Aurora	0	0	0	0	1	1	1	1	0
330400	Belleville	0	0	0	0	0	1	0	1	0
330500	Berwyn	0	0	0	0	0	1	1	1	0
330600	Bloomington	0	0	0	0	0	1	1	1	0
330700	Calumet City	0	0	0	0	1	0	0	0	0
330800	Champaign	0	0	0	1	0	0	1	0	0

Code number	City name	Edu	Wfa	Wga	Hos	Hea	San	Par	Sew	Jud
						Function				
330900	Chicago	0	0	1	1	1	1	1	1	0
331000	Chicago Heights	0	0	0	0	1	1	0	1	0
331100	Cicero	0	0	1	0	1	1	0	0	0
331200	Danville	0	0	0	0	1	1	1	1	0
331300	Decatur	0	0	0	0	0	0	1	1	0
331400	Des Plaines	0	0	0	0	1	1	0	1	0
331500	East St. Louis	0	0	0	0	0	1	0	1	0
331600	Elgin	0	0	0	0	1	1	1	0	0
331700	Elmhurst	0	0	0	0	1	0	0	1	0
331800	Evanston	0	0	0	0	1	1	1	1	0
331900	Freeport	0	0	0	0	0	1	0	1	0
332000	Galesburg	0	0	0	0	0	0	1	1	0
332100	Granite City	0	0	0	0	0	0	0	1	0
332200	Harvey	0	0	0	0	0	1	0	1	0
332300	Highland Park	0	0	0	0	0	0	1	1	0
332400	Joliet	0	0	0	0	0	0	0	0	0
332500	Kankakee	0	0	0	0	1	0	0	1	0
332600	Maywood	*NO DATA*								
332700	Moline	0	0	0	1	1	1	1	1	0
332800	Oaklawn	0	0	0	0	0	0	0	0	0
332900	Oak Park	0	0	0	0	1	1	1	1	0
333000	Park Forest	0	0	0	0	1	0	0	1	0
333100	Park Ridge	0	0	0	0	0	1	0	1	0
333200	Pekin	0	0	0	0	0	1	0	1	0
333300	Peoria	0	0	0	1	1	1	1	1	0
333400	Quincy	0	0	0	0	0	1	0	1	0
333500	Rockford	0	0	0	1	1	0	0	0	0
333600	Rock Island	0	0	0	0	1	1	1	1	0
333700	Skokie	0	0	0	0	1	1	0	1	0
333800	Springfield	0	0	0	0	1	1	1	1	0
333900	Urbana	0	0	0	0	0	1	0	1	0
334000	Waukegan	0	0	0	0	1	0	1	1	0
334100	Wilmette	0	0	0	0	1	1	1	1	0
340100	Allen Park, MI	0	0	0	0	0	0	1	0	0
340200	Ann Arbor	0	0	0	0	1	1	1	0	0
340300	Battle Creek	0	0	0	0	0	0	1	0	0
340400	Bay City	0	0	0	0	0	1	1	1	0
340500	Birmingham	0	0	0	0	0	0	1	1	0
340600	Dearborn	0	0	0	0	1	1	1	1	0
340700	Detroit	0	1	1	1	1	1	1	1	0
340800	East Detroit	0	0	0	0	0	1	1	1	0
340900	East Lansing	0	0	0	0	0	1	1	1	0
341000	Ferndale	0	0	0	0	0	1	0	1	0
341100	Flint	0	0	0	1	1	1	1	0	0
341200	Garden City	0	0	0	0	1	0	1	0	0
341300	Grand Rapids	0	0	0	0	1	1	1	1	0
341400	Hamtramck	0	0	0	0	1	1	0	1	0
341500	Hazel Park	0	0	0	0	0	0	1	0	0
341600	Highland Park	0	0	0	1	1	1	1	1	0
341700	Inkster	0	0	0	0	0	1	1	0	0

Code number	City name	Function Edu	Wfa	Wga	Hos	Hea	San	Par	Sew	Jud
341800	Jackson	0	0	0	0	1	0	1	1	0
341900	Kalamazoo	0	0	0	0	1	1	1	0	0
342000	Lansing	0	0	0	0	0	1	1	0	0
342100	Lincoln Park	0	0	0	0	0	0	1	0	0
342200	Livonia	0	0	0	0	0	0	1	1	0
342300	Madison Heights	0	0	0	0	0	0	1	0	0
342400	Midland	0	0	0	0	1	1	1	1	0
342500	Muskegon	0	0	0	0	0	1	1	0	0
342600	Oak Park	0	0	0	0	0	0	1	1	0
342700	Pontiac	0	0	0	1	1	1	1	1	0
342800	Port Huron	0	0	0	0	0	1	1	1	0
342900	Roseville	0	0	0	0	0	1	1	1	0
343000	Royal Oak	0	0	0	0	1	1	1	1	0
343100	Saginaw	0	0	0	0	1	1	1	0	0
343200	St. Clair Shores	0	0	0	0	0	1	1	1	0
343300	Southfield	0	0	0	0	0	0	0	0	0
343400	Southgate	0	0	0	0	0	0	0	0	0
343500	Warren	0	0	0	0	0	1	1	1	0
343600	Wyandotte	0	0	0	1	1	1	0	0	0
343700	Wyoming	0	0	0	0	0	0	1	0	0
350100	Appleton, WI	1	0	1	0	1	1	1	1	0
350200	Beloit	1	0	0	0	1	1	1	1	0
350300	Eau Claire	1	0	1	0	1	0	1	1	0
350400	Fond du lac	1	0	1	0	1	1	1	1	0
350500	Green Bay	1	0	1	0	1	1	1	1	0
350600	Janesville	1	0	0	0	1	1	1	1	0
350700	Kenosha	1	0	0	0	1	1	1	1	0
350800	LaCrosse	1	0	0	0	1	0	1	1	0
350900	Madison	1	0	1	0	1	1	1	1	0
351000	Manitowoc	1	0	1	0	1	0	1	1	0
351100	Milwaukee	0	0	0	1	1	1	1	1	0
351200	Oshkosh	1	0	1	0	1	1	1	1	0
351300	Racine	1	0	0	0	1	1	1	1	0
351400	Sheboygan	1	0	1	0	1	1	1	1	0
351500	Superior	1	0	1	0	1	1	1	1	0
351600	Waukesha	0	0	1	0	0	0	1	1	0
351700	Wausau	1	0	1	0	1	1	1	1	0
351800	Wauwatosa	1	0	0	0	1	1	1	1	0
351900	West Allis	1	0	0	0	1	1	1	1	0
410100	Austin, MN	0	0	0	0	1	0	1	1	0
410200	Bloomington	0	0	1	0	1	0	1	0	0
410300	Duluth	0	0	0	1	0	0	1	1	0
410400	Edina	0	0	0	0	1	0	1	0	0
410500	Minneapolis	0	0	1	0	1	1	1	1	0
410600	Minnetonka	0	0	0	0	1	0	0	0	0
410700	Richfield	0	0	0	0	1	0	0	0	0
410800	Rochester	0	0	0	0	1	1	1	1	0
410900	St. Cloud	0	0	1	0	1	1	1	1	0
411000	St. Louis Park	0	0	1	0	0	0	1	0	0

Code number	City name	Function								
		Edu	Wfa	Wga	Hos	Hea	San	Par	Sew	Jud
411100	St. Paul	1	0	1	0	1	1	1	1	0
420100	Ames, IA	0	0	0	1	1	0	1	1	0
420200	Burlington	0	0	0	0	1	1	1	1	0
420300	Cedar Rapids	0	0	0	1	1	1	1	1	0
420400	Clinton	0	0	0	0	0	0	1	1	0
420500	Council Bluffs	0	0	0	0	0	1	1	1	0
420600	Davenport	0	0	0	0	1	1	1	1	0
420700	Des Moines	0	0	0	0	1	1	1	1	0
420800	Dubuque	0	0	0	0	1	1	1	1	0
420900	Fort Dodge	0	0	0	0	0	1	1	0	0
421000	Iowa City	0	0	0	0	1	1	1	1	0
421100	Mason City	0	0	0	0	1	1	1	1	0
421200	Ottumwa	0	0	0	0	1	0	1	1	0
421300	Sioux City	0	0	0	0	1	1	1	1	0
421400	Waterloo	0	0	0	0	1	1	1	1	0
430100	Bismarck, ND	0	0	0	0	1	1	0	1	0
430200	Fargo	0	0	0	0	1	1	1	0	0
430300	Grand Forks	0	0	0	0	1	1	1	1	0
430400	Minot	0	0	0	0	1	1	1	1	0
440100	Rapid City, SD	0	0	0	0	0	1	1	1	0
440200	Sioux Falls	0	0	0	0	1	0	1	1	0
450100	Grand Island, NE	0	0	0	0	1	1	1	1	0
450200	Lincoln	0	0	0	1	1	0	1	1	0
450300	Omaha	0	0	0	0	1	1	1	1	0
510100	Billings, MT	0	0	0	0	1	1	1	1	0
510200	Butte	0	0	0	0	1	1	0	1	0
510300	Great Falls	0	0	0	0	1	1	1	1	0
510400	Missoula	0	0	0	0	1	0	1	1	0
520100	Boise City, ID	0	0	0	0	1	0	1	1	0
520200	Idaho Falls	0	0	0	0	1	1	1	1	0
520300	Pocatello	0	0	0	0	0	0	1	1	0
530100	Aurora, CO	0	0	0	0	0	0	1	1	0
530200	Boulder	0	0	0	0	1	0	1	1	0
530300	Colorado Springs	0	0	0	1	1	0	1	1	0
530400	Denver	0	1	1	1	1	1	1	1	1
530500	Englewood	0	0	0	0	0	0	1	1	0
530600	Fort Collins	0	0	0	0	1	0	1	1	0
530700	Greenley	0	0	0	0	0	0	1	1	0
530800	Pueblo	0	0	0	0	1	1	1	1	0
540100	Ogden, UT	0	0	0	0	0	1	1	0	0
540200	Provo	0	0	0	0	1	1	1	1	0
540300	Salt Lake City	0	0	0	0	1	1	1	1	0
550100	Casper, WY	0	0	0	0	1	1	1	0	0
550200	Cheyenne	0	0	0	0	1	1	1	0	0
560100	Mesa, AZ	0	0	0	0	0	1	1	1	0

Code number	City name	Function								
		Edu	Wfa	Wga	Hos	Hea	San	Par	Sew	Jud
560200	Phoenex	0	0	0	0	0	1	1	1	0
560300	Tucson	0	0	0	0	0	1	1	1	0
570100	Albuquerque, NM	0	0	0	0	1	1	1	1	0
570200	Carlsbad	0	0	0	0	1	1	1	1	0
570300	Hobbs	0	0	0	0	0	1	1	1	0
570400	Las Cruces	0	0	0	1	0	1	0	1	0
570500	Roswell	0	0	0	0	0	1	1	1	0
570600	Santa Fe	0	0	0	0	1	1	1	1	0
610100	Alameda, CA	0	0	0	0	1	0	1	1	0
610200	Alhambra	0	0	0	0	0	1	1	1	0
610300	Anaheim	0	0	0	0	0	1	1	1	0
610400	Arcadia	0	0	0	0	0	0	1	1	0
610500	Bakersfield	0	0	0	0	0	1	1	0	0
610600	Baldwin Park	0	0	0	0	0	0	0	0	0
610700	Bellflower	0	0	0	0	0	0	1	0	0
610800	Berkeley	0	0	0	0	1	1	1	1	0
610900	Beverly Hills	0	0	0	0	0	1	1	1	0
611000	Buena Park	0	0	0	0	0	0	1	0	0
611100	Burbank	0	0	0	0	0	1	1	1	0
611200	Chula Vista	0	0	0	0	0	0	1	1	0
611300	Compton	0	0	0	0	0	0	1	0	0
611400	Concord	0	0	0	0	0	0	1	0	0
611500	Costa Mesa	0	0	0	0	0	0	1	0	0
611600	Culver City	0	0	0	0	0	1	1	0	0
611700	Daly City	0	0	0	0	0	0	1	1	0
611800	Downey	0	0	0	0	0	0	0	1	0
611900	El Cajon	0	0	0	0	0	0	1	0	0
612000	El Cerrito	0	0	0	0	0	0	1	0	0
612100	Eureka	0	0	0	0	1	0	1	1	0
612200	Fremont	0	0	0	0	0	0	1	0	0
612300	Fresno	0	0	0	0	1	1	1	0	0
612400	Fullerton	0	0	0	0	0	0	1	1	0
612500	Gardena	0	0	0	0	0	0	1	0	0
612600	Garden Grove	0	0	0	0	0	0	1	0	0
612700	Glendale	0	0	0	0	1	1	1	1	0
612800	Hawthorne	0	0	0	0	0	0	1	0	0
612900	Hayward	0	0	0	0	0	0	1	1	0
613000	Huntington Park	0	0	0	0	0	1	1	0	0
613100	Inglewood	0	0	0	0	1	1	1	1	0
613200	La Habra	0	0	0	0	0	0	1	0	0
613300	Lakewood	0	0	0	0	1	0	1	0	0
613400	La Mesa	0	0	0	0	0	0	1	0	0
613500	Long Beach	0	0	0	0	1	1	1	1	0
613600	Los Angeles	0	0	0	1	1	1	1	1	0
613700	Lynwood	0	0	0	0	0	0	1	0	0
613800	Manhattan Beach	0	0	0	0	0	0	1	0	0
613900	Menlo Park	0	0	0	0	0	0	1	1	0
614000	Modesto	0	0	0	0	0	1	1	0	0
614100	Monrovia	0	0	0	0	0	0	1	1	0

Code number	City name	Function								
		Edu	Wfa	Wga	Hos	Hea	San	Par	Sew	Jud
614200	Montebello	0	0	0	0	0	0	1	0	0
614300	Monterey Park	0	0	0	0	0	0	1	1	0
614400	Mountain View	0	0	0	0	0	0	1	1	0
614500	National City	0	0	0	0	0	0	1	1	0
614600	Newport Beach	0	0	0	0	0	1	1	1	0
614700	Norwalk	0	0	0	0	0	0	0	0	0
614800	Oakland	0	0	0	0	1	1	1	1	0
614900	Ontario	0	0	0	0	0	1	1	1	0
615000	Orange	0	0	0	0	0	0	1	1	0
615100	Oxnard	0	0	0	0	0	1	1	1	0
615200	Palo Alto	0	0	0	0	0	1	1	1	0
615300	Paramount	0	0	0	0	0	0	1	0	0
615400	Pasadena	0	0	0	0	1	1	1	1	0
615500	Pico Rivera	0	0	0	0	0	0	1	0	0
615600	Pomona	0	0	0	0	1	1	1	1	0
615700	Redlands	0	0	0	0	0	1	1	1	0
615800	Redondo Beach	0	0	0	0	0	1	1	1	0
615900	Redwood City	0	0	0	0	0	1	1	1	0
616000	Richmond	0	0	0	0	1	0	1	1	0
616100	Riverside	0	0	0	0	1	1	1	1	0
616200	Sacramento	0	0	0	0	1	1	1	1	0
616300	Salinas	0	0	0	0	0	0	1	1	0
616400	San Bernardino	0	0	0	0	1	1	1	1	0
616500	San Bruno	0	0	0	0	0	0	1	1	0
616600	San Buenaventura	0	0	0	0	0	0	1	0	0
616700	San Diego	0	0	0	0	1	1	1	1	0
616800	San Francisco	0	1	1	1	1	1	1	1	1
616900	San Jose	0	0	0	0	1	1	1	1	0
617000	San Leandro	0	0	0	0	0	1	1	1	0
617100	San Mateo	0	0	0	0	0	1	1	1	0
617200	Santa Ana	0	0	0	0	0	0	1	1	0
617300	Santa Barbara	0	0	0	0	0	1	1	1	0
617400	Santa Clara	0	0	0	0	0	1	1	1	0
617500	Santa Cruz	0	0	0	0	1	1	1	1	0
617600	Santa Monica	0	0	0	0	0	1	1	1	0
617700	Santa Rosa	0	0	0	0	0	0	1	1	0
617800	South Gate	0	0	0	0	0	0	1	0	0
617900	S. San Francisco	0	0	0	0	0	0	1	1	0
618000	Stockton	0	0	0	0	1	1	1	1	0
618100	Sunnyvale	0	0	0	0	0	0	1	1	0
618200	Torrance	0	0	0	0	0	1	1	0	0
618300	Vallejo	0	0	0	0	0	0	1	1	0
618400	West Covina	0	0	0	0	0	0	1	0	0
618500	Westminster	0	0	0	0	0	0	1	0	0
618600	Whittier	0	0	0	0	0	1	1	1	0
620100	Eugene, OR	0	0	0	0	1	1	1	1	0
620200	Portland	0	0	0	0	1	1	1	0	0
620300	Salem	0	0	0	0	1	1	1	1	0

Code number	City name	Function								
		Edu	Wfa	Wga	Hos	Hea	San	Par	Sew	Jud
630100	Bellingham, WA	0	0	0	0	1	0	1	1	0
630200	Bremerton	0	0	0	0	1	0	1	0	0
630300	Everett	0	0	0	0	0	0	1	1	0
630400	Seattle	0	0	0	0	1	1	1	1	0
630500	Spokane	0	0	0	0	1	1	1	1	0
630600	Tacoma	0	0	0	0	1	1	0	1	0
630700	Vancouver	0	0	0	0	1	0	1	0	0
630800	Yakima	0	0	0	0	1	1	0	0	0
640100	Las Vegas, NV	0	0	0	0	1	0	1	1	0
640200	Reno	0	0	0	0	0	0	1	0	0
650100	Anchorage, AK	NO DATA								
660100	Hilo, HI	NO DATA								
660200	Honolulu	NO DATA								
710100	Abilene, TX	0	0	1	0	1	1	1	1	0
710200	Amarillo	0	0	0	0	1	1	1	1	0
710300	Arlington	0	0	0	0	1	0	1	1	0
710400	Austin	0	0	0	1	1	1	1	1	0
710500	Baytown	0	0	1	0	1	1	0	0	0
710600	Beaumont	0	0	1	0	1	1	1	1	0
710700	Big Spring	0	0	0	0	1	1	1	0	0
710800	Brownsville	0	0	0	0	1	1	1	0	0
710900	Bryan	1	0	0	0	1	1	1	1	0
711000	Corpus Christi	0	0	1	1	1	1	1	1	0
711100	Dallas	0	0	0	0	1	1	1	1	0
711200	Denton	0	0	0	1	1	1	0	0	0
711300	El Paso	1	0	0	0	1	1	1	1	0
711400	Fort Worth	0	0	0	0	1	1	1	1	0
711500	Galveston	0	0	1	0	1	1	1	0	0
711600	Garland	0	0	0	0	1	1	1	0	0
711700	Grand Prairie	0	0	0	0	1	0	1	1	0
711800	Harlingen	0	0	0	0	1	1	1	0	0
711900	Houston	0	0	0	0	1	1	1	1	0
712000	Irving	0	0	0	0	0	1	1	1	0
712100	Kingsville	0	0	0	0	1	1	1	1	0
712200	Laredo	0	0	1	0	1	1	1	1	0
712300	Longview	0	0	0	0	1	1	1	1	0
712400	Lubbock	0	0	1	0	1	1	1	1	0
712500	McAllen	0	0	1	1	1	1	1	1	0
712600	Mesquite	0	0	0	0	1	1	1	0	0
712700	Midland	0	0	0	0	1	1	1	0	0
712800	Odessa	0	0	0	0	1	1	0	0	0
712900	Orange	0	0	0	0	0	1	1	1	0
713000	Pasadena	0	0	0	0	1	1	1	1	0
713100	Port Arthur	0	0	0	0	1	1	1	1	0
713200	San Angelo	0	0	1	0	1	0	1	0	0
713300	San Antonio	0	0	1	0	1	1	1	1	0
713400	Temple	1	0	0	0	1	1	1	0	0
713500	Texarkana	0	0	0	0	1	0	1	0	0

Code	City	Function								
number	name	Edu	Wfa	Wga	Hos	Hea	San	Par	Sew	Jud
713600	Texas City	0	0	0	0	1	1	1	0	0
713700	Tyler	0	0	1	0	1	1	1	1	0
713800	Victoria	0	0	0	0	1	1	1	0	0
713900	Waco	0	0	0	0	1	1	1	1	0
714000	Wichita Falls	0	0	0	1	1	1	1	1	0
720100	Bartlesville, OK	0	0	0	0	1	1	1	1	0
720200	Enid	0	0	0	0	1	1	1	1	0
720300	Lawton	0	0	0	0	1	1	1	1	0
720400	Midwest City	0	0	0	1	0	1	0	0	0
720500	Muskogee	0	0	0	1	1	0	1	1	0
720600	Norman	0	0	0	1	0	1	1	0	0
720700	Oklahoma City	0	0	0	0	0	1	1	1	0
720800	Tulsa	0	0	0	0	0	1	1	1	0
730100	Hutchinson, KS	0	0	0	0	1	1	1	0	0
730200	Kansas City	0	0	0	0	1	1	1	0	0
730300	Lawrence	0	0	0	1	1	1	1	0	0
730400	Prairie Village	0	0	0	0	0	0	0	0	0
730500	Salina	0	0	0	0	1	1	1	0	0
730600	Topeka	0	0	0	0	1	1	1	0	0
730700	Wichita	0	0	0	0	1	1	1	1	0
740100	Columbia, MO	0	0	0	0	1	1	1	0	0
740200	Florissant	0	0	0	0	1	0	1	1	0
740300	Independence	0	0	0	0	1	0	1	0	0
740400	Jefferson City	0	0	0	0	0	0	1	0	0
740500	Joplin	0	0	0	0	1	1	1	0	0
740600	Kansas City	0	0	0	0	1	1	1	0	0
740700	Kirkwood	0	0	0	0	1	1	1	1	0
740800	St. Joseph	0	0	0	0	1	0	1	1	0
740900	St. Louis	0	1	1	1	1	1	1	1	1
741000	Springfield	0	0	0	1	1	1	1	1	0
741100	University City	0	0	0	0	0	1	1	1	0
741200	Webster Groves	0	0	0	0	0	0	1	1	0
750100	El Dorado, AR	0	0	0	0	0	1	0	1	0
750200	Fort Smith	0	0	0	0	1	1	1	0	0
750300	Hot Springs	0	0	0	0	1	0	0	0	0
750400	Little Rock	0	0	0	0	1	1	1	1	0
750500	N. Little Rock	0	0	0	0	1	1	1	1	0
750600	Pine Bluff	0	0	0	0	1	1	1	1	0
810100	Alexandria, LA	0	0	0	0	1	1	1	0	0
810200	Baton Rouge	0	0	0	0	1	1	1	1	0
810300	Bossier City	0	0	0	1	0	1	1	0	0
810400	Lafayette	0	0	0	0	0	1	1	0	0
810500	Lake Charles	0	0	0	0	0	1	1	1	0
810600	Monroe	0	0	0	0	0	1	1	0	0
810700	New Iberia	0	0	0	0	0	1	1	0	0
810800	New Orleans	0	0	1	0	1	1	1	1	1
810900	Shreveport	0	0	0	0	0	1	1	1	0

Code number	City name	Function								
		Edu	Wfa	Wga	Hos	Hea	San	Par	Sew	Jud
820100	Anniston, AL	0	0	0	1	1	1	1	0	0
820200	Bessemer	0	0	0	0	1	0	1	0	0
820300	Birmingham	0	0	0	0	1	1	1	1	0
820400	Decatur	1	0	0	1	1	1	0	0	0
820500	Dothan	1	0	0	0	1	1	1	0	0
820600	Florence	0	0	0	1	1	1	0	1	0
820700	Gadsen	0	0	0	0	1	1	1	1	0
820800	Huntsville	1	0	0	1	1	1	1	0	0
820900	Mobile	0	0	0	0	1	1	1	1	0
821000	Montgomery	0	0	0	0	1	1	1	1	0
821100	Phenix City	0	0	0	1	1	1	1	0	0
821200	Prichard	0	0	0	0	1	0	1	0	0
821300	Selma	0	0	0	0	1	1	1	0	0
821400	Tuscaloosa	0	0	0	1	1	1	1	0	0
830100	Biloxi, MS	0	0	0	0	0	1	1	1	0
830200	Greenville	0	0	0	0	1	1	1	0	0
830300	Gulfport	0	0	0	1	1	0	1	0	0
830400	Hattiesburg	0	0	0	0	1	1	1	1	0
830500	Jackson	0	0	0	0	1	1	1	1	0
830600	Laurel	0	0	0	0	1	1	1	0	0
830700	Meridian	0	0	0	0	1	1	1	1	0
830800	Vicksburg	0	0	0	0	1	1	1	1	0
840100	Clearwater, FL	0	0	0	0	0	1	1	1	0
840200	Coral Gables	0	0	0	0	0	1	1	1	0
840300	Daytona Beach	0	0	0	0	0	0	1	0	0
840400	Fort Lauderdale	0	0	0	0	1	1	1	1	0
840500	Fort Pierce	0	0	0	0	1	1	1	0	0
840600	Gainesville	0	0	0	0	1	1	1	1	0
840700	Hialeah	0	0	0	0	0	1	1	1	0
840800	Hollywood	0	0	0	0	1	1	1	1	0
840900	Jacksonville	0	0	0	0	1	1	1	1	0
841000	Key West	0	0	0	0	0	0	1	0	0
841100	Lakeland	0	0	0	0	1	1	1	1	0
841200	Miami	0	0	0	0	1	1	1	1	0
841300	Miami Beach	0	0	0	0	0	1	1	1	0
841400	North Miami	0	0	0	0	0	1	1	0	0
841500	Orlando	0	0	0	0	1	1	1	0	0
841600	Panama City	0	0	0	0	0	1	1	0	0
841700	Pensacola	0	0	0	0	1	1	1	1	0
841800	St. Petersburg	0	0	0	1	1	1	1	1	0
841900	Sarasota	0	0	0	0	0	1	1	1	0
842000	Tallahassee	0	0	0	1	1	1	1	0	0
842100	Tampa	0	0	0	0	1	1	1	1	0
842200	West Palm Beach	0	0	0	0	0	1	1	1	0
850100	Albany, GA	0	0	0	0	1	1	1	1	0
850200	Athens	0	0	0	0	1	1	1	1	0
850300	Atlanta	0	0	0	0	1	1	1	1	0
850400	Augusta	0	0	0	0	0	1	1	0	0
850500	Columbus	0	0	0	1	1	1	1	0	0

Code number	City name	Function								
		Edu	Wfa	Wga	Hos	Hea	San	Par	Sew	Jud
850600	East Point	0	0	0	0	0	1	1	1	0
850700	Macon	0	0	0	1	1	1	1	1	0
850800	Marietta	0	0	0	0	0	1	1	0	0
850900	Rome	0	0	0	0	0	1	1	1	0
851000	Savannah	0	0	0	0	1	1	1	1	0
851100	Valdosta	0	0	0	0	0	1	1	0	0
860100	Asheville, NC	0	0	0	0	1	1	1	1	0
860200	Burlington	0	0	0	0	0	1	1	0	0
860300	Charlotte	0	0	0	0	1	1	1	0	0
860400	Durham	0	0	0	0	0	1	1	0	0
860500	Fayetteville	0	0	0	0	0	1	1	0	0
860600	Gastonia	0	0	0	0	0	1	1	0	0
860700	Goldsboro	0	0	0	0	0	1	0	0	0
860800	Greensboro	0	0	0	0	0	1	1	1	0
860900	High Point	0	0	0	0	0	1	1	1	0
861000	Raleigh	0	0	0	0	0	1	1	0	0
861100	Rocky Mount	0	0	0	0	1	1	1	0	0
861200	Wilmington	0	0	0	0	1	1	1	0	0
861300	Wilson	0	0	0	0	1	1	1	0	0
861400	Winston-Salem	0	0	0	1	1	1	1	1	0
870100	Anderson, SC	0	0	0	0	0	1	1	0	0
870200	Charleston	0	0	0	0	0	1	1	0	0
870300	Columbia	0	0	0	0	1	1	1	0	0
870400	Greenville	0	0	0	0	1	1	1	1	0
870500	Rock Hille	0	0	0	0	1	1	1	0	0
870600	Spartanburg	0	0	0	0	0	1	1	0	0
910100	Alexandria, VA	1	1	1	0	1	1	1	1	1
910200	Charlottesville	1	1	1	0	1	1	1	1	1
910300	Danville	1	1	1	0	1	1	1	1	1
910400	Hampton	1	1	1	1	1	1	1	0	1
910500	Lynchburg	1	1	1	0	1	1	1	0	1
910600	Newport News	1	1	1	0	1	1	1	1	1
910700	Norfolk	1	1	1	1	1	1	1	1	1
910800	Petersburg	1	1	1	0	1	1	1	1	1
910900	Portsmouth	1	1	1	0	1	1	1	1	1
911000	Richmond	1	1	1	0	1	1	1	1	1
911100	Roanoke	1	1	1	0	1	1	1	1	1
920100	Charleston, WV	0	0	0	0	1	1	1	0	0
920200	Clarksburg	0	0	0	0	1	1	0	1	0
920300	Fairmont	0	0	0	1	0	0	0	0	0
920400	Huntington	0	0	0	0	1	1	0	Sew	0
920500	Parkersburg	0	0	0	1	1	1	1	0	0
920600	Weirton	0	0	0	0	0	1	1	1	0
920700	Wheeling	0	0	0	0	1	1	1	0	0
930100	Ashland, KY	0	0	0	0	1	1	0	1	0
930200	Bowling Green	0	0	0	1	1	1	0	0	0
930300	Covington	0	0	0	0	1	1	1	1	0
930400	Lexington	0	0	0	0	1	1	1	1	0

Code	City	Function								
number	name	Edu	Wfa	Wga	Hos	Hea	San	Par	Sew	Jud
930500	Louisville	1	0	0	1	1	1	1	1	0
930600	Newport	0	0	0	0	1	1	0	0	0
930700	Owensboro	0	0	0	1	0	1	1	0	0
930800	Paducah	0	0	0	0	1	1	1	0	0
940100	Chattanooga, TN	1	0	1	1	1	1	1	1	0
940200	Jackson	1	0	1	1	1	1	1	0	0
940300	Johnson City	1	0	1	0	1	1	1	0	0
940400	Kingsport	1	0	1	0	0	1	1	1	0
940500	Knoxville	1	0	1	1	1	1	1	1	0
940600	Memphis	1	0	1	1	1	1	1	1	0
940700	Nashville	1	0	1	1	1	1	1	1	0
940800	Oakridge	1	0	1	0	1	0	1	1	0

References

Adrian, C. R., and C. Press
1968   *Governing urban America.* New York: McGraw-Hill.
Agger, R. E., D. Goldrich, and B. E. Swanson
1964   *The rulers and the ruled.* New York: Wiley.
Aiken, M., and R. R. Alford
1968   Community structure and mobilization: The case of the war on poverty. Madison: Institute for Research on Poverty, Univ. of Wisconsin.
1970a   Community structure and innovation: The case of public housing. *American Political Science Review* **64**: 843–864.
1970b   Community structure and innovation: The case of urban renewal. *American Sociological Review* **35**: 650–665.
1970c   Comparative urban research and community decision-making. *The New Atlantis* **1**: 85–110.
Aiken, M., and J. Hage
1968   Organizational interdependence and intra-organizational structure. *American Sociological Review* **33**: 912–930.
Alford, R. R.
1969   *Bureaucracy and participation: Political cultures in four Wisconsin cities.* Chicago: Rand McNally.
1974   *Health care politics: Interest group and ideological barriers to reform.* Chicago: Univ. of Chicago Press.
Alford, R. R., and E. C. Lee
1968   Voting turnout in American cities. *American Political Science Review* **62**: 796–813.
Alford, R. R., and H. Scoble
1965   Political and socio-economic characteristics of American cities. In *The municipal yearbook 1965,* edited by O. F. Nolting and D. S. Arnold. Pp. 82–97. Chicago: International City Managers' Association.
Alwin, D. F., and R. M. Hauser
1975   The decomposition of effects in path analysis. *American Sociological Review* **40**: 37–47.
Bain, C. W.
1967   *A body incorporate: The evolution of city–county separation in Virginia.* Charlottesville: The Univ. Press of Virginia.

205

Banfield, E. C.
1961 *Political influence.* New York: Free Press of Glencoe.
1974 *The unheavenly city revisited.* Boston: Little, Brown.
Becker, S., and T. L. Whisler
1967 The innovative organization: A selective review of current theory and research. *Journal of Business* 40: 462–469.
Blalock, H. M., Jr.
1967 Causal inferences, closed populations, and measures of association. *American Political Science Review* 61: 130–136.
Blau, P. M.
1970 A formal theory of differentiation in organizations. *American Sociological Review* 35: 201–218.
Bohrnstedt, G. W.
1969 A quick method for determining the reliability and validity of multiple-item scales. *American Sociological Review* 34: 542–548.
Bollens, J. C.
1957 *Special-district governments in the United States.* Berkeley, Calif.: Univ. of California Press.
Bollens, J. C., and H. J. Schmandt
1970 *The metropolis.* New York: Harper and Row.
Boskoff, A.
1970 *The sociology of urban regions.* New York: Appleton-Century-Crofts.
Boskoff, A., and H. Ziegler
1964 *Voting patterns in a local election.* Philadelphia: Lippincott.
Brazer, H. E.
1959 *City expenditures in the United States.* Washington, D. C.: National Bureau of Economic Research.
Brewer, G. D.
1973 *Politicians, bureaucrats, and the consultant.* New York: Basic Books.
Bridenbaugh, C.
1955 *Cities in revolt: Urban life in America, 1743–1776.* New York: Knopf.
Broom, L., and P. Selznick
1973 *Sociology.* New York: Harper and Row.
Burns, T., and G. M. Stalker
1961 *The management of innovation.* London: Travistock.
Burt, R. S.
1974 Power in a social structure. A paper presented at the VIIIth World Congress of the International Sociological Association, August.
Cain, G. C., and H. Watts
1969 Problems in making policy inferences from the Coleman report. *American Sociological Review* 35: 228–242.
Campbell, A., and S. Sacks
1967 *Metropolitan America: Fiscal patterns and governmental systems.* New York: Free Press.
Carter, R. F., and J. Sutthoff
1960 *Voters and their schools.* Stanford: Stanford Univ. Press.
Cion, R. M.
1971 Accomodation par excellence: The Lakewood plan. In *Metropolitan politics,* edited by M. D. Danielson. Pp. 224–231. Boston: Little, Brown.

Clark, B. R.
1970   *The distinctive college.* Chicago: Aldine.
Clark, T. N.
1971   Community structure, decision-making, budget expenditures, and urban renewal in 51 American communities. In *Community politics,* edited by C. M. Bonjean, R. L. Lineberry, and T. N. Clark. Pp. 291–313. New York: Free Press.
Cochran, T. C.
1963   The historian's use of social role. In *Generalization in the writing of history,* edited by L. Gottschalk. Chicago: Univ. of Chicago Press.
Committee for Economic Development
1970   *Reshaping government in metropolitan areas.* New York: Committee for Economic Development.
Connolly, W. E.
1969   The challenge to pluralist theory. In *The bias of pluralism,* edited by W. E. Connolly. Pp. 3–34. New York: Atherton.
Crain, R. L., E. Katz, and D. B. Rosenthal
1969   *The politics of community conflict: The fluoridation decision.* Indianapolis: Bobbs-Merrill.
Crecine, J. P. (Editor)
1970   *Financing the metropolis.* Beverly Hills, Calif.: Sage Publications.
Dahl, R. A.
1961   *Who governs?* New Haven: Yale Univ. Press.
Dorfman, R.
1970   The functions of the city. In *Thinking about cities* edited by A. H. Pascal. Pp. 32–40. Belmont, Calif.: Dickenson.
Duncan, O. D.
1966   Path analysis: Sociological examples. *American Journal of Sociology* 72: 1–16.
Durkheim, E.
1933   *The division of labor in society.* Glencoe, Ill.: Free Press.
Emery, F. E., and E. L. Trist
1965   The causal texture of organizational environments. *Human Relations* 18: 21–32.
Etzioni, A.
1968   *The active society.* New York: Free Press.
Eulau, K., and K. Prewitt
1973   *Labyrinths of democracy.* New York: Bobbs-Merrill.
Evan, W. M.
1966   The organization set: Toward a theory of interorganizational relations. In *Approaches to organizational design,* edited by J. D. Thompson. Pp. 173–191. Pittsburgh: Univ. of Pittsburgh Press.
Fairlie, J. A.
1898   *The centralization of administration in New York State.* New York: Columbia Univ. Press.
Friesema, H. P.
1966   The metropolis and the maze of local government. *Urban Affairs Quarterly* 2: 68–90.
Gilbert, C. W.
1966   *Community power structure: A study in the sociology of knowledge.* Evanston, Ill.: Ph.D. dissertation, Northwestern University.
Gist, N. P., and Fava, S. F.
1969   *Urban society.* New York: Thomas Y. Crowell.

Glaab, C. N., and A. T. Brown
1967   *A history of urban America.* New York: Macmillan.
Gold, D.
1969   Statistical tests and substantive significance. *American Sociologist* 4: 42–46.
Gordon, D. N.
1970   Immigrants and municipal voting turnout: Implications for the changing ethnic impact on urban politics. *American Sociological Review* 35: 665–681.
Gottschalk, S. S.
1975   *Communities and alternatives: An exploration of the limits of planning.* New York: Schenkman.
Gouldner, A. W.
1954   *Patterns of industrial bureaucracy.* New York: Free Press.
Government Affairs Foundation

1958   *Metropolitan surveys: A digest.* Chicago: Public Administration Service.
Greenstein, F. I.
1964   The changing pattern of urban party politics. *Annals* 353 (May): 1–13.
Greer, S.
1962a   *The emerging city.* New York: Free Press.
1962b   *Governing the metropolis.* New York: Wiley.
1965   *Urban renewal and American cities.* Indianapolis: Bobbs-Merrill.
1972   *The urbane view.* New York: Oxford Univ. Press.
Greer, S., D. L. McElrath, D. W. Minar, and P. Orleans (Editors)
1968   *The new urbanization.* New York: St. Martin's Press.
Griffith, E. S.
1938   *History of American city government: The colonial period.* New York: Oxford Univ. Press.
Gutman, R., and D. Popenoe (Editors)
1970   *Neighborhood, city, and metropolis.* New York: Random House.
Hage, J.
1972   Organizational permeability, boundary spanners, and organizational structure. Paper presented at the annual American Sociological Association meetings, New Orleans, August.
Hage, J., and M. Aiken
1967   Program change and organizational properties: A comparative analysis. *American Journal of Sociology* 72: 503–519.
1970   *Social change in complex organizations.* New York: Random House.
Hage, J., and R. Dewar
1971   The prediction of organizational performance: The case of program innovation. Paper presented at the annual American Sociological Association meetings, Denver, August.
Haller, A. O., and A. Portes
1973   Status attainment processes. *Sociology of Education* 46: 51–91.
Hauser, P. M.
1967   On the impact of urbanism on social organization, human nature, and the political order. In *Politics of metropolitan areas,* edited by P. B. Coulter. Pp. 3–13. New York: Thomas Y. Crowell.
Hawley, A. H.
1957   Metropolitan population and municipal government expenditures in central cities.

In *Cities and society,* edited by P. K. Hatt and A. J. Reiss, Jr. Pp. 773–782. New York: Free Press.

Hawley, A. H., and B. G. Zimmer
1970 *The metropolitan community: Its people and government.* Beverly Hills, Calif.: Sage.

Hawley, W. D.
1973 *Nonpartisan elections and the case for party politics.* New York: Wiley.

Heise, D. R., and G. W. Bohrnstedt
1970 Validity, invalidity, and reliability. In *Sociological methodology, 1970,* edited by E. F. Borgatta and G. W. Bohrnstedt. San Francisco: Jossey-Bass.

Hillery, G. A., Jr.
1968 *Communal organizations.* Chicago: Univ. of Chicago Press.

Hoover, E. M., and R. Vernon
1962 *Anatomy of a metropolis.* Garden City, N. Y.: Doubleday.

Iannaccone, L.
1967 *Politics in education.* New York: The Center for Applied Research in Education.

Jacob, P. E., and H. Teune
1964 The integrative process: Guidelines for analysis of the bases of political community. In *The integration of political communities,* edited by P. E. Jacob and J. V. Toscano. Pp. 1–45. Philadelphia: Lippincott.

Jensen, A. L.
1963 *The maritime commerce of colonial Philadelphia.* Madison: State Historical Society of Wisconsin.

Jones, V., R. L. Forstall, and A. Collver
1963 Economic and social characteristics of urban places. In *The municipal year book 1963,* Chicago: International City Managers' Association.

Kasarda, J. D.
1972 The impact of suburban population growth on central city service functions. *American Journal of Sociology* **77**: 1111–1124.

Katz, M. B.
1968 *The irony of early school reform.* Cambridge: Harvard Univ. Press.
1970 *Class, bureaucracy, and schools.* Boston: Beacon.

Kerr, C.
1963 *The uses of the university.* New York: Harper and Row.

Klatzky, S. R.
1970 Organizational inequality: The case of public employment agencies, *American Journal of Sociology* **76**: 474–491.

Kotter, J. P., and P. R. Lawrence
1974 *Mayors in action.* New York: Wiley.

Ladd, E. C., Jr.
1969 *Ideology in America: Change and response in a city, a suburb, and a small town.* Ithaca: Cornell Univ. Press.

Land, K. C.
1969 Principles of path analysis. In *Sociological methodology 1969,* edited by E. F. Borgatta. Pp. 3–37. San Francisco: Jossey-Bass.

Laumann, E. O., and F. U. Pappi
1973 New directions in the study of elites. *American Sociological Review* **38**: 212–230.

Lee, E. C.
1963 City elections: A statistical profile. In *The municipal yearbook, 1963,* edited by

O. F. Nolting and D. S. Arnold. Pp. 74–84. Chicago: International City Managers' Association.

Levine, S., and P. E. White
1961 Exchange as a conceptual framework for the study of interorganizational relationships. *Administrative Science Quarterly* **5**: 583–601.

Liebert, R. J.
1974a Municipal functions, structure, and expenditures: A reanalysis of recent research. *Social Science Quarterly* **54**: 765–783.
1974b Theory construction and measurement error in city expenditure analysis: Response to Clark. *Social Science Quarterly* **55**: 791–794.
1975 The partial eclipse of community government: The trend toward functional specialization. *Social Science Quarterly* **56**: 210–224.

Lineberry, R. L., and E. P. Fowler
1967 Reformism and public policies in American cities. *American Political Science Review* **61**: 701–716.

Lipset, S. M.
1950 *Agrarian socialism*. Berkeley, Calif.: Univ. of California Press.
1959 *Political man: The social bases of politics*. Garden City, N.Y.: Doubleday.
1970 *Revolution and counter-revolution: Change and persistence in social structures*. Garden City, N. Y.: Doubleday.

Long, N. E.
1958 The local community as an ecology of games. *American Journal of Sociology* **64**: 251–261.

Lynd, R. S., and H. M. Lynd
1929 *Middletown*. New York: Harcourt Brace.
1937 *Middletown in transition*. New York: Harcourt.

Maclear, A. B.
1967 *Early New England towns: A comparative study of their development*. New York: AMS Press.

McKenzie, R. D.
1933 *The metropolitan community*. New York: McGraw-Hill.

Maass, A. (Editor)
1959 *Area and power*. Glencoe, Ill.: Free Press.

Martin, M. (Editor)
1966 *The public welfare directory*. Chicago: American Public Welfare Association.

Mechanic, D.
1962 Sources of power of lower participants in complex organizations. *Administrative Science Quarterly* **7**: 349–364.

Michels, R.
1949 *Political parties*. Glencoe, Ill.: Free Press.

Miller, D. C.
1975 *Leadership and power in the Bos-Wash megalopolis*. New York: Wiley.

Mills, C. W.
1940 Methodological consequences of the sociology of knowledge. *American Sociological Review* **46**: 316–330.

Morgan, E. S.
1956 *The birth of the republic, 1763–89*. Chicago: Univ. of Chicago Press.

Morrison, D. E., and R. E. Henkel
1969 Significance tests reconsidered. *American Sociologist* **4**: 131–139.

Mumford, L.
1961   *The city in history.* New York: Harcourt.
National Municipal League
1930   *The government of metropolitan areas in the United States.* New York: National
        Municipal League.
Neenan, W.
1970   The suburban-central city exploitation thesis: One city's tale, *National Tax
        Journal* **23**: 117–139.
Nisbet, R. A.
1962   *Community and power.* New York: Oxford Univ. Press.
Nolting, O. F.
1969   *Progress and impact of the council-manager plan.* Chicago: Public Administration
        Service.
Nolting, O. F., and D. S. Arnold (Editors)
1963   *The municipal yearbook, 1963.* Chicago: International City Managers' Associa-
        tion.
1965   *The municipal yearbook, 1965.* Chicago: International City Managers' Asso-
        ciation.
Nuquist, A. E.
1964   *Town government in Vermont.* Burlington, Vt.: Univ. of Vermont Press.
O'Conner, J.
1973   *The Fiscal Crisis of the State.* New York: St. Martin's Press.
Park, R. E.
1952   *Human communities.* Glencoe, Ill.: Free Press.
Paullin, C. O.
1932   *Atlas of the historical geography of the United States.* Washington, D. C.:
        American Geographical Society of New York.
Perrow, C.
1967   A framework for comparative organizational analysis. *American Sociological Re-
        view* **32**: 194–208.
Phillips, J. C.
1954   *State and local government in America.* New York: American Book Company.
Pinard, M.
1963   Structural attachments and political support in urban politics: A case of a
        fluoridation referendum. *American Journal of Sociology* **68**: 513–526.
Piven, F. F., and R. A. Cloward
1971   *Regulating the poor.* New York: Random House.
Porter, K. H.
1922   *County and township government in the United States.* New York: Macmillan.
Richards, A. R.
1954   Local government research: A partial evaluation. *Public Administration Review*
        14: 271–277.
Riesman, D.
1958   *Constraint and variety in American education.* Lincoln, Nebr.: Univ. of Nebraska
        Press.
Rogers, D.
1967   Obstacles to school desegregation in New York City: A benchmark case. In
        Educating an urban population, edited by M. Gittell. Pp. 155–184. Beverley Hills,
        California: Sage.

Rogers, E. M.
1962   Diffusion of innovations. New York: Free Press of Glencoe.
Rossi, P. H.
1960   Power and community structure, Midwest Journal of Political Science 4: 390–
        401.
Rossi, P. H., and A. S. Rossi
1973   An historical perspective on the functions of local politics. In Social change and
        urban politics, edited by D. N. Gordon. Pp. 49–60. Englewood Cliffs, N. J.:
        Prentice-Hall.
Sayre, W. S., and H. Kaufman
1960   Governing New York City. New York: Russell Sage.
Sayre, W. S., and N. W. Polsby
1965   American political science and the study of urbanism. In The study of urbaniza-
        tion, edited by P. M. Hauser and L. F. Schnore. Pp. 115–156. New York: Wiley.
Schnore, L. F.
1965   The urban scene. New York: Free Press.
Schnore, L. F., and R. R. Alford
1963   Forms of government and socioeconomic characteristics of suburbs. Administra-
        tive Science Quarterly 8: 1–17.
Seasongood, M.
1943   Cases on municipal corporations. Chicago: Callaghan.
Selznick, P.
1949   TVA and the grass roots. Berkeley, Calif.: Univ. of California Press.
1969   Rejoinder to Wolin. In A sociological reader on complex organizations, edited by
        A. Etzioni. Pp. 149–154. New York: Holt-Rinehart-Winston.
Sennett, R.
1969   Classic essays on the culture of cities. (Editor) New York: Appleton-Century-Crofts.
1970   The uses of disorder. New York: Knopf.
Stein, M. R.
1964   The eclipse of community: An inperpretation of American studies. New York:
        Harper and Row.
Stephan, E. G.
1972   Variation in county size: A theory of segmental growth. American Sociological
        Review 36: 451–461.
Stephenson, C.
1933   Borough and town: A study of urban origins in England. Cambridge, Mass.: The
        Medieval Academy of America.
Stinchcombe, A. L.
1965   Social structure and organizations. In Handbook of organizations, edited by J. G.
        March. Pp. 142–193. Chicago: Rand-McNally.
Stone, H. D., K. Price, and K. Stone
1940   City manager government in the United States. Chicago: Public Administration
        Service.
Turk, H.
1970   Interorganizational networks in urban society: Initial perspectives and compara-
        tive research. American Sociological Review 35: 1–19.
1973a   Comparative urban structure from an interorganizational perspective. Administra-
        tive Science Quarterly 18: 37–55.
1973b   Interorganizational activation in urban communities: Deductions from the con-

cept of system. Washington, D. C.: American Sociological Association Rose Monograph Series.

Updyke, F. A.
1913   County government in New England. *Annals of the American Academy of Political and Social Science* **47**: 26–38.

U. S. Bureau of the Census
1957   *U. S. Census of governments.* Washington, D. C.: U. S. Government Printing Office.
1962   *U. S. Census of governments,* Vol. I–VI. Washington, D. C.: U. S. Government Printing Office.
1967   *U. S. Census of governments,* Vol. I–VI. Washington, D. C.: U. S. Government Printing Office.
1950   *U. S. Census of housing,* Vol. I. Washington, D. C.: U. S. Government Printing Office.
1960   *U. S. Census of the population.* Washington, D. C.: U. S. Government Printing Office.
1962   *County and city data book, 1962.* Washington, D. C.: U. S. Government Printing Office.
1967   *County and city data book, 1967.* Washington, D. C.: U. S. Government Printing Office.
1972   *County and city data book, 1972.* Washington, D. C.: U. S. Government Printing Office.

U. S. Department of Housing and Urban Development
1966a   *Low rent project directory.* Report S-11A, June 30, 1966. Washington, D. C.: U. S. Department of Housing and Urban Development.
1966b   *Urban renewal directory.* June 30, 1966. Washington, D. C.: U. S. Department of Housing and Urban Development.

U. S. Senate Subcommittee on Executive Reorganization
1966   *The federal role in urban affairs.* Washington, D. C.: U. S. Government Printing Office.

Walton, J.
1966   Substance and artifact: The current status of research on community power structure. *American Journal of Sociology* **71**: 430–438.
1968   Differential patterns of community power structure: An explanation based on interdependence. In *Community structure and decision making,* edited by T. N. Clark. Pp. 441–462. San Francisco: Chandler.

Warner, W. L. (Editor)
1963   *Yankee city.* New Haven: Yale Univ. Press.

Warren, R. L.
1963   *The community in America.* Chicago: Rand-McNally.
1967   The interorganizational field as a focus for investigation. *Administrative Science Quarterly* **12**: 396–419.
1970   Toward a non-utopian normative model of the community. *American Sociological Review* **35**: 219–228.
1971   The sociology of knowledge and the problems of the inner cities. *Social Science Quarterly* **52**: 469–491.

Warren, R. L., S. M. Rose, and A. F. Bergunder
1974   *The structure of urban reform.* Lexington, Mass.: Heath.

Washburn, E.
  1840   *Sketches of the judicial history of Massachusetts from 1630 to the revolution in 1775.* Boston: Little-Brown.
Weber, M.
  1946   *From Max Weber: Essays in sociology,* edited by H. H. Gerth and C. W. Mills. New York: Oxford Univ. Press.
  1947   *The theory of social and economic organization.* Glencoe, Ill.: Free Press.
  1949   *The methodology of the social sciences.* New York: Free Press.
  1958   *The city.* Glencoe, Ill.: Free Press.
Weisman, S. R.
  1975   How New York became a fiscal junkie. *The New York Times magazine,* August 17, 8ff.
Wilensky, G.
  1970   Determinants of local government expenditures. In *Financing the metropolis,* edited by J. P. Crecine. Pp. 197–218. Beverly Hills, Calif.: Sage.
Wilensky, H. L., and C. N. Lebeaux
  1965   *Industrial society and social welfare.* New York: Free Press.
Willbern, Y.
  1966   *The withering away of the city.* Bloomington, Ind.: Indiana Univ. Press.
Williams, O. P., H. Herman, C. S. Liebman, and T. R. Dye
  1965   *Suburban differences and metropolitan policies: A Philadelphia story.* Philadelphia: Univ. of Pennsylvania Press.
Wilson, J. Q. (Editor)
  1966   *Urban renewal: The record and the controversy.* Cambridge, Mass.: M.I.T. Press.
Winch, R. F., and D. T. Campbell
  1969   Proof? No. Evidence? Yes. The significance of tests of significance. *American Sociologist* 4: 140–143.
Winter, W. O.
  1969   *The urban polity.* New York: Dodd, Mead.
Wolfinger, R. E., and J. O. Field
  1966   Political ethos and the structure of city government. *American Political Science Review* 60: 308–326.
Wolin, S. S.
  1960   *Politics and vision.* Boston: Little, Brown.
Wood, R. C.
  1964   *1400 governments: The political economy of the New York metropolitan region.* Garden City, N. Y.: Doubleday.
Wynne, E.
  1972   *The politics of school accountability.* Berkeley, Calif.: McCutchan.
Zald, M. N.
  1969   The structure of society and social service integration. *Social Science Quarterly* 50: 557–567.
  1970   Political economy: A framework for comparative analysis. In *Power in organizations,* edited by M. N. Zald. Pp. 221–261. Nashville, Tenn.: Vanderbilt Univ. Press.

Zimmer, B. G., and A. H. Hawley
  1968   *Metropolitan area schools: Resistance to district reorganization.* Beverly Hills, Calif.: Sage.
Zuckerman, M.
  1970   *Peaceable kingdoms: New England towns in the eighteenth century.* New York: Knopf.

Author Index

217

Subject Index

QUANTITATIVE STUDIES IN SOCIAL RELATIONS

Consulting Editor: Peter H. Rossi

UNIVERSITY OF MASSACHUSETTS
AMHERST, MASSACHUSETTS

Seymour Sudman, APPLIED SAMPLING

James D. Wright, THE DISSENT OF THE GOVERNED: *Alienation and Democracy in America*

Roland J. Liebert, DISINTEGRATION AND POLITICAL ACTION: *The Changing Functions of City Governments in America*

Walter Williams and Richard F. Elmore, SOCIAL PROGRAM IMPLEMENTATION

Edward O. Laumann and Franz U. Pappi, NETWORKS OF COLLECTIVE ACTION: *A Perspective on Community Influence Systems*

In Preparation

Richard A. Berk, Harold Brackman, and Selma Lesser, THE MEASURE OF JUSTICE: *An Empirical Study of Criminal Law Change*

Eric Hanushek and John Jackson, INTRODUCTION TO ESTIMATION THEORY